Faultlines

Debating the Issues in American
Politics

Faultlines

Debating the Issues in American Politics

David T. Canon
University of Wisconsin—Madison

John J. Coleman
University of Wisconsin—Madison

and

Kenneth R. Mayer
University of Wisconsin—Madison

W • W • NORTON & COMPANY NEW YORK • LONDON

W. W. Norton & Company has been independent since its founding in 1923, when William Warder and Mary D. Herter Norton first published lectures delivered at the People's Institute, the adult education division of New York City's Cooper Union. The Nortons soon expanded their program beyond the Institute, publishing books by celebrated academics from America and abroad. By mid-century, the two major pillars of Norton's publishing program—trade books and college texts—were firmly established. In the 1950s, the Norton family transferred control of the company to its employees, and today—with a staff of four hundred and a comparable number of trade, college, and professional titles published each year—W. W. Norton & Company stands as the largest and oldest publishing house owned wholly by its employees.

Composition by PennSet, Inc.
Manufacturing by Maple-Vail Book Group

Library of Congress Cataloging-in-Publication Data
Faultlines : debating the issues in American politics / David T. Canon, John J. Coleman, and Kenneth R. Mayer.
    p.   cm.
Includes bibliographical references.

ISBN 0-393-92485-8 (pbk.)

1. United States—Politics and government. I. Canon, David T. II. Coleman, John J., 1959– III. Mayer, Kenneth R., 1960–

JK31.F37 2004
320.973—dc22

                                                              2003070213

W. W. Norton & Company, Inc., 500 Fifth Avenue, New York, N.Y. 10110
www.wwnorton.com

W. W. Norton & Company Ltd., Castle House,
75/76 Wells Street, London W1T 3QT

1 2 3 4 5 6 7 8 9 0

Contents

Faultlines

Debating the Issues in American
Politics

1   Political Culture:
A Place for Religion in Politics?

For a country of great prosperity and wealth, the United States is unusually religious. Around the world, the pattern is clear: the more economically developed a country is, the fewer the number of people who say that religion is an important part of their lives. The United States stands out as a striking exception to that rule. Religious belief has been an important part of American political culture since the colonial days and, indeed, was part of the reason individuals fled to America in that formative era. In the Constitution, religion is protected in two ways: the First Amendment guarantees freedom of religious expression and prohibits any official government establishment of religion. Both parts of this formulation have been the focus of substantial debate.

In recent American history, religious belief has been central to political discourse. Reverend Martin Luther King often invoked religious language and principles in support of the civil rights movement, and religious belief has motivated many activists in the anti-abortion movement. Political party coalitions have historically differed in their religious composition—most recently, in the 1980s and 1990s Americans with more conservative religious beliefs became an important part of the Republican party coalition. Presidents and presidential candidates have also wrestled with the place of religion in politics. Presidential candidate John F. Kennedy, a Catholic, defended himself against accusations that he had "divided loyalties" and that his decision making would be directed from Rome. Speaking to a group of Protestant ministers in Houston in September 1960, Kennedy stated that he believed firmly in the separation of church and state. "I do not speak for my church on public matters—and the church does not speak for me," he declared. At the same time, Kennedy pointed out that he wouldn't simply abandon his beliefs: "I do not intend to apologize for these views . . . nor do I intend to disavow either my views or my church in order to win this election." In November, he was narrowly elected president, and was the first Catholic elected to that office.

Over thirty years later, religious references in public life were commonplace. President Bill Clinton, by one accounting, was not only personally a believer who often included religious references in his speeches, but his administration enacted a number of laws intended to strengthen religious institutions. Presidential candidate George W. Bush spoke openly about his turn to faith at around age forty and the importance of religious belief in his life and views. He frequently noted the importance of faith for the country: "For too long, some in government believed there was no room for faith in the public square. I guess they've forgotten the history of this great country. . . . Every expansion of justice in American history received inspiration from men and women of moral conviction and religious belief."

President Bush has continued and expanded former President Clinton's efforts to increase the role of religious institutions in American public life. One of his chief proposals was the Faith-Based Initiative. The goal of this program, in short, was to allow faith-based organizations more access to federal funds in the area of social service provision. Bush had difficulty passing his initiative through Congress, so in December 2002, he signed an executive order that directed federal agencies to treat faith-based organizations equally to secular organizations.

In this chapter, Stanley Carlson-Thies and Barry Lynn debate the propriety of this initiative. Carlson-Thies, the former White House Associate Director for Cabinet Affairs in the Bush administration, supports the initiative and places it in historical context. He argues that the initiative is part of a continuing effort to renegotiate the boundaries between government and faith, a negotiation that has been going on for decades and not only in the United States. In this sense, the initiative is more evolutionary than revolutionary. Carlson-Thies also contends that the initiative is fundamentally about reorganizing government and making government more efficient and effective than it is about promoting any particular religious worldviews. To him, the initiative is simply common sense: if there are social service programs that are working and accomplishing goals the government wishes to accomplish, why prohibit government from supporting these programs? Barry Lynn, the Executive Director of Americans United for Separation of Church and State, takes a different stand. To Lynn, the initiative fails on a number of grounds. It inevitably uses government funds to promote the spiritual message of the recipients of the funds, in violation of the First Amendment. Lynn also suggests that the initiative will lead to job discrimination, to favored religions receiving aid while minority religions are excluded, and to particular theological views being advantaged over others. He also contends that the process has a political undercurrent, that it is being used to further the political interests of the president and the Republican party. Given the deeply intertwined nature of religious belief and American political culture, the points raised in the debate between Carlson-Thies and Lynn may well produce a series of contentious court cases in the near future.

STANLEY CARLSON-THIES AND BARRY LYNN

The Faith-Based Initiative Two Years Later: Examining the Potential, Progress and Problems

STANLEY CARLSON-THIES:

We are now two years into President Bush's initiative to "rally the armies of compassion." So what's going on and what's next? I'll talk first about the larger context of the initiative, and then about the path or trajectory that it's following.

* * *

So let me sketch some parts of this bigger picture, and I will mention four points.

Point one: Government funding of expressly religious social service providers did not start with the Bush administration. We all know about Jewish Family Services, about Catholic Charities, and so on, but many people say the government funded only the secular programs that were run by these groups that might be religiously affiliated. After all, the rule used to be and ought to be that anything government does or funds has to be secular—isn't that the constitutional requirement?

Well, the truth is that actual practice has not been nearly that spiritless. Stephen Monsma's 1996 study, *When Sacred and Secular Mix*, showed that long before Bush's faith-based initiative, the government was funding child- and family-serving agencies that were expressly faith-based, in terms of what they displayed on their walls, prayers over meals, encouraging discussion of religious matters, and giving preference to staff of the same faith, and so on.

So despite the theory, even before the Bush faith-based initiative, there was considerable, though inconsistent, history of government funding of expressly faith-based organizations.

Point two: Deliberate efforts to promote consistency—to make both government policy and government practice hospitable to faith-based organizations—did not start with the Bush administration.

Take federally funded childcare for low-income families. More than a dozen years ago, Congress wrote the rules in such a way that churches and other expressly faith-based organizations can take part without sacrificing their faith commitments and characteristics.

And of course, there is Charitable Choice. Since Bush became president, there has been bitter opposition to Charitable Choice in Congress from many, but during the previous administration, Congress and President Bill Clinton four times wrote this language into federal law. So in some key federal programs right now—welfare, community action agencies, and drug treatment—when state and local governments get this federal money, they are required to spend it according to new rules to protect the religious character of faith-based organizations and the religious liberty of people seeking help.

* * *

And according to a range of studies, faith-based organizations that in the past never were partners with government now in many places are receiving government support for their good works, and the sky has not fallen. There have been some problems, some contracts have not been written the way they should be, some organizations have not done everything the way they should do it, but the experience has been positive rather than negative, as far as I can see. The widely voiced fears about religious coercion, massive fraud, and worthless groups displacing expert services have proven to be just that—fears and not realities.

Point three: Initiatives to connect government and civil society in new ways and to give a more prominent place to faith are not unique to the United States, as if such things were simply the product of the Religious Right and the politicians they've managed to lead astray.

* * *

Point four: Conceptions of the proper relationship between church and state, between religious organizations and government, have been in flux in the United States for many decades. That is, there was no long-settled consensus which the Bush administration arbitrarily started to overturn. The U.S. Constitution, of course, forbids the establishment of religion, but on into the twentieth century,

Protestantism was informally established, as the historians say. After World War II, as the nation became more religiously diverse and the federal courts increasingly acted to secure national constitutional values, that informal Protestant establishment was replaced by the concept of no aid to religion and a strict separation between church and state. The government was not to support anything religious.

However, as we've seen, practice was not as rigid as that theory, and the Supreme Court has been notoriously of multiple minds about church-state questions.

And there is a problem with the no-aid idea. After all, while many social service organizations are secular, many are inspired and shaped by religion. The no-aid concept tells government to support only secular programs no matter which ones are most effective, but such a secular bias violates equal treatment and can't be readily squared with the constitutionally required respect for religious liberty—or with good social policy, in my view.

Thus, for several decades we've been in the midst of debate and experimentation about how to go beyond no-aid, strict separationism. * * * And I think that's exactly the setting of the Bush faith-based initiative—our current stage of church-state relations in which the boundaries are being renegotiated. That's a process that started before the Bush administration and, in my view, will continue after it. Renegotiating the church-state boundaries is one key part of renegotiating the relationship between government and civil society, and such renegotiations are taking place in many countries.

In other words, we can best understand the Bush faith-based initiative if we see it as part of this decades-long, multi-nation process of reconfiguring how government responsibilities are carried out, what the appropriate place of religion is in the public square, what kind of policy is required in a nation comprised of multiple religions as well as secular convictions, and how government services can best be related to private efforts to help needy neighbors.

* * *

Now on to my second major theme about the trajectory or path of the faith-based initiative—a way to think about what's going on and what will happen next.

Many people, and not least many reporters, think the Bush faith-based initiative is a series of laws and programs designed to benefit religious organizations. So we get a picture of the faith-based initiative proceeding by fits and starts: Now there's a faith-based initiative because the House is battling over H.R. 7, and now the faith-based initiative has disappeared because the Senate decided not to take up the CARE Act last year; but wait, there's the faith-based initiative again because the CARE Act has been reintroduced in the Senate, and on and on. But in fact, the Bush faith-based initiative, I think, is more accurately regarded as a government reform effort that has a legislative agenda.

The Washington Post backed into the right idea in an editorial about the announcement in the State of the Union speech about federal funds for vouchers for drug treatment services. Here's what the editorial said: "Slowly we are seeing Mr. Bush's new strategy for his faith-based initiative. Once, he tackled it head-on, as a centerpiece of his compassionate conservatism. He did it by supporting, say, increased funding for faith-based groups or tax deductions for charitable contributions. Now he seems to have retreated to something more like a 'reinventing government' strategy, using executive orders and rule changes. For him, this has the advantage of tackling bureaucratic hostility to faith-based groups." * * * In my view, the initiative has always been a reinventing government strategy. There is no retreat, but the *Post* editorial was right to call attention to government reform in place of the conventional focus on legislative agenda.

For sure, government reform is not the whole story. One goal has always been to use the bully pulpit to encourage greater private giving to charities—partly through law and partly through his speeches. This part of the initiative has turned outward instead of inward to improve government's own operations. And the administration, of course, has promoted particular programs—the voucherized drug treatment idea, mentoring the children of prisoners, the compassion capital fund grants to expand the ability of technical assistance intermediaries to equip small groups to improve their fundraising, management, and programs.

Yet from the start, the primary focus of the Bush faith-based initiative has been on improving government operations. That means it's not a movement to trash government or simply to dump federal responsibilities on the doorsteps of churches and charities. Instead, it aims at reform, at improving the government's operations and impact. Our federal, state, and local governments spend hundreds of billions of dollars on programs to uplift communities, divert youth from crime and drugs, move individuals to self-sufficiency and so on. How well are we doing? Well, clearly there is much room for improvement.

The president has proposed that one reason these programs have not been more effective is because they have ignored or not adequately taken account of some of the most important forces in civil society—groups that already, on their own, using their own resources, with few resources—labor hard on behalf of their neighbors. These groups that he calls "neighborhood healers"—both faith-based and secular—are intimately involved in the lives of families and neighborhoods that need assistance, and they go beyond material needs to address values and hopes, and habit, morals, and the spirit. So one aim of the faith-based initiative is to make sure these kinds of groups can partner with federal efforts.

There is a related motivation: The administration's conviction that the exclusion or uncertain inclusion of faith-based groups from federally funded programs is due to a mistaken and obsolete reading of the constitutional requirements. Equal treatment and a level playing field—these concepts better implement the twin constitutional requirements of no establishment and religious liberty than does the old idea of no aid to religion. In this sense, something like the faith-based movement is not only permitted by the Constitution, but required by it.

So, how to build better connections between government programs and neighborhood groups, how to ensure equal treatment of faith-based organizations—these are not so much questions of grand legislative strategies as of government reform, of reinventing the way the federal government works across the sweep of its social service programs and reaching into how state and local governments use federal funds to provide services.

* * *

So what's been going on with the faith-based initiative and what will happen next? Well, since I left the White House Office of Faith-Based and Community Initiatives, I'm not privy to their specific plans—you'll have to ask them—but the trajectory of action, I think, is plain. When federally funded programs obstruct participation by faith-based and community groups; when federally funded programs don't share information, like technical assistance, effectively to such groups; when the design of federal programs disregards the good works done all across the nation by religious and secular neighborhood healers, then Bush's faith-based initiative will be working to identify the specific causes of these obstructions and to propose solutions. Reform may require legislation. There has been some; there will be more. It may require changed regulations, as we've seen. Perhaps just new guidelines instead of updated legal advice, or administrative program redesign, or the inclusion of fresh expertise on grant review committees, and so on.

The focus is improving governmental operations, making sure that federal social service spending actually makes a positive difference in the lives of people who need the help of others. Making the government faith-friendly is a major part of that strategy—faith-friendly, not biased towards faith and against secular providers. Being faith-friendly is important because that's what the Constitution demands, and government ought to be faith-friendly because so much social service work is performed by faith-based organizations. If government is going to do well, it needs to partner with others who are doing well out in the community.

BARRY LYNN:

Two years ago, when President Bush first announced his faith-based initiative, I told an interviewer that it was the worst idea since they took King Kong from Skull Island and brought him to New York. And I would now like to apologize to King Kong, because the president's program is infinitely worse. Now having achieved a cheap laugh, I'd like to try to prove that what I've just said is correct.

Even though the president's program was never implemented legislatively, never passed Congress, it certainly is being implemented in a kind of stealth atmosphere. Virtually everything, though, that has happened in the program demonstrates what I'd consider unfortunate—either intended or unintended—effects of any government-funded religion program. All the particular problems find their genesis in a fundamental design flaw, which is the idea that you can protect constitutional interests by simply proclaiming that public funds may go to religious groups so long as they are not used for religious instruction, worship, or proselytization. The kind of magic formula, as often phrased by administration officials, is that tax dollars, they say, will be used to buy bread, not Bibles. This conveniently ignores, though, that the government does fund religion when it funds some loaves of bread for the church-based hunger program, because it also, in the process, frees up more church funds to buy scriptures or to increase the salary of the pastor.

Moreover, it's not possible for most religious groups to turn off the religious element of what they are doing when a federal dollar floats by, but turn the spiritual spigot back on when it is a voluntarily contributed dollar. So the matter, in practical effect, in most cases, is that grants or contracts with pervasively religious groups do aid, do promote, do foster religion with tax dollars, violating a core principle of the First Amendment. And in the process, those funds promote the theological assumptions, the spiritual message, and the biases of the recipients.

* * *

The first major problem is this: The administration has made every effort to legitimize the funding of invidious job discrimination. In every set of proposed regulations, in the president's December executive order there is clear language that permits a recipient to hire persons to run taxpayer-funded programs solely on the basis of their religious affiliation or beliefs. This means that a Roman Catholic provider can refuse to hire or fire at will a pregnant, single mother. It effectively permits a fundamentalist Christian church to put the words "No Muslim Need Apply" on top of its employment form.

The president asserts this is designed to protect the integrity of the religious identity of the organization, and, of course, private religious groups can make such employment decisions with privately solicited funds. However, the constitutional and, I'd argue, the moral calculus changes when tax dollars enter the equation. It was wrong to create a system where you can be taxed to help pay for a job you cannot get even if you are the most eminently qualified person for that position. I've never found that a Methodist ladles out the stew in a soup kitchen differently from a Hindu, nor do Baptists change the bed sheets in a homeless shelter using a different methodology than do, let's say, non-believers.

The administration has literally poisoned the employment pool, aiding and abetting state officials who want to dole out tax dollars to discriminating organizations. * * * Folks, that is morally wrong. If you get government money, you have to be open to hiring the best-qualified person without regard to your religious opinion of him or her or the life he or she lives.

Second, there is a growing doubt about who will, in fact, be getting funds in this program. When George Bush was campaigning for the presidency, you may remember, he said that groups promoting hate would not be eligible, specifically mentioning the Nation of Islam. White House official Stephen Goldsmith has said that Wiccans could not get funding because they were not, in his words, "humane" enough to provide childcare services.

In America, we can personally have all kinds of biases about other religions based on our own theological differences. We know that just by listening to Jerry Falwell. I mean, he, on a regular basis, has opinions about everybody—Mohammed is a terrorist, Mohammed is a virulent man of war. I once had to remind Jerry Falwell on *Hardball* that there are actually people in America who thought that he was a virulent and hateful person. We can do that as individuals, but as government, we don't have an opinion and we shouldn't.

I cringe at the very idea that the government will put together lists of acceptable and unacceptable religions on the basis of the passion of the rhetoric or the idiosyncratic nature of their beliefs. Government seals of approval for faith serve as just one exemplar of how little this administration understands about the First Amendment to begin with.

The third trend is that the faith-based initiative is becoming a perfect example of how the government tries to palm off on private groups the problems they can't or won't fix themselves. I used to predict, as Stanley reminded us, that this plan would amount to dumping the poor on the church steps one day, dumping a small bag of money there the next day, and then praying that the two find each other.

I didn't think that was a wise idea, but from the very outset the president's program contained little, if any, new money. He wants to pit the current providers against a raft of new faith-based providers for the crumbs from an increasingly small sliver of pie of federal funding for human needs. In the first year of his presidency, some of you know, he zeroed out an entire program for inner-city development. Nothing has changed. In the new budget, about 400,000 people may be kicked off the low-income fuel subsidy program, which of course primarily helps people heat their homes in the winter. Now think about this. If it's too cold in your apartment because you have lost your home heating subsidy, why should we be impressed if a small percentage of the newly homeless will be taken in by a federally funded, faith-based homeless shelter? That is not compassion; that is just stupid.

Fourth, the blatantly political nature of this whole effort is now abundantly clear. * * * The administration has been setting up how-to seminars to lure people, particularly African American pastors, into hearing about this faith money, as one of their spokesmen calls it, and actually trying to convince them they might get some of it.

There was an overwhelmingly suspicious pattern about these meetings in advance of the recent elections. They were overwhelmingly being held in congressional districts deemed pivotal in the Republican effort to retain control of the House, or in states like Florida, with highly competitive gubernatorial races. In South Carolina, where this faith-based event was actually co-sponsored by the state Republican Party, the Democratic Party's invitation apparently got lost in the mail.

* * *

Fifth, the administration is already paving the way for implicit and explicit restrictions on the content of religious programs that will be eligible for funding. For example, several grants have now gone to Christian groups for strengthening marriage. Marriage is a sacrament in most religious faiths. When a government funds a program that teaches that divorce is never acceptable in the eyes of God, doesn't this, in fact, give some kind of government blessing to certain theological beliefs? It's absolutely inevitable that grants will eventually be awarded after a review process which includes consideration of the theologies which under-gird the potential recipients' programs. That's a bad idea.

It's already occurring in regard to other programs. Outside the religious arena, funding for community-based sex education programs, of course, only goes to those that preach abstinence only before marriage, not just that abstinence is preferable. One program in Louisiana has been successfully challenged in federal court because tax dollars are paying for a blatantly fundamentalist curriculum. But if we go one step further and restrict the content of a program run by a faith-based group, you are effectively giving preferential treatment and funding to some theological viewpoints over others.

It's not only liberals who worry about this. Joseph Farrah, a pretty conservative columnist, complained recently that some faith-based money might end up going through the Department of Energy to religious groups that have left-wing environmental views. After all, he said, many denominational structures actually believe in global warming. Can you believe that!? The National Council of Churches got behind that "What Would Jesus Drive?" campaign, which of course was a challenge to the auto industry's apparent belief in the God-given right of every man, woman, and driving-age child to own and operate an SUV. They were behind that stuff.

* * *

We now know that the president wants to help more people with vouchers who happen to be addicted. They can use the vouchers so they can go to any treatment program they want, including those that believe that addiction is sin, pure and simple, and reject even a medical component to their programs. The Louisiana-based group the president praised in the State of the Union address is in that category. Again, though, we cannot afford, and constitutionally are not permitted, to fund religious conversions, even if that has a temporary side benefit of stopping a person from abusing an illicit substance. The successful court challenge of one of Wisconsin's "faith works" programs makes that very clear.

Of course, we don't know whether these untested programs even have that secondary effect of helping people, but to this administration, the facts really don't seem to matter very much to begin with.

* * *

Sixth, and finally, we have mounting evidence that significant damage is being done to current ecumenical efforts and other community initiatives. * * * In [one] incident, a homeless shelter for veterans west of Boston was told that its federal grant was being cut so substantially that almost 50 percent of the beds would be eliminated. Their lost funds were now going to be going to several faith-based shelters—not near Boston, although one was in Utah and one was in North Carolina. A veterans' activist told *The Boston Globe* bluntly that this meant more people in Massachusetts would be out in the cold and, "more people will die."

This is what happens when you look at the wrong problem in the first place. The problem in America is the crying need of human beings for help from somebody. It is not the false claim that faith-based organizations have not had a level playing field so we should make up for it by punishing secular groups that are doing their job. The whole program is so tempting, though—even if you believe everything I've said. The State of the Union address made it clear when the president started talking about some of the unmet needs—AIDS projects in Africa, hydrogen-powered cars. We know that the American people are never going to support the level of taxation necessary to pay for all of those programs and all of the programs all of us want, and therefore we must keep private philanthropy alive and well.

I remain very concerned that one of the unintended consequences of the faith-based initiative will actually be a reduction in voluntary faith-community giving to others. If Uncle Sam is paying for the Wednesday night dinner for the homeless in your church, won't a few of your parishioners think about skimping on their pledge next year? And how do you get it back when Uncle Sam likes the Methodist program across the street more next year than he likes your program this year?

DISCUSSION QUESTIONS

1. *What would you do?* If a case concerning the faith-based initiative reaches the federal courts, it will most likely be on the grounds that the initiative violates the constitutional prohibition of government establishing religion (the "establishment clause"). The Supreme Court has established the "Lemon test" to determine whether a government action or law violates the establishment clause. The three-part Lemon test will find an action or law constitutionally acceptable if it (a) has a plausible secular purpose, (b) has a primary effect that is neither to advance nor prohibit religion, and (c) does not foster "excessive entanglements" between government and religion. With this standard in mind, you have been asked to submit an opinion column to the editor of a local newspaper indicating whether you would find the faith-based initiative constitutionally acceptable or constitutionally problematic.

2. Where would you draw the line between the appropriate and inappropriate use of religious belief and religious references by an elected public official? Are you comfortable with the use of religious language and imagery in public debate? Is it more problematic if a public official defends his or her actions by explicitly referring to religious beliefs rather than making secular references to "the values" that drive his or her decision making?

3. Carlson-Thies argues that the faith-based initiative is primarily about providing effective government services. Assuming he is correct, do Lynn's arguments retain or lose their persuasiveness? That is, if we were to find that a particular organization was exceptionally effective in combating drug use, should the government not be allowed to assist this organization because of its hiring practices or the possibility that certain theological messages would be conveyed to program beneficiaries?

2 Constitutional Amendments and Structural Change

In just the first six months of 2003, there were almost fifty proposals in Congress to amend the U.S. Constitution. Some of the proposed amendments reflect efforts to overturn particularly controversial Supreme Court decisions: pending are amendments to prohibit abortion, guarantee the right to obtain an abortion, make flag desecration a crime, and permit schools to offer voluntary prayer. Some amendments are designed to change the government's basic structure and process: to replace the electoral college with a direct popular vote, require federal judges to be reconfirmed every ten years, choose presidential electors at the congressional district level, limit amounts spent in election campaigns, repeal the Twenty-second Amendment (which limits presidents to two terms), require a two-thirds congressional vote to raise taxes, require a balanced budget, impose term limits on representatives and senators, or repeal the Sixteenth Amendment (which permits income taxes). And some would guarantee specific benefits or create new classes of constitutionally guaranteed rights: to affordable housing, quality health care, a clean environment, or full employment. Others are an attempt to preempt developments that proponents fear are foreshadowed by state action or recent Supreme Court decisions. One example in this category is H.J.Res.56, which states that marriage and the legal benefits accruing to marriage would only be available to a union of one man and one woman. This proposal is designed to forestall the possibility of same-sex marriage or marriage equivalents such as "civil unions."

Whether or not these amendments are, individually, good ideas, law professor Kathleen Sullivan is critical of efforts to alter the Constitution. The Constitution has been amended only twenty-seven times in over two hundred years (seventeen if you count the Bill of Rights as a single instance), and the amendments have tended to arise during times of crisis or to redefine basic political rights. Amendments that are intended to impose a particular policy, or which arise out of short-term forces, are usually not revered in the same way as, say, the Fourteenth or Nineteenth Amendments (which, respectively, guaranteed equal protection of the laws, and gave women the right to vote). Sullivan notes that the one attempt to impose a particular policy via constitutional amendment (prohibition of alcohol, enacted in the Eighteenth Amendment and repealed in the Twenty-first), was a dismal failure. Constitutional principles should not, she concludes, be "up for grabs" or politicized, but should be slow to change; amendments should be reserved for setting out the basic structure of government and defining "a few fundamental political ideals."

George Allen, a former governor of Virginia, disagrees with Sullivan. In Allen's view, the problem with the amendment process is that it is too difficult or, more specifically, too limited in its options. As the system has evolved, the federal government has intruded on the affairs of the states and mandated what state governments do. At the same time, the constitutional amendment process has, as Allen sees it, been monopolized by Congress. The one route that allows state initiation of amendments—calling of a constitutional convention—has been delegitimized in political discourse because of fears that a "runaway convention" would emerge and propose drastic change in the Constitution. To restore a balance of power in federalism, Allen writes on behalf of a constitutional amendment that would allow amendments to be more easily initiated from the states. Under this new process, if two-thirds of the states passed a resolution supporting a particular proposed amendment—for example, prohibiting flag burning—the proposal would then go to Congress. If two-thirds or more of the members of Congress voted *against* the anti-flag-burning amendment, it would die; otherwise it would return to the states for final approval. At that point, three-fourths of the states would need to approve the anti-flag-burning amendment for it to enter the Constitution. Allen contends that there are changes in national politics that are being obstructed by Congress but that have wide support in the states and among the people. The clear implication of Allen's commentary is that more amendments would result from this process, though he states that the number would not be large.

KATHLEEN M. SULLIVAN
What's Wrong with Constitutional Amendments?

Most things Congress does can be undone by the next election. Amendments to the U.S. Constitution cannot. And yet recent Congresses have been stricken with constitutional amendment fever. More constitutional amendment proposals have been taken seriously now than at any other recent time. Some have even come close to passing. An amendment calling for a balanced budget passed the House twice and came within one and then two votes of passing in the Senate. An amendment allowing punishment of flag burners easily passed the House and fell just three votes short in the Senate. These and other proposed amendments continue to circulate—including amendments that would impose term limits on members of Congress, permit subsidies for religious speech with public funds, confer procedural rights upon crime victims, denaturalize children of illegal immigrants, or require a three-fifths vote to raise taxes, to name a few.

Many of these amendments are bad ideas. But they are dangerous apart from their individual merits. The Constitution was, as Chief Justice John Marshall once wrote, "intended to endure for ages to come." Thus, it should be amended sparingly, not used as a chip in short-run political games. This was clearly the view of the framers, who made the Constitution extraordinarily difficult to amend. Amendments can pass only by the action of large supermajorities. Congress may propose amendments by a two-thirds vote of both houses. Or the legislatures of two-thirds of the states may request that Congress call a constitutional convention. Either way, a proposed amendment becomes law only when ratified by three-fourths of the states. Once an amendment clears these hurdles into the Constitution, it is equally difficult to remove.

Not surprisingly, the Constitution has been amended only twenty-seven times in our history. Half of these arose in exceptional circumstances. Ten made up the Bill of Rights, added in one fell swoop by the First Congress and ratified in 1791 as part of a bargain that induced reluctant states to accept the Constitution. And the Thirteenth, Fourteenth, and Fifteenth amendments, which abolished slavery and gave African Americans rights of equal citizenship, were passed by the Reconstruction Congress in the wake of the Civil War.

The remaining amendments have tinkered little with the original constitutional design. Four extended the right to vote in federal elections to broader classes of citizens: the Fifteenth to racial minorities, the Nineteenth to women, the Twenty-fourth to voters too poor to pay a poll tax, and the Twenty-sixth to persons between the ages of eighteen and twenty-one. Only two amendments ever tried to impose a particular social policy: the Eighteenth Amendment imposed Prohibition and the Twenty-first repealed it. Only two amendments changed the original structure of the government: the Seventeenth Amendment provided for popular election of senators, and the Twenty-second imposed a two-term limit on the presidency. And only four amendments have ever been enacted to overrule decisions of the Supreme Court. The remaining handful of amendments were national housekeeping measures, the most important of which was the Twenty-fifth Amendment's establishment of procedures for presidential succession. We have never had a constitutional convention.

Our traditional reluctance to amend the Constitution stands on good reason today, the will of the framers aside. This is not because the Constitution deserves idolatry—Thomas Jefferson cautioned in 1816 that we should not treat it "like the ark of the covenant, too sacred to be touched." It is rather because maintaining stable agreement on the fundamental organizing principles of government has a number of clear political advantages over a system whose basic structure is always up for grabs. As James Madison cautioned in *The Federalist* No. 43, we ought to guard "against that extreme facility" of constitutional amendment "which would render the Constitution too mutable." What are the reasons this might be so?

First, it is a bad idea to politicize the Constitution. The very idea of a constitution turns on the separation of the legal and the political realms. The Constitution sets up the framework of government. It also sets forth a few fundamental political ideals (equality, representation, individual liberties) that place limits on how far any temporary majority may go. This is our higher law. All the rest is left to politics. Losers in the short run yield to the winners out of respect for the constitutional framework set up for the long run. This makes the peaceful conduct of ordinary politics possible. Without such respect for the constitutional framework, politics would degenerate into fractious war. But the more a constitution is politicized, the less it operates as a fundamental charter of government. The more a constitution is amended, the more it seems like ordinary legislation.

Two examples are instructive. The only modern federal constitutional amendment to impose a controversial social policy was a failure. The Eighteenth Amendment introduced Prohibition, and, fourteen years later, the Twenty-first Amendment repealed it. As Justice Oliver Wendell Holmes, Jr., once wrote, "a constitution is not meant to embody a particular economic theory," for it is "made for people of fundamentally differing views." Amendments that embody a specific and debatable social or economic policy allow one generation to tie the hands of another, entrenching approaches that ought to be revisable in the crucible of ordinary politics.

Thus it is not surprising that the only amendment to the U.S. Constitution ever to impose such a policy is also the only one ever to be repealed.

Now consider the experience of the states. In contrast to the spare federal Constitution, state constitutions are typically voluminous tomes. Most state constitutions are amendable by simple majority, including by popular initiative and referendum. While the federal Constitution has been amended only twenty-seven times in more than two hundred years, the fifty state constitutions have suffered a total of nearly six thousand amendments. They have thus taken on what Marshall called in *McCulloch v. Maryland* "the prolixity of a legal code"—a vice he praised the federal Constitution for avoiding. State constitutions are loaded with particular provisions resembling ordinary legislation and embodying the outcome of special interest deals. As a result, they command far less respect than the U.S. Constitution.

A second reason to resist writing short-term policy goals into the Constitution is that they nearly always turn out to have bad and unintended structural consequences. This is in part because amendments are passed piecemeal. In contrast, the Constitution was drafted as a whole at Philadelphia. The framers had to think about how the entire thing fit together. Not so for modern amendments. Consider congressional term limits, for example. Term limits amendment advocates claim that rotating incumbents out of office would decrease institutional responsiveness to special interests and make the federal legislation more responsive to popular will. But would it? There's a better chance that term limits would shift power from Congress to the permanent civil service that staffs the executive branch and agencies, where special interest influence would remain untouched.

To take another example, advocates of the balanced budget amendment focus on claims that elimination of the deficit will help investment and growth. But they ignore the structural consequences of shifting fiscal power from Congress to the president or the courts. The power of the purse was intentionally entrusted by the framers to the most representative branch. As Madison wrote in *The Federalist* No. 58, the taxing and spending power is "the most complete and effectual weapon with which any constitution can arm the immediate representatives of the people." The balanced budget amendment, however, would tempt the president to impound funds, or at least threaten to do so in order to gain greater leverage over Congress. And it would tempt the courts to enter a judicial quagmire for which they are ill-equipped. When is the budget in balance? Whose estimates should we use? What if growth turns out faster than expected? Lawsuits over these questions could drag on for years. Such redistribution of power among the federal branches surely should not be undertaken lightly, especially not under the pressure of an election year.

A third danger lurking in constitutional amendments is that of mutiny against the authority of the Supreme Court. We have lasted two centuries with only twenty-seven amendments because the Supreme Court has been given enough interpretive latitude to adapt the basic charter to changing times. Our high court enjoys a respect and legitimacy uncommon elsewhere in the world. That legitimacy is salutary, for it enables the Court to settle or at least defuse society's most ideologically charged disputes.

Kathleen M. Sullivan

Contemporary constitutional revisionists, however, suggest that if you dislike a Supreme Court decision, mobilize to overturn it. If the Court holds that free speech rights protect flag burners, just write a flag-burning exception into the First Amendment. If the Court limits student prayer in public schools, rewrite the establishment clause to replace neutrality toward religion with equal rights for religious access instead. Such amendment proposals no doubt reflect the revisionists' frustration that court packing turns out to be harder than it seems—Presidents Reagan and Bush, as it turned out, appointed more moderate than conservative justices. But undermining the authority of the institution itself is an unwise response to such disappointments.

In any event, it is illusory to think that an amendment will somehow eliminate judicial discretion. Most constitutional amendment proposals are, like the original document, written in general and open-ended terms. Thus, they necessarily defer hard questions to ultimate resolution by the courts. Does the balanced budget amendment give the president impoundment power? Congress settled this matter by statute with President Nixon, but the amendment would reopen the question. Does splattering mustard on your Fourth of July flag napkin amount to flag desecration? A committee of senators got nowhere trying to write language that would guarantee against such an absurd result. Would unisex bathrooms have been mandated if the Equal Rights Amendment had ever passed? Advocates on both sides debated the issue fiercely, but only the Supreme Court would ever have decided for sure.

For the most part we have managed to keep short-term politics out of the rewriting of the fundamental charter. Now is no time to start. Of course, on rare occasions, constitutional amendments are desirable. We have passed various structural amendments to tie our hands against short-term sentiments, for example, through the amendments expanding the right to vote. But unless the ordinary give-and-take of our politics proves incapable of solving something, the Constitution is not the place to go to fix it.

GEORGE ALLEN

Submitted Statement before the Subcommittee on the Constitution, March 28, 1998

57–226

1999
Proposing an Amendment to the Constitution of the United States to Provide a Procedure by which the States May Propose Constitutional Amendments.

Hearing

before the

Subcommittee on the Constitution

of the
Committee on the Judiciary
House of Representatives

One Hundred Fifth Congress

Second Session
on
H.J. Res. 84

March 25, 1998

Prepared Statement of Hon. George Allen, Former Member of Congress and Former Governor of Virginia

Thank you, Mr. Chairman.

I appreciate the opportunity to be here today. I have fond memories of this committee, on which I had the pleasure of serving when I was in the House.

And it is indeed a privilege to join my good friend, Chairman Tom Bliley, an outstanding leader in the fight for a balanced federal system. He is to be commended for introducing H.J. Res. 84, which embodies the concept that we in Virginia have been calling the States' Initiative. This constitutional amendment is a necessary structural change if we are to reinvigorate our federalist system and restore the balance between the federal government and the states.

As a former Governor of Virginia, I approach this subject of federal-state relations with a perspective very similar to that of two of my early and esteemed predecessors—Patrick Henry and Thomas Jefferson. Like them—and like many governors who have served since their time, not only in Virginia but around the country—I have a healthy distrust of centralized power, especially power centralized in Washington.

Our country was founded on notions of individualistic liberty and limited government, and with the expectation that people would be free to chart their own course and control their own destiny through self-government based in their local communities and their states.

The founders pledged their lives, fortunes, and sacred honor to achieve freedom and independence from an oppressive monarchy in England. With that hard-fought victory won, they were not about to surrender their liberties to an all-powerful central government—this one, on the north banks of the Potomac.

Instead, they took pains to guard against centralized power through an elaborate constitutional system of checks and balances. For the federal government, power was divided among three branches of government and the legislative powers further split between the House and Senate.

At least as important, if not more so, was the shared sovereignty between the states and the federal government. As Patrick Henry concluded, "If there be a real check intended to be left on Congress, it must be left in the State Governments."

The power of the federal government was to be limited and enumerated, with all remaining powers reserved by the Tenth Amendment to the states and to the people. The onus was on the states to jealously guard their freedoms.

Almost from the beginning of our country's history, however, the federal government began to encroach upon the authority and freedoms intended for the states. As early as 1825, Thomas Jefferson observed:

> I see, as you do, and with the deepest affliction, the rapid strides with which the federal branch of our government is advancing towards the usurpation of all the rights reserved to the States, and the consolidation in itself of all powers, foreign and domestic, and that, too, by constructions which, if legitimate, leave no limits to their power. Take together the decisions of the Federal Court, the doctrines of the President, and the misconstructions of the constitutional compact acted on by the legislature of the federal branch, and it is but too evident that the three ruling branches of that department are in combination to strip their colleagues, the State authorities, of the powers reserved by them, and to exercise themselves all functions foreign and domestic.

Today, there is virtually no area of public responsibility or private activity in which federal bureaucrats do not assert the power to override the will of the people in the states, through federal mandates, edicts, and rulings.

The Framers intended the states to be jealous guardians of their responsibilities and power, but, historically, the states have faced a dilemma in resisting the growth of federal power at their expense. On the one hand, questions regarding the scope of the federal government's jurisdiction are resolved by federal courts, which generally have favored more expansive interpretations of federal power. On the other hand, the states' recourse to the constitutional amendment process has been impeded by Congress's virtual monopoly over the initiation of constitutional amendments.

Use of the Article V "convention" method of amendment, intended by our founders to allow direct state action, has never been used because of fear that a constitutional convention called by the states would become a "runaway" assemblage that would seek to rewrite our entire national charter.

So the power has gravitated almost inexorably to Washington, and we have paid a heavy price. While there are winners and losers from issue to issue, the truth is that all of our citizens enjoy less freedom and less opportunity for self-government as a result. Instead of decisions being made in our states and our local communities—where citizens can make their voices and views heard—more and more of the decisions that affect our lives are being made by unelected and unaccountable bureaucrats here in Washington, D.C.

This condition breeds a sense of powerlessness and unconnected distance among our citizens with their government. That feeling of powerlessness in turn breeds apathy and cynicism about the political process. And that apathy and cynicism about the political process can shake the very foundations of our free society and the rule of law on which it is based. They may threaten a society in which, for the first time in the long history of mankind, people were to be regarded as the masters, and government as the servants—not the other way around.

The most insightful framers of the Constitution feared this centralization of power and the resulting loss of freedom and self-determination by the American people. In vain, they fashioned the Tenth Amendment as a "parchment barrier," to borrow James Madison's term. But Madison foresaw what we now know from experience: that the Tenth Amendment alone could not restrain federal power. The people in the states must have the means to defend their own ideals and prerogatives. A new, workable avenue for the states and the people to change their Constitution must be crafted. Fears of a "runaway" constitutional convention have rendered impractical the state's existing constitutional means of self-defense.

That was the conclusion reached in Virginia by the Governor's Council on Self-Determination and Federalism, which I established by Executive Order in Virginia in 1994. I would like to submit for the record the report of the Subcommittee on Constitutional Amendments. This distinguished panel included, among others, State Senator (now Congressman) Virgil Goode, former Congressman Caldwell Butler, Judge Robert Bork, and Professor Nelson Lund, from whom you will hear shortly.

It was the conclusion reached by the five leading state government organizations at the bipartisan Federalism Summit in Cincinnati in 1995.

It was the conclusion reached by thirty Republican governors who convened in historic Williamsburg in 1994. At that eventful meeting, we adopted a statement known as the Williamsburg Resolve, making clear our determination to reclaim the states' prerogatives and to restore the constitutional checks and balances that stand guard in defense of our liberties.

Joined in Williamsburg by the newly elected leadership of the House and Senate, we charted a new course in relations between the federal and state governments. Certainly, some of the results have been heartening.

Almost immediately, the 104th Congress adopted the Unfunded Mandates Reform Act. That legislation has produced a new awareness of and accountability for intergovernmental mandates.

The sweeping welfare reform legislation signed into law the following year marked a turning point, devolving unprecedented authority back to the states to design and run their own welfare systems. Unfettered, the states are proving themselves to be the successful laboratories of democracy our founders envisioned. In Virginia, where we have built our Virginia Initiative for Employment not Welfare on the twin pillars of the work ethic and personal responsibility, welfare roles are down by more than 42 percent, thousands of families are on the ladder to self-sufficiency, some earning a paycheck for the first time, and taxpayers are saving millions of dollars.

But these actions must be seen for what they are—promising first steps on the long road back to a true federalist system of shared sovereignty and limited central power. The policy gains of the moment—indeed of this Congress, and its new leadership since 1994—in no way diminish the urgency or the need for permanently correcting the structural imbalance and enabling the states again to become full and equal partners in a federal system of dual sovereignty.

Already the states are struggling to preserve our forward momentum. A recent report by the General Accounting Office concludes that the Unfunded Mandates Reform Act has done little to stem the mandates coming out of federal agencies. Interpretations have exempted some of the costliest mandates (such as Medicaid) as well as significant edicts by regulators at the EPA and elsewhere. Recently published regulations from the Department of Health and Human Services threaten to take away by regulation the flexibility Congress granted the states through legislation over their welfare programs.

Indeed, without structural change, the many positive reforms emanating from Washington in recent years will be in jeopardy of being reversed by a succeeding Congress, by bureaucratic edict, or by judicial fiat. And the people of the states will be no better equipped than they have been in the past to fend off these retrenchments or federal hobbles.

Now, we all recognize the practical limits of constitutional change as a remedy for federal policy afflictions. Not every state grievance or misguided federal law or regulation will be corrected by affording states the practical ability to initiate constitutional changes. Indeed, the instances in which a large majority of state legislatures will agree on identical amendatory language undoubtedly will be quite few, and will be reserved for major questions of national importance.

In short, our freedoms will never be safe when they exist only at the sufferance of federal legislators, federal courts, and federal bureaucrats.

Yet, the means will be there, and that alone will change the relationship between the states and the federal government. The states will have a lever to force change upon a future Congress or future administration that may have fallen far out-of-touch with the decency, values, and concerns of the people of the United States.

By allowing the States to initiate constitutional changes without having to depend on Congress or holding a constitutional convention, the States' Initiative reflected in H.J. Res. 84 would give the nation's governors and state legislatures a seat at the table. Not a seat from which to impose national policy, but a seat from which to voice the perspective that the people of America, the true owners of this government, are not being heeded. It is the principle that people should be free to chart their own course in their local communities and in their states.

Now, this is not a Republican or a Democratic idea. It enjoys broad bipartisan support.

Eight years ago, when I was a member of the Virginia House of Delegates and our state had a Democrat governor and a Democrat majority in the legislature, our General Assembly adopted a resolution recommending this reform.

Then, when I was Governor in 1995, our legislature gave overwhelming bipartisan endorsement to a similar resolution sponsored by Virgil Goode, now a member of Congress.

Just this past year, the governors of the western states adopted a call for a new process for amending the Constitution along the lines of H.J. Res. 84, in order to "give states the ability to act in a meaningful way rather than merely complaining, writing letters and pleading their case before Congress and the media."

The States' Initiative remains true to the spirit and genius of the United States

Constitution as our founders envisioned it. It does not confer new powers upon the states; it simply restores to the states the ability to initiate the amendment process which fear of a runaway convention has rendered virtually ineffective.

If you think about it, the real significance of H.J. Res. 84 is that it will empower the people through their state legislatures to propose constitutional amendments that are broadly supported across the land—everywhere in fact except in the Congress of the United States. And, in that very limited sense, I know that we are asking Congress to commit what may be an act still disfavored in Washington—the voluntary surrender of a bit of power.

Yet, I believe you and the other members of this Congress have sufficient faith in the people of America to put them and their freedom first. And that is the message you will send if you approve House Joint Resolution 84.

I respectfully encourage you to take that action. The United States is still young—still an optimistic experiment in human freedom—still defying the odds. Centuries of dark world experience favored the enslavers over the liberators, the mighty over the just, the privileged few over the downtrodden many. For a comparatively short time here in America, we have been busy changing all that. We are perfecting a system of representative democracy that is a beacon for the world and the hope of humanity.

Let us not miss this chance to make our freedom more firm, our liberty more lasting, and our people more in control of their lives and their destiny. You can trust the people of our nation.

DISCUSSION QUESTIONS

1. *What would you do?* Allen tries to deflect criticism that the proposed constitutional amendment will make amendments so easy to enact that amendments that are really about policy choices will end up in the Constitution, a scenario feared by Sullivan. Are both authors too cautious about constitutional change? Imagine that you are writing a policy memo for a member of Congress. A new proposal would allow proposed amendments to be voted on by the public on a national ballot. A second proposal would allow the public to add proposed amendments to this ballot by collecting the signatures of 3 percent of the voting age population (approximately 6.5 million signatures). What would you recommend in your policy memo?

2. In the changed amendment process favored by Allen, as long as just over one-third of Congress supports a proposed amendment, it would go back to the states for final approval. Does this reduce the role of Congress too much?

3. Sullivan is worried about the Constitution becoming "politicized." If the change favored by Allen were enacted into the Constitution, would the risk of the Constitution becoming politicized increase, decrease, or stay about the same? Why?

3 New Federalism and Devolution

From welfare reform to health care, educational funding to inner-city redevelopment, state governments have sought more control over public policy within their borders. In the 1970s and 1980s, when this devolution of power to the states was called "New Federalism," the debate was pretty simple. Republicans favored devolution because state governments were "closer to the people" and could better determine their needs. Democrats resisted the transfer of power from Washington, fearing that many states would not adequately care for and protect minorities and poor people or protect the environment without prodding from Washington. To the extent that the courts got involved in the debate, they tended to favor the transfer of power to the states.

The debate over devolving power from the national government to the states has grown increasingly complicated in the past several years: the partisan nature of the debate shifted, the courts have played a larger but inconsistent role, and the "states' rights" rhetoric may be losing its appeal. While Republicans continued to favor greater state control, a Democratic president, Bill Clinton, supported devolution to the states in several areas, especially welfare policy. The Supreme Court, Jeffrey Rosen argues, has played a central role in the shift of power to the states, but their decisions often seem more motivated by a desire to increase their own power than an attempt to devolve power from Washington. Although a series of important Court decisions limited Congress's power to address problems of guns in school, violence against women, and age discrimination, several other recent cases involving voting rights and employment discrimination show that the Court may be just as willing to strike down a state law or uphold a national law if it furthers its views on discrimination, as in the recent decision upholding the 1993 Family Leave Act. *Bush v. Gore*, the case involving the contested election returns from Florida in the 2000 presidential election, is the most famous example of the Court asserting its views. In this case the Court imposed its own definition of a fair recount procedure, even though the Florida State Supreme Court and Florida law pointed in the other direction. Rosen argues that the Court should not be inserting itself so forcefully in the federalism debate, but rather the elected institutions should determine the relative balance of power between the states and national government when it comes to defining anti-discrimination laws.

Marci Hamilton argues that liberals' concerns with federalism are overblown: "The States and the people of the States no longer are the evil attackers of civil rights while the federal government is the savior." There are variations across states in the degree to which various civil rights are protected, but all abide by the established federal standards. Traditionally, this variation is seen as having two important virtues: it allows American citizens to "vote with their feet" and means that states are the "laboratories of democracy." The former is not discussed by Hamilton, but refers to the ability of Americans to decide what kind of state they want to live in. For example, citizens can choose a state with low taxes or one with more extensive government programs and higher taxes. Hamilton alludes to the benefits of having states be the "laboratories of democracy"—that is, trying out various policies to see which ones work the best. Later in this chapter, she argues that it is because the states have improved in the protection of civil rights that they are now trusted to do more. Hamilton also develops another important point concerning the hypocrisy by liberals and conservatives on federalism: liberals generally favor national power and conservatives favor state power, but the positions are reversed on issues such as gay marriage, medical marijuana, and assisted suicide.

JEFFREY ROSEN
Our Discriminating Court

Last week, the Supreme Court held that a Circuit City employee in California who claimed he had suffered race discrimination couldn't sue the electronics dealer under the state's anti-discrimination law. When he'd applied for the job, the employee had agreed to resolve employment disputes through arbitration. And last week the five conservative justices announced that the Federal Arbitration Act of 1925 requires judges to enforce arbitration agreements even when they conflict with state law. The case may seem like an anomaly: The Court's conservative majority is famous for limiting Congress's power in the name of states' rights. Here it did the opposite, expanding the scope of federal law in a way that curtailed states' rights. The ruling was particularly striking since, as the four liberal justices pointed out, employment contracts are explicitly exempted from the Federal Arbitration Act, which was intended to apply only to disputes arising from commercial and maritime contracts. But the *Circuit City* ruling wasn't an anomaly. It was the latest—and clearest—evidence that the Supreme Court's so-called federalism revolution isn't really about states' rights at all. Instead, it's about the determination of the five conservative justices to claim exclusive authority to decide what counts as illegal discrimination in America. If any other governmental body—Congress, a state legislature, or a lower court—comes to a different conclusion, the justices will overturn it. And so in February those five held that state employees couldn't sue for damages when the states violated the Americans with Disabilities Act. The justices didn't think discrimination on the basis of disability was a national problem, so they nullified the clear will of Congress. In December the same five held that the Florida Supreme Court couldn't order a recount in the presidential race. The justices said counting the ballots according to different standards would discriminate against certain voters—or was it certain ballots?—even though the Florida legislature had reached the opposite conclusion, reasoning that different counting standards for different ballots were necessary to avoid discrimination. And last year, in striking down the Violence Against Women Act, the Court dismissed Congress's conclusion that the states weren't responding adequately to gender-motivated violence—treating Congress more like a lower court than an equal branch of government. These cases show that what's at stake in the Court's recent acts of self-aggrandizement is not simply the New Deal legacy of a powerful federal government. What's at stake, even more importantly, is the legacy of the civil rights era and the idea that democratically elected bodies, rather than unelected judges, should have the main responsibility for determining what constitutes illegal discrimination in America.

These days, there's not much political support for the proposition that Congress lacks the power to prohibit private business from discriminating on the basis of gender, disability, or anything else. But a generation ago it was a different story. In 1963 Robert Bork argued in this magazine that the 1964 Civil Rights Act was unconstitutional because outlawing discrimination by motels and other privately owned spaces of public accommodation violated the free-assembly rights of racist businessmen. "The danger is that justifiable abhorrence of racial discrimination will result in legislation by which the morals of the majority are self-righteously imposed upon a minority," Bork wrote in a burst of youthful libertarianism. But, even then, Bork's was a minority view: In 1964 the Supreme Court unanimously rejected his reasoning and upheld the public-accommodations provisions of the Civil Rights Act. The justices reasoned that Congress, which has the constitutional authority to regulate interstate commerce, could plausibly conclude that racial discrimination by motel owners might affect interstate commerce.

For the next thirty years the Court interpreted Congress's power under the commerce clause very broadly, refusing to invoke its limits to strike down a single federal law. But in 1995, in the opening shot of the federalism revolution, a 5–4 conservative majority struck down the Gun-Free School Zones Act, reasoning that the connection between guns in schools and interstate commerce was too tenuous to pass constitutional muster. And last year, in striking down the Violence Against Women Act, the Court held that Congress couldn't use its commerce power to regulate noneconomic activities—such as violence—that didn't clearly affect interstate commerce.

These judicial efforts to adapt eighteenth-century limits on Congress's power to the twenty-first century might be viewed as a creative return to the pre-New Deal era—when most people agreed that Congress could pass laws regulating economic, but not social and moral, behavior. But they're also part of a more radical and far less defensible project: to usurp Congress's right to define illegal discrimination. The Fourteenth Amendment, passed in 1868, was intended to give Congress, rather than the courts, primary responsibility for enforcing equal protection of the laws. And when Congress passed the Violence Against Women Act in 1994, it reviewed what the Court later acknowledged was "voluminous" evidence that state courts and prosecutors were refusing to respond adequately to violence against women. But in striking down the law last year, the Court summarily dismissed Congress's conclusions. In parts of their opinion, the five conservatives came close to resurrecting Bork's view that Congress lacks the power to regulate discrimination by private parties—except in cases where Congress is responding to acts of discrimination that the Court itself views as unconstitutional. The five conservatives extended this view in another case last year when they held that states can't be sued for violating federal laws prohibiting age discrimination. Because the Court doesn't view age discrimination as a problem deserving heightened constitutional scrutiny, it prevented Congress from reaching a contrary conclusion.

This lack of deference to Congress is indefensible under any definition of judicial restraint. Unlike its efforts limiting Congress's power to regulate the economy, the Court has no authority to reserve for itself exclusive power to define illegal discrimination. As Alexis de Tocqueville recognized, ideas about what kinds of discrimination should be illegal change dramatically in response to the inexorable logic of democracy. As society becomes more democratic, public pressure to forbid discrimination becomes harder for politicians to resist. This is why, over the past two decades, Congress has decided that more and more forms of discrimination should be illegal—adding discrimination on the basis of age and disability to a list that originally included only race and gender. You may not like the expansion of anti-discrimination law into every corner of American life—my own view is that it fulfills Tocqueville's fears about the soft despotism of the nanny state—but there is no doubt that Congress is better equipped than the Court to represent the people's will.

Indeed, if the Court had taken a similarly self-aggrandizing view of its exclusive power to define discrimination a generation ago, it might have struck down Congress's decision in 1972 to extend federal prohibitions on gender discrimination to the states. And if it continues to take this view, it may prevent a future Congress from requiring the states to pay damages when they discriminate on the basis of sexual orientation. But when it comes to recognizing new forms of discrimination, the Court has historically followed Congress. For the Court to prevent Congress from responding to changing social understandings is as great an affront to democracy as any episode of judicial activism ventured by the Warren Court.

The best response to charges that the Rehnquist Court is engaging in unprincipled conservative judicial activism came from Chief Judge J. Harvie Wilkinson III of the U.S. Court of Appeals in Virginia, at a lecture at the American Enterprise Institute in March. Wilkinson, one of the most thoughtful and nuanced conservative judges, argued that the Rehnquist Court, unlike the Warren and Burger Courts, is acting not as an ideological combatant but as a "structural referee" among the federal government, the states, and the private sector. While the Warren and Burger Courts focused on the extremes of the political spectrum, he said—expanding federal power at one end and individual rights at the other—the Rehnquist Court is correctly protecting the interests of the intermediate organizations—states, local governments, and private groups—that Tocqueville considered necessary to "mediate between the otherwise isolated individual, and the rather awesome and remote array of national institutions."

Wilkinson argues convincingly that as the autonomy of states and civic organizations erodes, society may become "a less stable, less vital, and less nurturing place." But ultimately Wilkinson is defending the Rehnquist Court on policy grounds, not constitutional ones. Whether or not you agree that the expansion of anti-discrimination laws lead to social polarization, the Constitution explicitly empowers Congress to enforce the equal protection of the laws, and this includes the power to make empirical judgments about what kind of discrimination requires a national response.

Moreover, despite Wilkinson's provocative defense, the Supreme Court's devotion to the autonomy of states and private organizations is not always consistent or ideologically neutral. Voting-rights cases like *Bush v. Gore* and *Shaw v. Reno* show that the conservative justices are willing to overrule efforts by state legislatures to redress discrimination when they conflict with the justices' own views of what constitutes discrimination. The Court construes Congress's power narrowly when Congress subjects states to anti-discrimination suits; but, as last week's *Circuit City* ruling showed, the Court is equally prepared to construe Congress's power broadly when it exempts business from anti-discrimination suits.

If the conservative justices want to protect the autonomy of local organizations without usurping the power of Congress to define discrimination, they should rely not on the Fourteenth Amendment but on the First Amendment. In the Boy Scouts case last year, for example, the Court properly held that the First Amendment protects the right of private organizations like the Boy Scouts to discriminate on the basis of sexual orientation. And, in a welcome and important opinion last month, Judge Samuel Alito, a federal appellate judge in Philadelphia, held that a public school's antisexual-harassment policy violated the First Amendment.

But here, too, some conservative judges have proved inconsistent—willing to discard free speech when it clashes with, rather than supports, big business. For example, the U.S. Court of Appeals in Washington, D.C., recently upheld the Sonny Bono Copyright Term Extension Act, which extends by twenty years existing copyrights as well as copyrights in the future. The Bono bill was designed as a windfall for the Walt Disney Company, which wants to keep milking profits from Mickey Mouse. A group of lawyers led by Lawrence Lessig of Stanford Law School argued that it violates free speech and Congress's constitutional power to secure copyrights "for limited Times." After extending the terms of existing copyrights eleven times in the past thirty-six years, Congress now protects copyright for the life of the author plus seventy years—which in the case of Irving Berlin is 171 years. This is more than ten times longer than the initial copyright term endorsed by the first Congress. But two conservative judges on the D.C. appellate court rejected Lessig's argument that the Framers of the Constitution meant to limit terms of copyright because of the powerful public interest in free expression. Judge David Sentelle wrote a powerful dissent, invoking the Supreme Court's federalism decisions and insisting that Congress has no power to grant copyright extensions retroactively. If the conservatives on the Supreme Court refuse to reconsider this decision, they will appear less concerned with imposing principled limitations on Congress's power than with protecting the interests of business above all.

It was precisely this kind of economic partisanship that discredited conservative judicial activism in the past. During the New Deal and Progressive eras, judicial attacks on the power of Congress and the states to regulate the economy prompted FDR to retaliate with his court-packing plan. So far, popular reaction to the Rehnquist Court's imperiousness has been muted, perhaps because the federal laws the Court has struck down so far are largely symbolic. But by asserting an exclusive power to define discrimination, the Court has embarked on a battle it is likely, over the long term, to lose. In a democracy, discrimination is the greatest sin; not even Republican politicians will be able to resist pressure to forbid it in all its forms. During the previous Bush administration, for example, when the Court reduced the scope of federal discrimination laws, Congress promptly overruled the justices with the Civil Rights Act of 1991. Now the Court has grown even more arrogant, insisting that Congress lacks the constitutional power to define discrimination more broadly than the Court. The only way for Congress to defend its prerogatives is to ensure that future justices take a more deferential view of Congress's power and a more modest view of their own.

MARCI HAMILTON
Are Federalism and the States Really Anti–Civil Rights as Liberals Often Claim?

Brace yourself for an onslaught of kvetching over the Supreme Court's federalism jurisprudence. You will see it in the judicial confirmations soon to come—especially Jeff Sutton's nomination to a seat on the U.S. Court of Appeals for the Sixth Circuit. And if there is a 2003 Supreme Court vacancy, as seems likely, it will only get more intense. Listen carefully, for much of what is said about the Court's federalism cases is going to be misguided, unfair, or just plain inaccurate. Newspapers, Senate Democrats, and liberal law professors will all offer you the following spin: They will say, with all apparent sincerity, that the revival of States' rights is a disaster for civil rights. The National Organization of Women and other liberal lobbying groups are taking this message to all fifty States. The anti-civil-rights States the liberals are decrying, however, don't really exist anymore—as is evidenced by the fact that the problems liberals point to are decades old. It's true that in the pre-civil rights era, States were the source of some of the ugliest civil rights violations, and the federal government was one of the most effective protectors of civil rights. But no longer. Yet liberals keep dredging up what is now ancient history, as if these wrongs—terrible as they were in their time—were still ongoing. Syndicated columnist E. J. Dionne took this very path this week, pointing to the Trent Lott embarrassment as a reminder of the evils of the southern States, and the evil of States' rights in general [editors' note: this refers to the firestorm that was created when Senator Lott spoke approvingly of Senator Strom Thurmond's views, which were widely interpreted as longing for the days of racial segregation. Lott was forced to step down as Majority Leader of the Senate because of the flap]. This anachronistic approach is deeply unpersuasive: Where is the current evidence for the claim that federalism, and States' rights, are anti-civil rights? The truth is, there is little to no such evidence, but the claim is repeated over and over, nonetheless.

EQUATING THE STATES WITH CIVIL RIGHTS VIOLATIONS IS ANACHRONISTIC

In truth, times have changed—dramatically. The States and the people of the States no longer are the evil attackers of civil rights while the federal government is the savior. Remember, the groups that lobbied at the federal level for civil rights lost little time moving into the States and obtaining civil rights laws in the States as well. As a result, there are a plethora of equal opportunity statutes in the states, offering protections from race, gender, disability, and other forms of discrimination. Indeed, when the Supreme Court recently addressed Congress's power to apply the Americans with Disabilities Act and the Age Discrimination in Employment Act to the States—in *Board of Trustees of Univ. of Alabama v. Garrett* and *Kimel v. Florida Bd. of Regents*—it noted that both federal laws were mirrored in laws passed by the vast majority of States. Indeed, it is a rare civil rights claim that is not brought under both federal and state constitutional and statutory law. And at times, this occurs because state law is more expansive and more protective of rights than federal law; state civil rights law can and does at times go beyond federal civil rights law. You wouldn't know this, however, from the way liberals talk about civil rights issues.

FEDERALISM IS NOT RESULTS-ORIENTED: IT CAN HELP CIVIL RIGHTS

It's important to remember, too, that federalism is just a formal rule that determines which entity rules in a particular arena—the states or the federal government. It does not govern what policy either must adopt. And, as explained above, when responsibility for civil rights issues falls to the states, not the federal government, it hardly falls into a vacuum: states are now very active in civil rights matters. One thing is true: If responsibility in a particular area of the law falls solely to the states, laws will vary state-by-state. But that doesn't necessarily mean less protection. If the states are permitted to experiment in rights protections within constitutional boundaries, some will have expansive protections—indeed, more expansive protections than the federal government—and some will have fewer. We have already seen this kind of variation with abortion, where there is a great variety in abortion laws from state-to-state (within the federal constitutional framework of the Supreme Court's decisions in *Roe v. Wade* and *Planned Parenthood v. Casey*, of course). The truth is that there are arenas where—if the Supreme Court has held, or were to hold in the future, that states have exclusive latitude—liberals, not conservatives, will be able to win the policy debate. Medical use of marijuana, and assisted suicide, are two possible examples to add to abortion law. Certainly liberal states would take much more liberal positions than the current federal government on numerous issues, if left to themselves. And some more conservative states will take more conservative positions. Given these realities, how can one say, as liberals often do, that States' rights, as a concept, is conservative? At most, it is a neutral idea; the policy choice is filled in by the state whose right it is, according to the Court, to resolve it.

ASHCROFT AND LOTT'S ACTIONS HAVE MADE IT UNFAIRLY HARDER TO DEFEND FEDERALISM

The Bush Administration must now defend federalism to get its favored candidates through. Unfortunately, its task has been made significantly harder by the fact that Attorney General John Ashcroft and former Senate Majority Leader Trent Lott have muddied the waters considerably. First, for federalism purposes, John Ashcroft would have been better off leaving Oregon to enforce its liberal assisted-suicide law. Instead, he insisted that the federal government intervene. In debate after debate, I have heard critics of federalism claim, based on Ashcroft's decision, that the Bush Administration is only committed to states' rights when it serves a conservative agenda—not as a fundamental constitutional principle. Ashcroft should not have provided them with grist for this mill. But of course, the politicians are doing what politicians do—turn everything into politics. A liberal administration would doubtless have decried federalism and at the same time, deferred to Oregon—in a different kind of hypocrisy. Again, though, the problem is the hypocrisy—not states' rights as a general principle. Meanwhile, Trent Lott did more damage, by taking us back to the era when the word "state" meant "civil rights violators" and "federal" meant "protect us from these evil states." It is easy to fall into familiar ideas, and one could see liberals, witnessing the Lott saga, nostalgically reaching back to a time when they had a deep message, a resonant message. But that message no longer is based on factual reality: Now, as noted above, states protect civil rights, too. States have been the object of lobbyists from both sides of the aisle on civil rights for decades and given the Supreme Court's federalism cases, they will continue to be. Sometimes liberals will win; sometimes conservatives will. But federalism concerns the choice of forum; the result reached in the forum is up to the people of the state, acting through their representatives.

THE FEDERALISM CASES' RESULTS LEGALLY DEPEND ON THE STATES BEING PRO-CIVIL RIGHTS

Here is the deepest irony: the Supreme Court's federalism cases are actually predicated on the fact that the states did not continue to engage in widespread and persisting constitutional violations, as they did prior to the Civil Rights Era. In other words, it is the states' improved record that laid the framework for the federalism decisions. Thus, the reality that states' rights cannot be equated with anti-civil-rights policy is no coincidence. Instead, it is a direct result of Constitutional law. But again, this is little discussed, and not widely known to the public; thus, again, the result is the distortion of the states' rights debate. Section 5 of the Fourteenth Amendment gives Congress broad latitude to bring the states back within constitutional parameters when they do engage in widespread, persisting Constitutional violations. Thus, if the states had worse civil rights records than they do now, Congress would have far more power to assert its power in the civil rights area. Or, put another way, it is only—and precisely—because the states have turned a corner on civil rights that the Court has found the means of turning back a small portion of the ever-enlarging, ever-dominating power of the Congress. Section 5 should make civil rights supporters less leery of states' rights. Not only did it ensure that state power would only be restored when states began to consistently respect civil rights, it also ensures that if they ever stop, they will lose power to Congress as a result. Thus, suppose we someday were to return to the horrendous era when the states turned a blind eye to civil rights, and civil rights groups found no willing ear in the state legislatures. In that unlikely event, according to Supreme Court doctrine, Congress will again have the power necessary to bring the states, through federal civil rights legislation, back into the constitutional fold. That shouldn't be a surprise to anyone familiar with the Constitution—though liberal law professors often omit to note it. After all, this is simply what Section 5 says, and means. So when you start reading about the terrible things done in the name of federalism, ask this question: What exactly have the states done recently that makes them automatically suspect? Examples from the sixties and earlier should concern us as a matter of shameful American history, but not as a matter of contemporary policy. Then ask another question: Which policy does the speaker support, and why can't it be accomplished in the states, and not only at the federal level? Perhaps the answer may be that it is more convenient for lobbyists to have one office in Washington and not fifty in the fifty states (I have heard this response repeatedly). If so, tell the speaker that lobbying convenience is simply nowhere near a good enough reason to jettison a part of the Constitution's structure that has been there since the beginning and for very good reasons. Besides, lobbyists would no doubt benefit from going beyond the Beltway, and watching state policies in action; it would be all to the good for them to see how various policies actually affect those they are intended to help. A little loss of lobbying convenience may lead to a great gain in education for lobbyists. That would be an ultimate good for the people.

DISCUSSION QUESTIONS

1. *What would you do?* If you were "voting with your feet," as defenders of a state-centered federalism urge us to do, what kind of state would you seek out and why?

2. What are the advantages and disadvantages of having states as the center of policy making on some issues rather than the national government?

3. What standards should be used when deciding whether an issue should be primarily handled at the national level or the state level? Should civil rights policy be formed at the national or state level?

4. What role should the Supreme Court play in helping to define the boundaries of the balance of power between the state and national governments? Should the definition of those boundaries be left up to the elected institutions as Rosen argues?

4 Civil Liberties: The Tradeoff between Security and Freedom

One of the central purposes of any government is to provide security for its citizens. However, if a nation places too much emphasis on security it will have to limit freedom. Since the terrorist attacks of September 11, the United States government has been tipping the balance toward security and away from freedom by strengthening the police and surveillance powers of the state. A majority of Americans (78 percent according to a poll cited in the *Progressive* article) support these policies, and they passed by very large margins in the House and Senate. However, defenders of civil liberties and those who fear the power of the state are very concerned about the recent changes. It is sometimes said that the political continuum from left to right is not a line, but a circle. The debate over the balance between security and freedom is one of those instances in which the left and right are on one side of the debate against the middle. In fact, one of the articles that we considered using for its critique of the Patriot Act was in a journal that is published by the John Birch Society, one of the most conservative political groups in the nation. The American Civil Liberties Union, which is one of the most liberal, could have easily authored the article.

The editorial in *The Progressive* outlines many of the concerns about the Patriot Act and other threats to civil liberties since 9/11. The editorial lays out in very strong terms the "breathtaking assault" on our civil liberties, citing the vague language of the Patriot Act that permits the government broader access to monitor the activity of suspected terrorists on the Internet, in libraries, and in homes. The law also alters the attorney-client relationship to allow the government to listen in on conversations with suspected terrorists, allows the detention of designated "enemy combatants" without normal due process protections, and broadens powers for "material witness" wiretaps, warrants, and searches. Attorney General John Ashcroft is described as the central threat to civil liberties as he aggressively interprets the Patriot Act to enhance the nation's police powers.

Many of these claims are rebutted by Ramesh Ponnuru, who argues that our nation is not going to turn into a version of George Orwell's *1984,* in which Big Brother is watching our every move. Ponnuru's central argument is that many of the surveillance powers outlined in the Patriot Act simply extend existing police powers to fight terrorism and in some cases, such as Internet surveillance, clarified the law so that the government is now restrained in a way that it may not have been in the past (because existing law was not clear). Ponnuru argues that other aspects of the Patriot Act, such as roving wiretaps, are "common-sense measures" that will make the task of fighting terrorism easier.

The conflicting points of views on this issue may be explained, in part, by different interpretations of the law's language: Ponnuru applies a "best case" interpretation while *The Progressive* explores the worst case scenarios. Ultimately, the courts will have to sort out the meaning of the law, a process that has already begun. In some instances the federal courts have decided that the Patriot Act goes too far in limiting the civil liberties of suspected terrorists, in other cases the courts have upheld the government's position. The most widely publicized blows to the government came with the federal appeals courts' decision in December 2003 that the United States could not indefinitely detain a citizen as an "enemy combatant" or deny legal rights to 660 noncitizens captured in Afghanistan. On June 23, 2003, a New Jersey state court ruled that suspected terrorists must be allowed to confront the evidence against them. In this case, Mohamed Atriss spent six months in a county jail based on accusations that he was a terrorist. However, the judge ruled that the charges were based on faulty evidence that could have been easily rebutted by the suspect if his lawyers had access to the evidence. On the other hand, in a victory for the Bush administration on June 17, 2003, a federal appeals panel ruled that the identities of hundreds of people detained after 9/11 may be concealed, saying disclosure of even one name could endanger national security. This is an extremely contentious issue that will continue to be debated over the next several years.

THE PROGRESSIVE [EDITORS]

Casualties of War

Oh, it was too easy for a nation to turn its back on 1,200 detainees, mostly Muslim, rounded up since September 11 and held in secret. The terrorist attack was so shocking that many Americans were able to condone this violation of due process, thinking perhaps that the government would stop there. But now the government of the people has turned its attention to the rest of the people, and the war on terrorism goes from murky to muddy.

Welcome to the era of Total Information Awareness and other tomfoolery.

We're now at a time of perhaps unprecedented spying and secrecy. Richard Nixon could only dream of such powers. More than a year after the events of September 11, 2001, we are seeing the best of America—the Constitution and Bill of Rights—shredded by President George Bush and Attorney General John Ashcroft. To comprehend this breathtaking assault, we need to look back at how it all began.

The Ashcroft confirmation hearing was a bitter fight for the soul of the Justice Department. Amidst the cantankerous rhetoric and blow-hard posturing from both sides of the narrow fence, there was some plainspoken eloquence from Senator Richard Durbin, Democrat of Illinois.

"The Attorney General, more than any other Cabinet officer, is entrusted with protecting the civil rights of Americans," Durbin said. "We know from our history that defending those rights can often be controversial and unpopular. I find no evidence in the public career or voting record of Senator Ashcroft that he has ever risked any political capital to defend the rights of those who suffer in our society from prejudice and discrimination."

How right Durbin was.

Since 9/11, our top law enforcement officer has gone to great lengths to rewrite and dismantle civil liberties in this country. For all the Attorney General's singing about patriotism and love of country, his odious record demonstrates that he does not respect the fundamental tenets of our democracy.

The opening act in this wretched tragedy started two nights after the 9/11 attack when the Senate swiftly voted, by voice, to approve an attachment to an appropriations bill that made it easier for the government to wiretap the computers of terrorism suspects without having to go through due process. That was just the beginning of what would eventually become the USA Patriot Act, an omnibus anti-terrorism law that was supposed to pacify Americans so they would return to shopping malls and sporting events.

The USA Patriot Act is full of lax language that gives the government expansive powers to peep into the lives of Americans they deem dissenters and subversives. This is the kind of law a nation gets when 78 percent of its citizens, in an NBC/Wall Street Journal poll, say they're willing to sacrifice rights to fight against extremists. It's simply one of the most regressive acts in American history.

Even the definition of a terrorist in the act is flimsy and transparent. For instance, you're a domestic terrorist if you're breaking a law at the same time that you're doing something that appears "to be intended to influence the policy of government by intimidation." Under this definition, Martin Luther King was a domestic terrorist in Birmingham.

The act lets the FBI and other law enforcement agents enter your home when you're not there, ransack your files, use your computer and search your e-mails, and place a "magic lantern" on your computer to record your every keystroke. Then they can leave without telling you they were there.

In addition, the Patriot Act lets law enforcement find out what books you're buying at stores or checking out at libraries. And it then gags the bookstores and libraries so they can't tell anyone that they've had to fork over your name.

But this lunacy goes beyond reading material. A story in the December 10 edition of *The New York Times* reports that last summer the FBI, concerned about a terrorist attack involving scuba divers, "set out to identify every person who had taken diving lessons in the previous three years."

According to the *Times*, hundreds of dive shops and organizations willingly turned over the information.

"But just as the effort was wrapping up in July, the FBI ran into a two-man revolt," the *Times* says. "The owners of the Reef Seekers Dive Company in Beverly Hills, California, balked at turning over the records of their clients . . . even when officials came back with a subpoena asking for 'any and all documented and other records relating to all noncertified divers and referrals from July 1, 1999, through July 16, 2002.'"

The owners say they had several reasons to deny the FBI's request, primarily because terrorists would need to have far more sophisticated training than a few scuba lessons. The owners said they also worried the information would be passed on to other agencies. Some people called to say they hoped the shop would be blown up by terrorists.

"If we are going to decide as a country that because of our worry about terrorism that we are willing to give up our basic privacy, we need an open and full debate on whether we want to make such a fundamental change," Cindy Cohen, legal director of the Electronic Frontier Foundation, told the *Times*. The foundation represented Reef Seekers.

At about the same time Congress was ratifying the Patriot Act, Ashcroft issued an edict saying that prosecutors could eavesdrop on prisoner-lawyer conversations. And he rewrote Justice Department policy to allow a return to Cointelpro.

Bush himself jumped in with his military tribunal order, which allows the Pentagon to nab any noncitizens anywhere in the world and try them in military courts with lower standards of evidence and with no appeals possible to any judge or court anywhere in the world.

Again, the Bush Administration sold this to the American people as a necessary protection against foreign terrorists and assured the citizenry that they would not be victimized by it.

But then came the designation of "enemy combatants" and the holding of two U.S. citizens—Jose Padilla and Yasser Hamdi—in military brigs. Neither was charged with a crime. Neither was allowed counsel.

Padilla, also known as Abdullah Al-Mujahir, an ex-Chicago gang member, is being held under suspicion of being an Al Qaeda operative who was allegedly researching how to detonate a radioactive bomb.

Hamdi was taken into custody in Afghanistan and was interrogated there by a military screening team.

Neither Padilla nor Hamdi has been allowed to meet with an attorney, much less appear before a judge to contest the detention. The administration claims it can hold both of them (and others it may deem "enemy combatants" down the road) for as long as the war on terrorism goes on.

"This seems to me the classic case for habeas corpus," said Georgetown University law professor Mark Tushnet, who was quoted in the *Los Angeles Times*. "They don't get to say, 'This is a bad guy, and we can do with him what we want.'"

Federal District Court Judge Robert G. Doumar agreed. He heard a challenge by a public defender in Hamdi's case. "This case appears to be the first in American jurisprudence where an American citizen has been held incommunicado and subjected to an indefinite detention in the continental United States without charges, without any findings by a military tribunal, and without access to a lawyer," Judge Doumar wrote. When the government tried to defend Hamdi's detention, the judge asked the Attorney General's lawyer, "So, the Constitution doesn't apply to Mr. Hamdi?"

The American Civil Liberties Union has filed suit on behalf of Padilla and Hamdi. On December 4, U.S. District Judge Michael Mukasey gave civil libertarians a respite when he ruled that alleged "dirty bomber" Jose Padilla can have his status as an "enemy combatant" reviewed in a federal court and that he must have access to counsel in the interim.

"This ruling is a crucial rejection of the Bush Administration's claim of almost unbridled power to unilaterally detain American citizens and hold them indefinitely and incommunicado," said Lucas Guttentag, director of the American Civil

Liberties Union's Immigrant Rights Project, after the ruling. "The decision is a critical first step to providing a check on the government's use of the enemy combatant designation."

But not all courts have seen the light. On November 18, the Foreign Intelligence Surveillance Court of Review, established in 1978 to oversee domestic spying activities, gave the government even broader powers to snoop and sniff about the lives of ordinary Americans. What makes this new proclamation ghastly is that the court's proceedings are held in secret, its members are hand-picked by Chief Justice William Rehnquist, and the government is the only entity allowed to appear before it. Sounds like some ludicrous Stalinist-era kangaroo court, but it's right here in the good ol' U.S.A.

"The decision gives the government a green light to tear down the wall that has long existed between officials conducting surveillance on suspected foreign agents and criminal prosecutors investigating crimes," says a *New York Times* editorial from November 19. "Attorney General John Ashcroft has announced that he intends to use it to sharply increase the number of domestic wiretaps, and that he will add lawyers at the FBI and at federal prosecutors' offices around the country to hurry the process along."

The Bush Administration has constructed a repugnant parallel legal system for terrorism in which suspects, according to the *Washington Post*, could be "investigated, jailed, interrogated, tried, and punished without conventional legal protections."

The *Post* reports the new system includes indefinite detention for those—like Padilla and Hamdi—who are designated "enemy combatants." And it also includes a radically expanded use of "material witness" warrants, wiretaps, and searches.

Administration officials told the *Washington Post* that this parallel system is meant to be used selectively, "but is needed because terrorism is a form of war as well as a form of crime, and it must not only be punished after incidents occur, but also prevented and disrupted through the gathering of timely intelligence."

This is the biggest power grab since Attorney General A. Mitchell Palmer conducted his communist hunts under Woodrow Wilson!

The government wishes not to be disturbed in this war against terrorism. The government wishes not to be accountable to anyone, least of all the citizens it says it wishes to protect. Ashcroft's attitude is simple: If the government abuses some people in this fight, so be it. It's a war, and the casualties of a few are outweighed by the protection of the many.

It is this attitude that reduces the Constitution and the Bill of Rights to collateral damage.

RAMESH PONNURU
1984 in 2003?

Has the war on terrorism become a war on Americans' civil liberties? A coalition of left- and right-wing groups fears so, and has been working hard to restrain the law-and-order impulses of the Bush administration. It's a coalition that includes the ACLU and the American Conservative Union, Nat Hentoff and William Safire, John Conyers and Dick Armey.

The coalition started to form in 1996, when Congress passed an anti-terrorism bill. But it really took off after September 11. Members of the coalition believe that Washington's legislative response—called, rather ludicrously, the "USA Patriot Act," an acronym for "Uniting and Strengthening America by Providing Appropriate Tools to Intercept and Obstruct Terrorism"—was a too-hastily conceived, excessive reaction to the atrocities.

Since then, the coalition has regularly found new cause for alarm. It has protested the administration's plans for military tribunals, the president's designation of "enemy combatants," and the Pentagon's attempts to consolidate data under a program called "Total Information Awareness." This spring, the civil libertarians of left and right worked together again to block Sen. Orrin Hatch's attempt to make permanent those provisions of the Patriot Act which are set to expire next year. They have organized, as well, against the possibility that the Justice Department will propose another dangerous anti-terror bill ("Patriot II").

The civil libertarians have had some success. They forced modifications in the Patriot Act before its enactment. They have inspired some cities to pass resolutions banning their employees from cooperating with federal authorities to implement provisions of the act that violate the Constitution. (Officials in other cities are, presumably, free to violate the Constitution at will.) They imposed legislative restrictions on Total Information Awareness. They have inhibited the administration from proposing anti-terror measures that would generate adverse publicity.

They themselves have gotten favorable publicity. It's an irresistible story for the press: the lion and the lamb lying down together. The press has tended to marvel at the mere existence of the coalition. They have not been quick to note that there is a larger bipartisan coalition on the other side, which is why the civil libertarians have been losing most of the battles. The Patriot Act passed 357–66 in the House and 98–1 in the Senate. In early May, the Senate voted 90–4 to approve another anti-terror provision—making it easier to investigate "lone wolf terrorists" with no proven connection to larger organizations—that the civil libertarians oppose.

More important, the press has not adequately scrutinized the civil libertarians' claims. This has kept the debate mired in platitudes about liberty and security. It has also reduced the incentive for the civil libertarians to do their homework, which has in turn made their case both weaker and more hysterical than it might otherwise have been.

Take the attack on TIPS, the Terrorist Information and Prevention System. This abortive plan would have encouraged truckers, deliverymen, and the like to report suspicious behavior they observed in the course of their work. How effective this idea would have been is open to question. Most of the criticism, however, echoed former Republican congressman Bob Barr, who said that TIPS "smacks of the very type of fascist or communist government we fought so hard to eradicate in other countries in decades past."

But of all the measures the administration has adopted, it's the Patriot Act (along with the possible Patriot II) that has inspired the most overheated criticisms. When it was passed, the Electronic Frontier Foundation wrote that "the civil liberties of ordinary Americans have taken a tremendous blow with this law." The ACLU says the law "gives the Executive Branch sweeping new powers that undermine the Bill of Rights." But most of the concerns about Patriot are misguided or based on premises that are just plain wrong.

Roving wiretaps. Thanks to the Patriot Act, terrorism investigations can use roving wiretaps. Instead of having to get new judicial authorization for each phone number tapped, investigators can tap any phone their target uses. This is important when fighting terrorists whose MO includes frequently switching hotel rooms and cell phones. It's a common-sense measure. It's also nothing new: Congress authorized roving wiretaps in ordinary criminal cases back in 1986. It's hard to see Patriot as a blow to civil liberties on this score.

Internet surveillance. Libertarians have been particularly exercised about Patriot's green light for "spying on the Web browsers of people who are not even criminal suspects"—to quote *Reason* editor Nick Gillespie. This is a misunderstanding of Patriot, as George Washington University law professor Orin Kerr has demonstrated in a law-review article. Before Patriot, it wasn't clear that any statute limited the government's, or even a private party's, ability to obtain basic information about electronic communications (e.g., to whom you're sending e-mails). Patriot required a court order to get that information, and made it a federal crime to get it without one.

Kerr believes that the bar for getting a court order should be raised. But he notes that Patriot made the privacy protections for the Internet as strong as those for phone calls and stronger than for mail. Patriot's Internet provisions, he concludes, "updated the surveillance laws without substantially shifting the balance between privacy and security."

James Bovard traffics in another Patriot myth in a recent cover story for *The American Conservative*: that it "empowers federal agents to cannibalize Americans' e-mail with Carnivore wiretaps." Carnivore is an Internet surveillance tool designed by the FBI. Don't be scared by the name. The FBI's previous tool was dubbed "Omnivore," and this new one was so named because it would be more selective in acquiring information, getting only what was covered by a court order and leaving other information private. But even if Carnivore is a menace, it's not the fault of Patriot. As Kerr points out, "The only provisions of the Patriot Act that directly address Carnivore are pro-privacy provisions that actually restrict the use of Carnivore."

Hacking. Also in *Reason*, Jesse Walker writes that Patriot "expands the definition of terrorist to include such non-lethal acts as computer hacking." That's misleading. Pre-Patriot, an al-Qaeda member who hacked the electric company's computers to take out the grid could not be judged guilty of terrorism, even if he would be so judged if he accomplished the same result with a bomb. Hacking per se isn't terrorism, and Patriot doesn't treat it as such.

Sneak and peek. The ACLU is running ads that say that Patriot lets the government "secretly enter your home while you're away . . . rifle through your personal belongings . . . download your computer files . . . and seize any items at will." Worst of all, "you may never know what the government has done." Reality check: You will be notified if a sneak-and-peek search has been done, just after the fact—usually within a few days. The feds had the authority to conduct these searches before Patriot. A federal judge has to authorize such a search warrant, and the warrant has to specify what's to be seized.

Library records. Bovard is appalled that Patriot allows "federal agents to commandeer library records," and the American Library Association shares his sentiment. Patriot doesn't mention libraries specifically, but does authorize terrorism investigators to collect tangible records generally. Law enforcement has, however, traditionally been able to obtain library records with a subpoena. Prof. Kerr suggests that because of Patriot, the privacy of library records may be better protected in terrorism investigations than it is in ordinary criminal ones.

The civil libertarians deserve some credit. Their objections helped to rid Patriot of some provisions—such as a crackdown on Internet gambling—that didn't belong in an anti-terrorism bill. Armey added the Carnivore protections to the bill. The law, as finally enacted, places limits on how much officials may disclose of the information they gain from Internet and phone surveillance. Moreover, the civil libertarians make a reasonable demand when they ask that Patriot be subject to periodic re-authorizations, so that Congress can regularly consider making modifications.

The civil libertarians rarely acknowledge the costs of legal laxity: Restrictions on intelligence gathering may well have impeded the investigation of Zacarias Moussaoui, the "twentieth hijacker," before 9/11. David Cole, one of the movement's favorite law professors, goes so far as to lament that U.S. law makes "mere membership in a terrorist group grounds for exclusion and deportation."

And while civil libertarians may scant the value of Patriot, terrorists do not. Jeffrey Battle, an accused member of a terrorist cell in Portland, complained about Patriot in a recorded phone call that was recently released in court. People were less willing to provide financial support, he said, now that they were more likely to be punished for it.

Speaking of the administration's civil-liberties record, Al Gore said last year that President Bush has "taken the most fateful step in the direction of [a] Big Brother nightmare that any president has ever allowed to occur." Dick Armey worries about "the lust for power that these people in the Department of Justice have." The civil-liberties debate could use a lot less rhetoric of this sort—and a lot more attention to detail.

A calm look at the Patriot Act shows that it's less of a threat to civil liberties than, say, campaign-finance reform. A lot of the controversy is the result of confusion. Opponents of the Patriot Act are fond of complaining that few people have bothered to read it. No kidding.

DISCUSSION QUESTIONS

1. *What would you do?* You are a federal judge who must decide on the due process rights of suspected "enemy combatants." Should they have the same rights as all suspected criminals, or should the war on terrorism be given a different status in our legal system?

2. One of the authors was speaking to a community group shortly after the attacks of 9/11 about the tradeoff between security and freedom. After the presentation, a person in the audience made the following argument: "I have nothing to hide. I don't care if the government taps my phone or checks my email. I am happy to have them do that if we can catch some terrorists. These laws only infringe on the civil liberties of the guilty, not the innocent." What do you make of this argument? Could this logic be applied more broadly to police power more generally and fighting crime? If so, how much of an expansion of police power would be justified? Where does one draw the line between security and freedom?

3. President Bush has said that the government will not torture suspected terrorists who have been arrested to find out more about their terrorist operations. Do you think the government would ever be justified in torturing a suspect? What if he or she had information about a nuclear bomb that was about to be detonated in New York City, killing millions of people?

5   Affirmative Action in Higher Education

The Civil Rights Act of 1964 ensured, at least on paper, that all Americans would enjoy equality of opportunity. But even after the Act was passed, blacks continued to lag behind whites in socio-economic status because of enduring racism and gross inequalities in the distribution of income and the quality of education. Beginning in 1965, President Johnson tried to address these inequalities with a policy of affirmative action. By executive order, Johnson required all federal agencies and government contractors to submit written proposals to hire certain numbers of blacks, women, Asian Americans, and Native Americans within various job categories. Throughout the 1970s and 1980s, affirmative action programs grew in the private sector and throughout higher education as well. Through such programs, employers and universities sometimes gave preferential treatment to minorities and women, either to make up for past patterns of discrimination or to pursue the general goals of diversity.

Affirmative action in higher education has been a hotly contested area of the law in recent years. This was not always the case. The 1978 *Bakke* decision struck down racial quotas, but allowed race to be used in admissions decisions as a "plus factor" to promote diversity in the student body. This process was widely followed and largely unquestioned until 1996, when the Fifth Circuit Court of Appeals held that it was unconstitutional to consider race in law school admissions at the University of Texas. More recently a circuit court in Washington reached the opposite conclusion, and even more puzzling were two conflicting cases from the University of Michigan. A December 2000 district court case held that race-conscious undergraduate admissions was acceptable, but a decision a few months later in the same district court held that considering race in law school admissions was not constitutional. A deeply divided Supreme Court recently sorted out this mess in two decisions that upheld the *Bakke* principle of using race as a "plus factor" in admissions decisions (*Grutter v. Bollinger*), but struck down the point system used by the University of Michigan for undergraduate admissions for being too rigid in the application of affirmative action (*Gratz v. Bollinger*).

The crucial legal question was whether "viewpoint diversity," the idea that affirmative action brings diversity to classroom discussions, constituted a "compelling state interest" that allowed the university to make racial distinctions that would otherwise be barred by the Fourteenth Amendment's equal protection clause. There were differences of opinion on whether racial diversity produced viewpoint diversity and the validity of Michigan's argument about the "critical mass" necessary to produce viewpoint diversity. Justice Rehnquist pointed out that the necessary "critical mass" seemed to vary directly with the size of the applicant pool for a given racial group (e.g., the number of Native Americans needed to provide viewpoint diversity was much smaller than the number of African Americans), causing him to question the entire argument. Clarence Thomas's dissent in the *Grutter* case strongly rejects the viewpoint-diversity argument, claiming that racial classifications of any type should not be allowed unless there is a compelling state interest. Justice Thomas also decries the distinction between benign and invidious racial classifications, arguing that racial classifications of any type are bad. Much of his dissent is intensely personal; as the only African American on the Court, Justice Thomas is acutely aware that he benefited from affirmative action himself yet his strong objections to the practice come through loud and clear.

The Clinical Legal Education Association disagrees, saying that racial diversity is crucial to legal education because of the viewpoint diversity that it provides. While some of their arguments are specific to law-school clinics, their general points about the value of racial diversity was shared by scores of other parties who filed briefs on behalf of the University of Michigan. Many Fortune 500 corporations sided with the University, saying that affirmative action was necessary to provide them with the racially diverse workforce that is necessary to compete in the multicultural, international business environment. The CLEA brief also addresses the legal question of a "compelling state interest" and argues that the "critical mass" necessary to provide viewpoint diversity does not constitute arbitrary quotas. The Supreme Court has resolved the legal questions concerning affirmative action for now, but the issue remains controversial in higher education and the workplace.

JUSTICE CLARENCE THOMAS
Dissent in *Barbara Grutter v. Lee Bollinger, et al.* (2003)

JUSTICE THOMAS, with whom JUSTICE SCALIA joins as to Parts I-VII, concurring in part and dissenting in part.

Frederick Douglass, speaking to a group of abolitionists almost 140 years ago, delivered a message lost on today's majority:

> In regard to the colored people, there is always more that is benevolent, I perceive, than just, manifested towards us. What I ask for the negro is not benevolence, not pity, not sympathy, but simply justice. The American people have always been anxious to know what they shall do with us. . . . I have had but one answer from the beginning. Do nothing with us! Your doing with us has already played the mischief with us. Do nothing with us! If the apples will not remain on the tree of their own strength, if they are worm-eaten at the core, if they are early ripe and disposed to fall, let them fall! . . . And if the negro cannot stand on his own legs, let him fall also. All I ask is, give him a chance to stand on his own legs! Let him alone! . . . Your interference is doing him positive injury.

Like Douglass, I believe blacks can achieve in every avenue of American life without the meddling of university administrators. Because I wish to see all students succeed whatever their color, I share, in some respect, the sympathies of those who sponsor the type of discrimination advanced by the University of Michigan Law School (the "Law School"). The Constitution does not, however, tolerate institutional devotion to the status quo in admissions policies when such devotion ripens into racial discrimination. Nor does the Constitution countenance the unprecedented deference the Court gives to the Law School, an approach inconsistent with the very concept of "strict scrutiny."

No one would argue that a university could set up a lower general admission standard and then impose heightened requirements only on black applicants. Similarly, a university may not maintain a high admission standard and grant exemptions to favored races. The Law School, of its own choosing, and for its own purposes, maintains an exclusionary admissions system that it knows produces racially disproportionate results. Racial discrimination is not a permissible solution to the self-inflicted wounds of this elitist admissions policy. . . .

[Here Thomas examines the majority opinion and the legal standard of strict scrutiny.]

The Constitution abhors classifications based on race, not only because those classifications can harm favored races or are based on illegitimate motives, but also because every time the government places citizens on racial registers and makes race relevant to the provision of burdens or benefits, it demeans us all. "Purchased at the price of immeasurable human suffering, the equal protection principle reflects our Nation's understanding that such classifications ultimately have a destructive impact on the individual and our society" [*Adarand Construction, Inc. v. Pena*, 1995].

II

Unlike the majority, I seek to define with precision the interest being asserted by the Law School before determining whether that interest is so compelling as to justify racial discrimination. The Law School maintains that it wishes to obtain "educational benefits that flow from student body diversity." This statement must be evaluated carefully, because it implies that both "diversity" and "educational benefits" are components of the Law School's compelling state interest. Additionally, the Law School's refusal to entertain certain changes in its admissions process and status indicates that the compelling state interest it seeks to validate is actually broader than might appear at first glance.

Undoubtedly there are other ways to "better" the education of law students aside from ensuring that the student body contains a "critical mass" of underrepresented minority students. Attaining "diversity," whatever it means, is the mechanism by which the Law School obtains educational benefits, not an end of itself. The Law School, however, apparently believes that only a racially mixed student body can lead to the educational benefits it seeks. How, then, is the Law School's interest in these allegedly unique educational "benefits" not simply the forbidden interest in "racial balancing," that the majority expressly rejects?

A distinction between these two ideas (unique educational benefits based on racial aesthetics and race for its own sake) is purely sophistic—so much so that the majority uses them interchangeably. . . . The Law School's argument, as facile as it is, can only be understood in one way: Classroom aesthetics yields educational benefits, racially discriminatory admissions policies are required to achieve the right racial mix, and therefore the policies are required to achieve the educational benefits. It is the educational benefits that are the end, or allegedly compelling state interest, not "diversity."

One must also consider the Law School's refusal to entertain changes to its current admissions system that might produce the same educational benefits. The Law School adamantly disclaims any race-neutral alternative that would reduce "academic selectivity," which would in turn "require the Law School to become a very different institution, and to sacrifice a core part of its educational mission." In other words, the Law School seeks to improve marginally the education it offers without sacrificing too much of its exclusivity and elite status.

The proffered interest that the majority vindicates today, then, is not simply "diversity." Instead the Court upholds the use of racial discrimination as a tool to advance the Law School's interest in offering a marginally superior education while maintaining an elite institution. Unless each constituent part of this state interest is of pressing public necessity, the Law School's use of race is unconstitutional. I find each of them to fall far short of this standard.

III

A

A close reading of the Court's opinion reveals that all of its legal work is done through one conclusory statement: The Law School has a "compelling interest in securing the educational benefits of a diverse student body." No serious effort is made to explain how these benefits fit with the state interests the Court has recognized (or rejected) as compelling, or to place any theoretical constraints on an enterprising court's desire to discover still more justifications for racial discrimination. In the absence of any explanation, one might expect the Court to fall back on the judicial policy of *stare decisis*. But the Court eschews even this weak defense of its holding, shunning an analysis of the extent to which Justice Powell's opinion in *Regents of Univ. of Cal. v. Bakke* (1978), is binding, in favor of an unfounded wholesale adoption of it.

Justice Powell's opinion in *Bakke* and the Court's decision today rest on the fundamentally flawed proposition that racial discrimination can be contextualized so that a goal, such as classroom aesthetics, can be compelling in one context but not in another. This "we know it when we see it" approach to evaluating state interests is not capable of judicial application. Today, the Court insists on radically expanding the range of permissible uses of race to something as trivial (by comparison) as the assembling of a law school class. I can only presume that the majority's failure to justify its decision by reference to any principle arises from the absence of any such principle. . . .

[Here Thomas develops the argument that Michigan does not have a "compelling state interest" in maintaining an elite public law school. He says that the Law

School could simply accept "all students who meet minimum qualifications" rather than engage in racial discrimination].

A

The Court bases its unprecedented deference to the Law School—a deference antithetical to strict scrutiny—on an idea of "educational autonomy" grounded in the First Amendment. In my view, there is no basis for a right of public universities to do what would otherwise violate the Equal Protection Clause. . . .

[Here Thomas develops his argument that First Amendment protections of academic freedom do not allow universities to violate the Equal Protection Clause of the Fourteenth Amendment].

B

1

The Court's deference to the Law School's conclusion that its racial experimentation leads to educational benefits will, if adhered to, have serious collateral consequences. The Court relies heavily on social science evidence to justify its deference. The Court never acknowledges, however, the growing evidence that racial (and other sorts) of heterogeneity actually impairs learning among black students.

At oral argument in *Gratz v. Bollinger*, counsel for respondents stated that "most every single one of [the Historically Black Colleges, HBCs] do have diverse student bodies." What precisely counsel meant by "diverse" is indeterminate, but it is reported that in 2000 at Morehouse College, one of the most distinguished HBCs in the Nation, only 0.1 percent of the student body was white, and only 0.2 percent was Hispanic. And at Mississippi Valley State University, a public HBC, only 1.1 percent of the freshman class in 2001 was white. If there is a "critical mass" of whites at these institutions, then "critical mass" is indeed a very small proportion.

The majority grants deference to the Law School's "assessment that diversity will, in fact, yield educational benefits." It follows, therefore, that an HBC's assessment that racial homogeneity will yield educational benefits would similarly be given deference. An HBC's rejection of white applicants in order to maintain racial homogeneity seems permissible, therefore, under the majority's view of the Equal Protection Clause. Contained within today's majority opinion is the seed of a new constitutional justification for a concept I thought long and rightly rejected—racial segregation.

2

Moreover, one would think, in light of the Court's decision in *United States v. Virginia* (1996), that before being given license to use racial discrimination, the Law School would be required to radically reshape its admissions process, even to the point of sacrificing some elements of its character. In *Virginia*, a majority of the Court, without a word about academic freedom, accepted the all-male Virginia Military Institute's (VMI) representation that some changes in its "adversative" method of education would be required with the admission of women, but did not defer to VMI's judgment that these changes would be too great. Instead, the Court concluded that they were "manageable." That case involved sex discrimination, which is subjected to intermediate, not strict, scrutiny. So in *Virginia*, where the standard of review dictated that greater flexibility be granted to VMI's educational policies than the Law School deserves here, this Court gave no deference. Apparently where the status quo being defended is that of the elite establishment—here the Law School—rather than a less fashionable Southern military institution, the Court will defer without serious inquiry and without regard to the applicable legal standard.

C

Virginia is also notable for the fact that the Court relied on the "experience" of formerly single-sex institutions, such as the service academies, to conclude that admission of women to VMI would be "manageable." Today, however, the majority ignores the "experience" of those institutions that have been forced to abandon explicit racial discrimination in admissions.

The sky has not fallen at Boalt Hall at the University of California, Berkeley, for example. Prior to Proposition 209's adoption of Cal. Const., Art. 1, § 31(a), which bars the State from "granting preferential treatment . . . on the basis of race . . . in the operation of . . . public education," Boalt Hall enrolled 20 blacks and 28 Hispanics in its first-year class for 1996. In 2002, without deploying express racial discrimination in admissions, Boalt's entering class enrolled 14 blacks and 36 Hispanics. University of California Law and Medical School Enrollments (available at http://www.ucop.edu/acadadv/ datamgmt/ lawmed/ law-enrolls-eth2.html.) Total underrepresented minority student enrollment at Boalt Hall now exceeds 1996 levels. Apparently the Law School cannot be counted on to be as resourceful. The Court is willfully blind to the very real experience in California and elsewhere, which raises the inference that institutions with "reputations for excellence," rivaling the Law School's have satisfied their sense of mission without resorting to prohibited racial discrimination.

V

Putting aside the absence of any legal support for the majority's reflexive deference, there is much to be said for the view that the use of tests and other measures to "predict" academic performance is a poor substitute for a system that gives every applicant a chance to prove he can succeed in the study of law. The rallying cry that in the absence of racial discrimination in admissions there would be a true meritocracy ignores the fact that the entire process is poisoned by numerous exceptions to "merit." For example, in the national debate on racial discrimination in higher education admissions, much has been made of the fact that elite institutions utilize a so-called legacy preference to give the children of alumni an advantage in admissions. This and other exceptions to a "true" meritocracy give the lie to protestations that merit admissions are in fact the order of the day at the nation's universities. The Equal Protection Clause does not, however, prohibit the use of unseemly legacy preferences or many other kinds of arbitrary admissions procedures. What the

Equal Protection Clause does prohibit are classifications made on the basis of race. So while legacy preferences can stand under the Constitution, racial discrimination cannot. I will not twist the Constitution to invalidate legacy preferences or otherwise impose my vision of higher education admissions on the nation. The majority should similarly stay its impulse to validate faddish racial discrimination the Constitution clearly forbids.

In any event, there is nothing ancient, honorable, or constitutionally protected about "selective" admissions. The University of Michigan should be well aware that alternative methods have historically been used for the admission of students, for it brought to this country the German certificate system in the late-nineteenth century. Under this system, a secondary school was certified by a university so that any graduate who completed the course offered by the school was offered admission to the university. The certification regime supplemented, and later virtually replaced (at least in the Midwest), the prior regime of rigorous subject-matter entrance examinations. The facially race-neutral "percent plans" now used in Texas, California, and Florida, are in many ways the descendents [sic] of the certificate system.

Certification was replaced by selective admissions in the beginning of the twentieth century, as universities sought to exercise more control over the composition of their student bodies. Since its inception, selective admissions has been the vehicle for racial, ethnic, and religious tinkering and experimentation by university administrators. The initial driving force for the relocation of the selective function from the high school to the universities was the same desire to select racial winners and losers that the Law School exhibits today. Columbia, Harvard, and others infamously determined that they had "too many" Jews, just as today the Law School argues it would have "too many" whites if it could not discriminate in its admissions process.

Columbia employed intelligence tests precisely because Jewish applicants, who were predominantly immigrants, scored worse on such tests. Thus, Columbia could claim (falsely) that "'we have not eliminated boys because they were Jews and do not propose to do so. We have honestly attempted to eliminate the lowest grade of applicant [through the use of intelligence testing] and it turns out that a good many of the low grade men are New York City Jews.'"

Similarly, no modern law school can claim ignorance of the poor performance of blacks, relatively speaking, on the Law School Admissions Test (LSAT). Nevertheless, law schools continue to use the test and then attempt to "correct" for black underperformance by using racial discrimination in admissions so as to obtain their aesthetic student body. The Law School's continued adherence to measures it knows produce racially skewed results is not entitled to deference by this Court. The Law School itself admits that the test is imperfect, as it must, given that it regularly admits students who score at or below 150 (the national median) on the test (between 1995 and 2000, the Law School admitted 37 students—27 of whom were black; 31 of whom were "underrepresented minorities"—with LSAT scores of 150 or lower). . . .

Having decided to use the LSAT, the Law School must accept the constitutional burdens that come with this decision. The Law School may freely continue to employ the LSAT and other allegedly merit-based standards in whatever fashion it likes. What the Equal Protection Clause forbids, but the Court today allows, is the use of these standards hand in hand with racial discrimination. An infinite variety of admissions methods are available to the Law School. Considering all of the radical thinking that has historically occurred at this country's universities, the Law School's intractable approach toward admissions is striking.

The Court will not even deign to make the Law School try other methods, however, preferring instead to grant a twenty-five-year license to violate the Constitution. And the same Court that had the courage to order the desegregation of all public schools in the South now fears, on the basis of platitudes rather than principle, to force the Law School to abandon a decidedly imperfect admissions regime that provides the basis for racial discrimination.

VI

The absence of any articulated legal principle supporting the majority's principal holding suggests another rationale. I believe what lies beneath the Court's decision today are the benighted notions that one can tell when racial discrimination benefits (rather than hurts) minority groups, and that racial discrimination is necessary to remedy general societal ills. This Court's precedents supposedly settled both issues, but clearly the majority still cannot commit to the principle that racial classifications are per se harmful and that almost no amount of benefit in the eye of the beholder can justify such classifications.

Putting aside what I take to be the Court's implicit rejection of *Adarand*'s holding that beneficial and burdensome racial classifications are equally invalid, I must contest the notion that the Law School's discrimination benefits those admitted as a result of it. The Court spends considerable time discussing the impressive display of amicus support for the Law School, in this case from all corners of society. But nowhere in any of the filings in this Court is any evidence that the purported "beneficiaries" of this racial discrimination prove themselves by performing at (or even near) the same level as those students who receive no preferences.

The silence in this case is deafening to those of us who view higher education's purpose as imparting knowledge and skills to students, rather than a communal, rubber-stamp, credentialing process. The Law School is not looking for those students who, despite a lower LSAT score or undergraduate grade point average, will succeed in the study of law. The Law School seeks only a facade—it is sufficient that the class looks right, even if it does not perform right.

The Law School tantalizes unprepared students with the promise of a University of Michigan degree and all of the opportunities that it offers. These overmatched students take the bait, only to find that they cannot succeed in the cauldron of competition. And this mismatch crisis is not restricted to elite institutions. Indeed, to cover the tracks of the aestheticists, this cruel farce of racial discrimination must continue—in selection for the Michigan Law Review, and in hiring at law firms and for judicial clerkships—until the "beneficiaries" are no longer tolerated. While these students may graduate with law degrees, there is no evidence that they have received a qualitatively better legal education (or become better lawyers) than if they had gone to a less "elite" law school for which they were better prepared. And the aestheticists will never address the real problems facing "underrepresented minorities," instead continuing their social experiments on other people's children.

Beyond the harm the Law School's racial discrimination visits upon its test subjects, no social science has disproved the notion that this discrimination "engenders attitudes of superiority or, alternatively, provokes resentment among those who believe that they have been wronged by the government's use of race. These programs stamp minorities with a badge of inferiority and may cause them to develop dependencies or to adopt an attitude that they are 'entitled' to preferences" (quoted in *Adarand*).

It is uncontested that each year the Law School admits a handful of blacks who would be admitted in the absence of racial discrimination. Who can differentiate between those who belong and those who do not? The majority of blacks are admitted to the Law School because of discrimination, and because of this policy all are tarred as undeserving. This problem of stigma does not depend on determinacy as to whether those stigmatized are actually the "beneficiaries" of racial discrimination. When blacks take positions in the highest places of government, industry, or academia, it is an open question today whether their skin color played a part in their advancement. The question itself is the stigma—because either racial discrimination did play a role, in which case the person may be deemed "otherwise unqualified," or it did not, in which case asking the question itself unfairly marks those blacks who would succeed without discrimination. Is this what the Court means by "visibly open"?

Finally, the Court's disturbing reference to the importance of the country's law schools as training grounds meant to cultivate "a set of leaders with legitimacy in the eyes of the citizenry" through the use of racial discrimination deserves discussion. As noted earlier, the Court has soundly rejected the remedying of societal discrimination as a justification for governmental use of race. For those who believe that every racial disproportionality in our society is caused by some kind of racial discrimination, there can be no distinction between remedying societal discrimination and erasing racial disproportionalities in the country's leadership caste. And if the lack of proportional racial representation among our leaders is not caused by societal discrimination, then "fixing" it is even less of a pressing public necessity. . . .

[Here Justice Thomas agrees with the majority opinion on two relatively minor points: that discrimination among preferred groups (such as Hispanics and African Americans) is unconstitutional and that after twenty-five years an admissions plan such as the Law School's would no longer be "narrowly tailored" (though Thomas argues that is true today as well).]

* * *

For the immediate future, however, the majority has placed its imprimatur on a practice that can only weaken the principle of equality embodied in the Declaration of Independence and the Equal Protection Clause. "Our Constitution is color-blind, and neither knows nor tolerates classes among citizens" (*Plessy v. Ferguson*, 1896).

It has been nearly 140 years since Frederick Douglass asked the intellectual ancestors of the Law School to "do nothing with us!" and the nation adopted the Fourteenth Amendment. Now we must wait another twenty-five years to see this
principle of equality vindicated. I therefore respectfully dissent from the remainder
of the Court's opinion and the judgment.

TIMOTHY A. NELSEN, FRANCES P. KAO, ERIC J. GORMAN, AND AMY M. GARDNER

Brief of the Clinical Legal Education Association as Amicus Curiae
Supporting Respondents, in *Barbara Grutter v. Lee Bollinger*, et al.
(2003)

BARBARA GRUTTER, Petitioner, v. LEE BOLLINGER, et al., Respondents

No. 02-241

2002 U.S. Briefs 241

February 18, 2003

Brief of the Clinical Legal Education Association as Amicus Curiae Supporting
Respondents[1]

Timothy A. Nelsen, Counsel of Record, Frances P. Kao, Eric J. Gorman, Amy M.
Gardner

INTEREST OF AMICUS CURIAE

The Clinical Legal Education Association (CLEA) is a nonprofit organization dedicated to expanding and improving clinical legal education; encouraging, promoting,
and supporting clinical legal research and scholarship; and fostering communication among clinical law professors. CLEA works cooperatively with other organizations interested in improving clinical and legal education, as well as the legal
system itself. CLEA currently counts as members more than 600 clinical law professors nationwide, who teach at approximately 180 of the 186 law schools accred-
ited by the American Bar Association (ABA).

Personal experience, student feedback, and the academic analyses and writings
of CLEA's members demonstrate that viewpoint diversity and racial diversity are
critically important in training young lawyers to be effective advisors and advocates, both while studying in the legal clinics of America's law schools, and after

[1]Legal citations and references for quotes are omitted. For the sources of internal quotations see the ori-
ignal document at clrn.law.cuny.edu/clea/clea%20grutter.pdf.

graduation, when new lawyers enter the increasingly multicultural, multijurisdictional, and global practice of law.

CLEA believes that, should admissions practices such as the one adopted by The University of Michigan Law School (the "Law School") be forbidden, it would be extremely difficult, if not impossible, to achieve the necessary diversity in the student bodies of our law schools. As this brief explains, diverse law school student bodies aid all law students, majority and minority alike, by enhancing their exposure to people from different backgrounds and perspectives. This exposure to different backgrounds and perspectives, in turn, better equips students to render competent, ethical representation to all of their clients. . . .

ARGUMENT

To be constitutional, the Law School's consideration of race in its admissions process must (1) be a narrowly tailored measure and (2) serve a compelling governmental interest. This brief will address only the compelling state interests served by the Law School's policy as it affects law school clinics and their clients.

I. The State Has a Compelling Interest in Enrolling a Diverse Law School Student Body

A. All Law Students Benefit from Racially and Ethnically Diverse Student Bodies

All students, regardless of ethnic origin, benefit from a diverse law school student body because it provides exposure to people different from themselves. A diverse law school student body allows all students opportunities to learn to work with people of different backgrounds—a critical skill as the practice of law becomes more multicultural. Indeed, some estimates predict that the percentage of persons of color in the United States population will roughly equal the percentage of Caucasians as early as the year 2030. As a result of the demographic shift, the need for clinical educators to prepare law students to represent all clients and to understand their points of view fully will become increasingly important, "because that pluralism often introduces an extra layer of complexity to legal disputes and may create special challenges in representing diverse clients."

Further, a diverse collection of law students creates opportunities for those students, in their clinical, classroom, journal, and social interactions, to confront their own stereotypes and prejudices, and gain the ability to better critically analyze their own views. These benefits are particularly important in the clinical setting, where student-lawyers see firsthand how their own stereotypes and assumptions may impede their obligation to render ethically competent representation to, and to communicate with, clients as required by ethics rules.

B. The Focus of Clinical Legal Education Is to Prepare Student-Lawyers to Enter into a Multicultural, Global Legal Profession

In explaining why diversity is so critical to clinical legal education, there first must be an assessment of the goal for which law schools in general and clinical educators in particular are preparing students. Clearly, that goal is to become highly skilled, effective, and responsible attorneys, whether in private practice, business, government, or in some other capacity.

Since the United States is multicultural, and is becoming increasingly so, the practice of law must take this fact into account. As an objective and practical matter, the legal profession also is increasingly becoming global. Regardless of the context, lawyers are more and more faced with arrays of problems that involve multicultural considerations, from traditional constructs of contract or tort law, to providing assistance to individuals from different racial and ethnic backgrounds to enforce consumer rights or procure housing, to the criminal prosecution or defense of people of different racial backgrounds. As for private law firms, the multicultural practice is even more significant. "The question is not . . . whether or not diversity is 'good for business' but rather whether global law firms can successfully adapt to a competitive environment that will by any measure be more multicultural, multidisciplinary, and multidimensional than anything that these firms have ever faced before."

As both society and the profession become more diverse, "it will be incumbent upon lawyers to seek out and give voice to a range of viewpoints in stating legal problems and fashioning their solutions." Proper clinical education must equip students to do just this in order to practice effectively, both as student-lawyers and as future lawyers. It is from this pragmatic clinical education goal that the need for diversity arises. * * *

[Here the brief cites the importance of clinical education, quoting Justice O'Connor.]

1. Law School Clinics Serve a Predominantly Minority Client Base

American law school clinics generally represent underprivileged clients. Depending on the law school program, student-lawyers in law clinics may be expected to defend indigent criminal defendants, or to work on cases involving child advocacy, poverty law, low-income housing, civil rights, and asylum and refugee law. The reality is that, in most instances, 60 percent or more of the underprivileged clients who use the services of law clinics consist of minorities with cultural and economic backgrounds, education levels, viewpoints, and sensibilities different from the student-lawyer. This exposure to a largely minority client base is frequently the first step in preparing young lawyers to enter the multicultural national legal market and the growing global legal profession in which they may routinely be faced with clients and problems that require a genuine ability to understand diverse cultural and racial sensibilities.

2. Student-Lawyers are Better Able to Provide Effective Client-Centered Counseling with Exposure to a Diverse Population of Law Students

(a) Client-Centered Counseling Demands Genuine Understanding of Each Client's Interests and Objectives

Over the last decade, the vast majority of law school clinical programs have concluded that the lawyer-client relationship requires a client-centered approach. A central tenet of this approach is for lawyers to communicate—and connect—with clients in a manner that elicits disclosure of complete and accurate information. Armed with this information, lawyers are better able to understand their clients' motives and best pursue their clients' true interests and objectives, not simply interests or objectives that lawyers may believe their clients have or should have.

(b) Viewpoint and Racial Diversity Are Critical to Student-Lawyers' Self-Evaluation of Biases that Might Hinder Effective Client Representation

For client-centered counseling to be successful in a law school clinic setting, student-lawyers need fully and accurately to understand their clients' viewpoints within the clients' own contextual experiences. This understanding is essential for student-lawyers to formulate case strategies designed to achieve the goals that are most important to their clients. Moreover, without such understanding, student-lawyers are unable to convey their clients' viewpoints and experiences accurately to opposing counsel and parties, as well as judges and juries.

The achievement of these objectives is almost necessarily predicated on the presence in the law school of a truly diverse student body. Student-lawyers working in the areas of, for example, poverty law, welfare law, child advocacy, immigration, and refugee law meet many clients who have backgrounds and experiences totally foreign to, and often difficult even to comprehend by, many or most law students.

With backgrounds that fall all along the spectrum of privilege, many law students may also have subconscious biases regarding race, culture, social status, wealth, and poverty. To understand and communicate effectively with clients from backgrounds vastly different from their own, student-lawyers must first be able to identify their own biases. They must then attempt to set aside their biases and to consider the actions and objectives of their clients from the perspectives of their clients and in the context of their clients' racial, cultural, and socio-economic backgrounds.

For the student-lawyer, the process of self-identification and analysis often begins and progresses through discourse with a racially, culturally, and socio-economically diverse mix of fellow student-lawyers. It is through this discourse that students test their own perceptions about race, poverty, and culture against those of their peers. This discourse enables student-lawyers to understand how race and culture can form clients' (and their own) worldviews and influence clients' (and their own) actions and objectives. Such a discourse also enables student-lawyers to understand that there is no single, uniform minority viewpoint held generally by members of a minority group, just as there is no single "white" viewpoint. In essence, having a diversity of viewpoints teaches student-lawyers to recognize personal bias, eliminate reliance on stereotypes, and undertake an unencumbered evaluation of each client's background and problems to achieve each client's unique objective.

Studies have shown that members of minority groups often view a given set of facts differently than do non-minorities. Furthermore, race can even play a role in the way employees perceive feedback from their superiors. Clinical law professors believe it imperative for this discourse and self-identification to begin early in lawyers' training. Indeed, where student-lawyers enter into attorney-client relationships without being aware of their own cultural perspectives, whatever they might be, myriads of harm can result to clients.

Additionally, early exposure to diverse viewpoints and discourse enhances the abilities of student-lawyers to consider and resolve problems and teaches students to reexamine assumed solutions and develop creative approaches to clients' unique needs. The benefits conferred by a racially diverse law student body thus far outweigh the benefits of admitting only law students who, say, scored above 172 on the Law School Admissions Test (LSAT).

The consequences of failing to provide law students with a diverse student body, from a clinical law perspective, are real and immediate. When student-lawyers represent clients of different cultural backgrounds, and make judgments based on misinformation or inability to appreciate the clients' cultural norms, they run the risk of "misjudging a client or . . . providing differential representation based on stereotype or bias."

3. Law Students Have Experienced the Benefits of Racial Diversity

The benefits of racial diversity in law schools have been recognized not only by clinical law professors and admissions deans, but by law students themselves. Law students—the intended beneficiaries of both legal education and law school diversity—report that exposure to racial diversity has enhanced their abilities to analyze problems and find solutions to legal issues. Furthermore, law students recognize that a diverse law school student body can prepare them for the multicultural practice they will enter upon graduation. For example, in a survey of students at The University of Michigan Law School and Harvard Law School, 72 percent of students at Michigan, and 67 percent of students at Harvard, agreed that having a racially diverse law school student body had enhanced their abilities to work more effectively and get along better with individuals of other racial backgrounds.

"Confronting different opinions and taking ideas very seriously are hallmarks of a good education. This is all the more true for legal education, where students need to understand all sides of conflicts and how to argue difficult issues in contentious, high-stakes settings." Again, 68 percent of Harvard law students and 75 percent of Michigan law students believe that conflicts because of racial differences challenged them to rethink their own values. It is exactly this confrontation and reevaluation of beliefs that is so critical to properly training student-lawyers and, ultimately, enhancing their ability to promote fairness and work equity in the legal system.

D. Enrolling a Critical Mass of Minority Law Students Requires Law Schools to Consider Applicants as Complete Individuals, and to Weigh the Contributions Each Student Can Make to the Law School as a Whole

Close to two centuries of overt discrimination—including criminal sanctions for educating minorities, and enforced segregation—against disfavored minority groups in this country have resulted in an elementary and secondary educational system whose well-documented shortcomings fall disproportionately on the very minority groups the Law School's policy seeks to help admit. As petitioner's own amicus admits, there is an "enormous academic gap" between minority and majority secondary students, and "most black and Hispanic students operate at a huge academic disadvantage"—to the extent they stay in school at all.

Saddled with these obstacles, it is little wonder that applicants from disfavored minority groups often score lower on standardized tests than majority students. Consequently, an admissions system based solely on LSAT numbers and undergraduate grade-point averages (UGPA) may not yield a student body with a critical mass of minority students.

To realize the benefits of diversity, law schools must be allowed to consider applicants as complete individuals—individuals who, among other things, come from particular racial and ethnic backgrounds and experiences. Law schools must not, as petitioner urges, be restricted to considering only such limited and incomplete data as LSAT scores and UGPA. Although petitioner's argument assumes that such cramped criteria "objectively" measure so-called merit, that assumption, and the resulting argument, cannot withstand scrutiny. At best, such scores present a severely limited view of law school applicants, and the qualities each prospective student would bring to his law school studies, the student body, and the law school as a whole.

Heedless of the warnings provided by the very people who draft and administer petitioner's preferred tests, petitioner urges the Court to declare a legal rule forbidding law schools from considering applicants' racial and ethnic backgrounds. Petitioner's assumption that "merit" can be reduced to a series of numbers makes all the more ironic her effort to seize the mantle of equal protection and individual opportunity.

Petitioner assumes, without support, that barring law schools from considering individual applicants' racial and ethnic backgrounds, and the contributions such backgrounds make to legal education (especially clinical legal education), would allow for the enrollment of more qualified law students. While such a practice might result in higher average LSAT and UGPA numbers, however, higher numbers are not necessarily indicative of greater merit. Indeed, there is no suggestion, and no evidence, that minority students admitted as part of the Law School's critical mass approach are unqualified for the study or practice of law, or inadequate for admission to the Law School. On the contrary, the record below demonstrates that minority students perform well in law school, graduate, and go on to successful careers in the law.

As a result, donning the blinders demanded by petitioner would not result in the matriculation of more qualified law students. In fact, such a limited view of applicants would actually compromise the legal education applicants seek, by depriving all law students, and especially clinical law students and their clients, of the essential leavening factor of diversity.

II. The Benefits of Diversity Cannot Material Without a Critical Mass of Minority Students

A. Critical Mass Is Not a Quota

Petitioner and her amici strain to equate the concept of "critical mass" with a quota system. Quotas, they argue, cannot withstand constitutional scrutiny because they have the purpose and effect of directly benefitting members of a preferred group at the expense of others outside the preferred group.

These arguments mischaracterize the Law School's admissions practices. Critical mass is not a quota system. As the Law School discusses in its own submission, there are no seats set aside for minorities, nor was the critical mass goal designed to act as a functional equivalent of a quota.

In any event, petitioner's "quota" argument does not square with what CLEA understands and believes to be the rationale behind the Law School's admissions program, and is certainly inapplicable to the rationale behind CLEA's interest in significant diversity: to attain a critical mass of diverse students for purposes of clinical training.

B. A Critical Mass of Minority Students Is Necessary to Realize the Benefits of Diversity

The Law School's admissions policy was adopted to aid the school in achieving its stated goal of attaining a diverse student body, a goal whose legitimacy was explicitly approved in *Bakke*. Witnesses testified in the district court that "racial diversity is part of the diversity of perspectives needed to enhance the 'classroom dynamic.' " They testified that a "critical mass" of minority students is required to achieve this diversity of perspectives because minority students need to "feel free to express their views, rather than to state 'expected views' or 'politically correct views.' " Indeed, they testified that "when a critical mass of minority students are present, racial stereotypes are dismantled because non-minority students see that there is no 'minority viewpoint.' " Thus, based on the record below, it is apparent that the benefits to be obtained from a critical mass are by no means intended by the Law School to inure wholly to minority students. Rather, the concept of critical mass is designed to enhance the legal education of every student in the Law School.

From the perspective of CLEA, the benefit to minority students of having a critical mass of such students is no greater (and no less) than the benefit received by majority students. As explained above, a multiplicity of viewpoints helps each student to test his or her own viewpoints and perspectives by demonstrating both that minorities can and do have world views and experiences that are foreign to majority students, and vice versa, and that there is no single minority opinion or experience, just as there is no single majority view. The "robust exchange of ideas" brought about by diversity and exposure to diversity are particularly "central to clinical legal education which focuses on lawyering in an increasingly pluralistic and multicultural society and which usually entails small classes and interactive and collaborative educational experiences."

The issue then becomes whether these benefits can exist without a critical mass of minority students. Both academic research and the experiences of clinical law professors tend to show that they cannot.

In a more formal—classroom or clinical—setting, in the absence of a critical mass of minority students, minority students often feel a lack of support in voicing an opinion and, as a result, suppress their opinions. When this self-censoring takes place, the opportunity to hear, challenge, and learn from differing perspectives is lost. The educational experiences of all students are made immeasurably poorer by such suppression of divergent opinions.

A "critical mass" of minority students is also essential in order for all students to be able to be exposed to differing perspectives in the various informal settings that are central to the educational process. A small number of minority students is simply insufficient to provide the opportunities for interaction with much larger numbers of non-minority students on a routine basis in unstructured, relaxed settings. Such settings often provide the opportunity for much more open, frank, and intense discourses and learning than does a structured classroom (or even a clinical) setting, and in the views of many represents the paradigm of the university experience.

III. Enrolling a Critical Mass of Minority Law Students Is Essential to Fostering and Maintaining Public Confidence in America's Legal System

In a legal and political system, such as ours, that depends in large part on the consent of the governed, it is critically important to foster and maintain the public's sense that the law and the legal system are impartial, fair, and legitimate. Indeed, the effectiveness of the legal system, and legal service providers, depends on the trust, confidence, respect, and cooperation of this nation's citizens. Gaining that trust, confidence, respect, and cooperation, however, depends in large measure on building a legal system that includes judges, lawyers, jury members, and other participants of all races and backgrounds.

Attaining a diverse student body in the clinics of America's law schools can make important contributions in regaining trust and respect for the legal system among minorities. . . . [L]aw school clinics tend to serve a predominantly poor and minority client base. Serving that client base effectively, with a racially and ethnically diverse group of student-lawyers who represent their clients through the client-centered approach utilized by many law school clinics, is important in rebuilding minority clients' confidence and trust in the legal system. In addition to the representation provided directly by law school clinics, the graduates of those clinics also continue to play a role in serving the legal needs of minorities and the poor. For example, Justice O'Connor has cited the experiences of her former clerks who participated in law school clinical programs. "As my former clerks describe it, once they are in private practice, they miss the feeling of personal connection they got out of their clinical work in school. They recapture that feeling by taking on a steady stream of pro bono clients, which in turn benefits all of us."

Finally, it is axiomatic that to have a racially and ethnically diverse legal system, the law schools themselves—the only source of lawyers—must also reflect that diversity. Pluralism among federal and state judges, law professors, prosecutors, public defenders, lawyers for government agencies, corporate general counsel, and attorneys in private law firms necessarily depends on true diversity being achieved in America's law schools. It is equally true that for racial and ethnic diversity to seep into the highest, most prestigious positions in our legal system, minority law students must attain a critical mass at America's elite law schools, including the University of Michigan Law School, because the graduates of such law schools disproportionately occupy these positions. For these reasons, too, enrolling a critical mass of minority law students is a compelling state interest.

CONCLUSION

"Although the law is a highly learned profession . . . it is an intensely practical one. The law school, the proving ground for legal learning and practice, cannot be effective in isolation from the individuals and institutions with which the law interacts." For decades, clinical educators have known that they and the student-lawyers they teach, cannot, as a practical matter, properly deliver legal services to their predominantly minority client base if student-lawyers have not learned to evaluate their own biases and engage in value-neutral communication with clients. These skills do not develop in a vacuum. Indeed, they can be instilled only when there is a genuine, critical mass of diversity in the law school class—the people with whom law students relate on a day-to-day basis.

In the interests of properly and rigorously training the next generation of lawyers, CLEA respectfully requests that the Court affirm the decision of the Court of Appeals.

DISCUSSION QUESTIONS

1. *What would you do?* Sandra Day O'Connor was the pivotal vote in the decision to uphold the principle of affirmative action. There were four clear votes to uphold affirmative action in higher education and four votes to strike it down. If you were Justice O'Connor, how would you have decided this case? To what extent should race be used as a "plus factor" to promote racial diversity and viewpoint diversity, if at all? How would you justify your decision?

2. Is viewpoint diversity an important goal? Think of your own experiences from high school and college. Has racial diversity contributed to viewpoint diversity?

3. Do you think that "reverse discrimination" (that is, discrimination against whites because of affirmative action policies) is a problem? Should today's generation help compensate for past discrimination?

4. Justices Thomas and Rehnquist both made the argument that the state of Michigan does not have a compelling interest in having an elite law school. The simple answer, they argue, is to lower their admissions standards, applying a lottery if necessary to allocate slots to students who meet the lower standards. Would this be a good approach?

5. Some states have applied a "10 percent solution" to the issue of racial diversity in higher education. That is, any student who graduates in the top 10 percent of his or her high school class is admitted into the top public university in the state. What are the merits and disadvantages of this approach compared to using race as a "plus factor" in the admissions decision?

6 Representation in Congress:
The Politics of Pork

The articles in this chapter highlight the importance legislators place on serving their constituents by delivering specific benefits, such as a new highway overpass, water treatment plant, or veterans hospital. Although the strategy might work for re-election, it may undermine the capacity of Congress to deal effectively with national problems and priorities. The debate over "pork barrel politics" captures this institutional tension, and illustrates the difficulties of defining "national" interests rather than parochial or local interests.

Examples of pork barrel spending are plentiful. The airline bailout bill that passed in the weeks after the terrorist attacks of September 11, 2001, was viewed by its critics as nothing more than another example of wasteful government spending that rewarded an influential industry that hires high-paid lobbyists and makes generous campaign contributions. More recently, as David Firestone describes, the Senate "rolled a pork barrel" in the bill that appropriated money for the war in Iraq. The bill included amendments to fund a research station at the South Pole and repair a dam in Vermont. House leaders were outraged because their rules restrict "nongermane" amendments to bills. Editorial boards and political pundits around the country criticized the Senate for using the war for their parochial interests. A slightly different version of pork-motivated behavior was the recent effort by Sen. Larry Craig (R-ID) to force the Air Force to send four additional C-130 transport planes to an Air National Guard base in Boise by holding up more than eight hundred Air Force promotions, including fighter pilots who flew in Iraq. A *New York Times* editorial referred to this behavior as "so obnoxious that it calls the country's attention to one of the more repugnant aspects of Congress's normal operating procedures" (June 11, 2003).

Sean Paige and Jonathan Cohn view pork barrel politics from different perspectives. For Paige, the $520 billion spending bill passed in late 1998 tossed aside the "hard-won gains" of budget balancing achieved in 1997 and was "larded . . . with heapings of pork-barrel projects." Paige recognizes the difficulties of practicing fiscal discipline when all members of Congress want and need to provide something for their home districts. Nevertheless, he criticizes the practice of attaching last-minute pork barrel riders to the budget, something done even by members who built their careers on deficit reduction. The national interest in a balanced budget, according to Paige, should take priority over parochial projects.

Where Paige sees waste and abuse of the nation's resources, however, Cohn views pork as the "glue" of legislating. If it takes a little pork for the home district or state to get important legislation through Congress, so be it. Cohn also questions the motives of budget reform groups that call for greater fiscal discipline in Congress; most of these groups, in his view, are not truly concerned about waste, but are simply against government spending in general. The policies they identify as pork, he argues, can have important national implications: military readiness, road improvements for an Olympic host city, or the development of new agricultural and food products.

In other words, "pork" is in the eye of the beholder: one person's pork is another person's essential spending. From the latter perspective, national interests can be served by allowing local interests to take a dip into the pork barrel. Finally, Cohn argues that pork, even according to the critics' own definition, constitutes less that one percent of the overall federal budget.

DAVID FIRESTONE

A Nation at War: Paying for the War; Senate Rolls a Pork Barrel into War Bill

The hour was late, the war in Iraq was raging, and members of the Senate simply wanted to pass the $80 billion bill to pay for the war and go home for the night. In their haste, many senators never realized last week that they were also voting to send $10 million to a research station at the South Pole that had had a hard winter.

Or that they were approving $3.3 million to fix a leaky dam in Vermont.

Or allowing themselves to spend more money to send notices of town meetings to voters.

Or allowing the Border Patrol to accept donations of body armor for dogs.

In fact, there were dozens of pork-barrel projects and special interest provisions that were inserted at the last minute Thursday night into the bill to pay for the war in Iraq, and the lawmakers were not particularly shy about acknowledging what they did.

Senator Lisa Murkowski, Republican of Alaska, for example, sent out a news release to reporters in her home state, boasting of helping the Alaska seafood industry with a provision allowing wild salmon to be labeled as organic. The release does not even mention that the intention of the overall bill was to pay for the war and improve domestic security. The provision was inserted into the measure by Ms. Murkowski's Republican colleague from Alaska, Senator Ted Stevens, the chairman of the Appropriations Committee.

Members of the House, who thought they had an agreement with the Senate to keep the war bill "clean" and free of extraneous matter, were furious this week when they saw what the Senate had passed. Although the House bill includes a $3 billion aid package for the airlines, it is relatively free of the personal projects inserted by members of the Senate Appropriations Committee. House leaders say they are determined to keep it that way as they negotiate the final bill.

"I'm very concerned about that, because we had an agreement with the Senate leadership that we would try to keep this bill as clean as possible," Tom DeLay, the House majority leader, said today. "These things do nothing but slow down the process of getting the bill, and hopefully the conference committee can work out the differences and bring out a clean supplemental."

Even more exercised was Senator John McCain, Republican of Arizona, who berated his colleagues on the floor last week for approving dozens of nonwar projects, at a cost of hundreds of millions of dollars, without even reading them.

"I was really appalled," said Mr. McCain. "Here, in the name of fighting the war in Iraq, they loaded up the bill with pork-barrel spending. I mean, I didn't realize that Al Qaeda had reached all the way to the South Pole, but it's an example of a process that's simply out of control."

But members of the Appropriations Committee, who brought up most of the extraneous provisions after 10 P.M. on Thursday, about forty minutes before the bill would be passed, said many of the expenditures were vital and needed to be attached to a bill that was guaranteed approval. Although the president calls the measure a war bill, they said, it is really a wide-ranging appropriations bill that may be the only vehicle for months to enact important provisions.

"The administration itself has asked for funds in this bill that have nothing to do with Iraq, such as their request for aid to Colombia," said David Carle, a spokesman for Senator Patrick J. Leahy, Democrat of Vermont, who inserted several additions to the bill. "Each year there is a midyear course-correction bill like this to address issues like these that cannot or should not wait another year." Mr. Carle was referring to the $104 million in the bill the president requested for antinarcotics efforts in Colombia.

The Senate bill included these special items:

- An increase from $320 million to $330 million for a science research station at the South Pole. A spokesman for Senator Christopher S. Bond, Republican of Missouri, who inserted the provision, said Antarctica had had a difficult winter and the station needed to lay extra pipes to get oil from a tanker ship.

- A communications system for the metropolitan government of Louisville-Jefferson County in Kentucky, which will cost $5 million. A spokesman for Senator Jim Bunning, Republican of Kentucky, said he asked for the money as part of the domestic security section of the bill, because police radios in the area work on different frequencies and need to be upgraded.

- A provision that would make it easier for senators to send out postcards to constituents to notify them of town meetings. The amendment, sponsored by Senator Arlen Specter, Republican of Pennsylvania, would eliminate wording that limited the taxpayer-financed postcards to counties of fewer than 250,000 people.

  "This is directly related to the war effort," said Mr. Specter, who is preparing for a tough re-election battle. "Meeting with the people of Pennsylvania is an important part of our job, including informing them of the war effort. It's really laughable to suggest this is anything but a minuscule change."

- An amendment that would prohibit the German-owned DHL Worldwide Express delivery company from carrying American military cargo. The provision, sponsored by several senators, came after lobbying by Federal Express and United Parcel Service, according to Senate officials, and could hinder a proposed merger between DHL and Airborne Express.

- A provision to shift $3.3 million to repair a leaking dam in Waterbury, Vt. A spokesman for Mr. Leahy said the need to rebuild the dam was urgent and could not wait until the next appropriations bill.

- A provision to allow the Border Patrol to accept donations of body armor for patrol dogs, also inserted by Mr. Leahy. An eleven-year-old girl in Vermont has been raising money to buy a bulletproof vest for a patrol dog, but the current legislation does not allow the patrol to accept gifts.

All of these provisions were inserted into the bill by Mr. Stevens in an omnibus package of changes, known as a "manager's amendment," just before the final vote on the legislation. Mr. McCain could have objected to the package and held up the entire bill, but he said he decided not to do so because of the need to pay for the war. But he said he would not agree to any more manager's amendments in future spending bills.

Now and then a member of the House or Senate will do something so obnoxious that it calls the country's attention to one of the more repugnant aspects of Congress's normal operating procedures. Now it is Senator Larry Craig, a conservative Idaho Republican who advertises himself as a strong supporter of America's military. For the past month he has frozen hundreds of Air Force promotions, including those of pilots who risked their lives over Iraq, to bludgeon the Pentagon into transferring four additional C-130 transport planes to an Air National Guard base in Boise.

Senator Craig may set a new record for skewed priorities—even the Idaho Air National Guard is trying to distance itself from his little crusade. But his narrow-minded approach to military matters is disturbingly common on Capitol Hill. Congressional pressure to relocate military hardware, keep open unneeded bases and pad orders for local defense plants continually bloats the military budget. The Pentagon is directed to purchase items it never requested, and its efforts to cut obsolete and expensive weapons programs are regularly thwarted. This helps explain why America spends some $400 billion a year on the military and still underfinances promising new weapons systems like unmanned reconnaissance and combat aircraft.

Few customs are as entrenched in Washington as seeking Pentagon contracts to score political points at home. Trent Lott got the shipyard in Pascagoula, Miss., a contract for a $1.5 billion helicopter carrier the Navy had not even sought. John Warner, the Republican who is now the chairman of the Senate Armed Services Committee, looks out for the Northrop Grumman Newport News shipyard in Virginia, which continues to build attack submarines, weapons that lost much of their military rationale with the end of the Cold War.

Democrats have been as eager as Republicans to lobby for home-state contractors. One of the most flagrant current examples of distorted spending is a costly leasing deal for aerial tankers backed by Representative Norm Dicks of Washington. Leasing the craft instead of buying them helps the state's financially ailing Boeing Company but will ultimately cost the taxpayer billions. While the Air Force's wrongheaded F-22 fighter program is now rightly being questioned, actually pulling the plug on the project could be impossible as long as it is defended by Georgia's senators, Saxby Chambliss, a Republican, and Zell Miller, a Democrat. Much of the work on the plane is done by Lockheed Martin in Georgia.

America's defense dollars would go further if more legislators showed themselves true friends of the American military by joining military reformers like Senators John McCain and Charles Grassley and others working to pry apart the iron triangle of services, defense contractors, and parochial members of Congress that lards each year's military budget with billions of dollars of wasteful pork.

SEAN PAIGE

Rolling Out the Pork Barrel

The fall of 1997 was a triumphant time for deficit hawks in Congress: Step by laborious step they finally had maneuvered President Clinton into signing the first balanced-budget bill in two decades, a long-sought political grail. Yet only a year later, as Congress rushed to cram a year's worth of budget writing into the waning weeks before the midterm elections, the hard-won gains of 1997 vanished like a mirage and the madness of budget seasons past made a triumphant return.

"There's a lot of little things tucked away there that I wish weren't," the president said, talking not about the latest batch of White House interns but rather the $520 billion omnibus spending bill he was signing into law. "But on balance, it honors our values and strengthens our country and looks to the future."

Critics, however, say the values it honors most are political expediency, fiscal opportunism and the scruples of the horse trader—while the only future to which its politician authors looked was their own.

All but a few members of Congress claimed to hate the damned thing.

However, a majority in both chambers held their noses and voted for it, larded as it was with heapings of pork-barrel projects, the distribution of which remains a staple of the incumbency protection racket, and some breathtaking acts of budget wizardry. The more than $21 billion in spending that exceeded budget caps set only a year earlier was declared "emergency" spending, as members continued to exploit a loophole that threatens to make the U.S. Treasury a federal disaster area. And some $9.1 billion in additional spending was "forward funded"—which means that Congress will spend it now and figure out how to pay for it later.

Criticism of the bill was rancorous and bipartisan. But even the opposition was divided: One faction hated what it saw as a retreat from fiscal restraint and responsibility; the other was appalled by the opacity of the process, in which a handful of negotiators from the White House and Congress worked out the horse trades behind closed doors. "This is a sham," cried Republican Rep. Jon Christensen of Nebraska. "This Congress ought to be ashamed of itself," scolded Wisconsin Democrat Rep. David Obey.

Retiring Speaker Newt Gingrich—who hasn't been quite the same since the federal-government brownout of 1995, a game of chicken with the White House that went badly for Republicans—found himself fending off a rearguard action from the right, of all places, and had to put the ingrates (he called them "petty dictators" and the "perfectionist caucus") in their place. "It is easy to get up and say, 'Vote No!' Then what would you do?" shrugged a world-wizened Gingrich. "Those of us who have grown up and matured . . . understand that we have to work together on the big issues."

Even the old sausage-maker himself, Democratic Sen. Robert Byrd of West Virginia, was shocked at what he saw. Renowned for his own cagey use of the budget process to bring billions of dollars in pork back to the Mountain State (and perhaps a bit peeved at finding himself excluded from all the behind-the-scenes horse trading), Byrd condemned the bill as a "gargantuan monstrosity"—a "Frankenstein monster patched together from old legislative body parts that don't quite fit."

Members of both parties chafed at having to vote on legislation crafted in such haste that few actually knew what was inside the 40-pound, 16-inch, 4,000-page end product (except, of course, for that quick peek at page 2,216, Part B, subsection 3[a], just to be sure that a wastewater-treatment facility and $4 million grant for the alma mater made it in). But by now a bit more is known about how this particular sausage was made and what ingredients went into it. The measure included funding for eight unfinished spending bills, a $21 billion emergency-spending measure and a cornucopia of legislative riders ranging from the substantial (one resulted in a major reorganization of the State Department) to the trivial (another extended duck-hunting season in Mississippi for 11 days) to the ludicrous (still another bans nude sunbathing at a beach near Cape Canaveral, Fla.).

Fiscal conservatives, led by House Budget Committee Chairman John Kasich of Ohio, had entertained the notion of dusting off the old budget battle ax. But perennial targets for their imagined whacks, such as the National Endowment for the Arts and the Tennessee Valley Authority, sailed through unscathed. Moreover, even some old budget bogeymen—such as the wool, mohair and sugar subsidies—came roaring back from the brink of extinction.

If and when disputes arose between Democrats and Republicans, they invariably hinged not on where the ax might fall but on whom would be supping upon the larger ladle of gravy.

Clinton and the Democrats got $1.2 billion to begin hiring 30,000 of 100,000 new teachers (meaning much more money will be needed in the future); an $18 billion bailout for the International Monetary Fund; $1.7 billion in new home-health-care money for Medicare (reversing changes to the program made in 1996); and more than most Republicans wanted in farm aid (which even Senate Agriculture Committee Chairman Richard Lugar of Indiana said would "undermine" recent efforts to wean farmers off federal aid). Democrats also prevailed on a measure expanding coverage of the federal-employee health-insurance plan to include oral contraceptives; restored $35 million in food and oil shipments to North Korea; and turned back the Republican push for tax relief.

Republicans got $6.8 billion in increased military spending (some of which is classified), $1 billion for antimissile defense (although the Pentagon already is spending $3 billion annually on missile defense, with no deployment in sight) and $690 million for antidrug efforts (including the purchase of $40 million gulf-stream jets for law-enforcement agencies reportedly surprised by the windfall and $90 million for helicopters for Colombia). The GOP also was successful in its push to increase visa quotas for hightech workers and, striking a blow for peduncles everywhere, blocked a Department of Transportation move that would have mandated peanut-free zones on commercial airliners.

The standoff continued on the question of how the year-2000 census will be conducted—whether by actual head count, as Republicans and the Constitution demand, or statistical sampling, as Democrats prefer—with a settlement postponed until after the Supreme Court rules on the case early next year. Other interesting bill provisions, without any known partisan parentage, include: a cut in foreign aid to countries that haven't paid parking tickets in the District of Columbia; a measure allowing the Secretary of Agriculture to lend Russia money, which the Russians then can use to buy frozen chickens from Mississippi; $325 million inserted to buy enriched uranium from Russia; and $1 billion during the next five years to help the Tennessee Valley Authority refinance its debt.

Some of the $21.4 billion in "emergency" spending extras included: $3.35 billion to tackle the Y2K computer problem; $2.4 billion for antiterrorism activities; $6.8 billion to improve military readiness; and $5.9 billion in additional aid to farmers. Many items among them drew fire from budgetwatchers, including $100 million for a new visitors center for the U.S. Capitol—an idea entertained for years which received a boost following last summer's fatal shootings there—and $100 million for a buyout of fishermen working in the Bering Sea, where pollock stocks have plummeted.

Singled out for particular opprobrium, however, was the $5.9 billion in emergency farm relief. Citizens Against Government Waste (CAGW) President Tom Schatz called it a "bipartisan and cynical attempt to buy the farm vote before this fall's election," pointing to studies showing that actual farm losses because of drought or other disasters were much lower. The group also condemned increased subsidies to sugar, peanuts and mohair producers contained in the agriculture appropriations bill. Such subsidies, said CAGW, represented "a first step toward dismantling the 1996 farm bill"; which made history by beginning to phase out farm price supports that have been in place since the 1930s.

Of course, more pedestrian and parochial kinds of pork projects also were packed into the bill, a random sampling of which includes: $37.5 million for a ferry and docking facilities at King Cove, Alaska; $2 million for the National Center for Cool and Cold Water Aquaculture in West Virginia ("The seafood capital of Appalachia!" one wag said); $1 million for peanut quality research in Georgia;

$1.4 million for the Jimmy Carter National Historical Site; a $200,000 grant to Vermont's Center for Rural Studies; $1 million to restore a German submarine at a museum in Chicago (the project received $900,000 last year); $1.2 million for a project called "Building America"; $400,000 for another called "Rebuilding America"; and $67,000 for the New Orleans Jazz Commission.

Christmas came early to the nation's capital this year. The party was a hoot-and-a-half while it lasted, but the inevitable hangover followed as its fuller consequences have become clear.

The 1998 spending spree "has made it almost impossible to stay within the budget caps set in the 1997 [budget] agreement," Senate Budget Committee staff director G. William Hoagland told a gathering just weeks after the bill became law. The committee estimates that when everything is factored in, the extra spending in the omnibus bill will drain $38.2 billion from any future budget surplus. And as the bills for its "forward-funding" mechanisms come due, deep and painful cuts in next year's discretionary spending will be necessary. And that, Hoagland says, is "unlikely unless we can come up with more user fees or some quick gimmicks in the budget."

But even if such a plan fails and the fiscal restraint that took decades to muster caves in on itself like a black hole, sucking the rest of the republic in after it, one thing will be said of the ludicrous budget battle of 1998: At least the duck hunters of Mississippi are happy.

JONATHAN COHN

Roll Out the Barrel: The Case Against the Case Against Pork

On most days, the lobby of the U.S. Chamber of Commerce's Washington, D.C., headquarters has a certain rarefied air. But on this Tuesday morning it is thick with the smell of greasy, grilled bacon. The aroma is appropriate, since the breakfast speaker is Republican Representative Bud Shuster of Pennsylvania, chairman of the House Transportation Committee and, his critics say, one of the most shameless promulgators of pork-barrel spending in all of Congress. The odor seems even more fitting given that the topic of Shuster's address is the Building Efficient Surface Transportation and Equity Act, the six-year, $217 billion highway-spending package about to pass Congress—and, according to these same critics, the single biggest hunk of pork Washington has seen in a decade.

The critics, of course, are absolutely right. The House version of BESTEA, which hit the floor this week, contains at least $18 billion in so-called "demonstration" and "high-priority" projects. Those are the congressional euphemisms for pork—public works programs of dubious merit, specific to one congressional district, designed to curry favor with its voters. And Shuster's record for bringing home the bacon is indeed legendary. BESTEA's predecessor, which passed in 1991, included $287 million for 13 projects in Shuster's central Pennsylvania district. Today, visitors can see these and other shrines to his legislative clout by driving along the newly built Interstate 99, a shimmering stretch of asphalt the state has officially christened the Bud Shuster Highway.

None of this much bothers the suits at the Chamber of Commerce, who savor every line of Shuster's pitch as if it were just so much more fat-soaked sausage from the buffet table. Money for roads—whether in Shuster's district or anybody else's—means more ways to transport goods and more work for construction companies. But, outside the friendly confines of groups like this, a relentless chorus of high-minded watchdog groups and puritanical public officials complains that pork-barrel spending wastes government money. These critics also protest the way pork becomes law in the first place, as last-minute amendments designed to bypass the hearings and debate bills normally require.

To be sure, these arguments are not exactly novel. The very term "pork barrel" is a pre-Civil War term, derived from what was then a readily understandable (but, to modern ears, rather objectionable) analogy between congressmen gobbling up appropriations and slaves grabbing at salt pork distributed from giant barrels. "By the 1870s," William Safire writes in his *Political Dictionary*, "congressmen were regularly referring to 'pork,' and the word became part of the U.S. political lexicon." Criticizing pork, meanwhile, is just as venerable a tradition. Virtually every president from Abraham Lincoln to Ronald Reagan has promised to eliminate pork from the federal budget, and so have most congressmen, much to the satisfaction of muckraking journalists and similarly high-minded voters.

But rarely have the politicians actually meant it, and even more rarely have they succeeded. Until now. Thanks to an endless parade of media exposés on government waste, and a prevailing political consensus in favor of balanced budgets, pork critics have been gaining momentum. In 1994, anti-pork fervor nearly killed President Clinton's crime bill; in 1995, the same sentiment lay behind enactment of the line-item veto, something budget-balancers had sought in vain for more than a decade. A few years ago, a handful of anti-pork legislators took to calling themselves "pork-busters." Thanks to their vigilance, says the nonprofit group Citizens Against Government Waste, the amount of pork in the budget declined by about nine percent in 1998.

The influence of pork-busters reached a new peak in 1997, when they helped defeat a preliminary attempt at BESTEA. They probably won't be able to duplicate the feat this year—Shuster has nearly 400 votes behind his new pork-laden bill, which House Budget Chairman John Kasich has called an "abomination." But pork-busters won a major public relations victory last week when four House Republicans turned on Shuster and accused him of trying to buy them off with pet projects. "I told them my vote was not for sale," said Steve Largent of Oklahoma. "Shuster bought just about everyone," David Hobson of Ohio told *The Washington Post*. Three weeks ago, Republican Senator John McCain of Arizona, Capitol Hill's most determined pork-buster, won passage of an amendment that could cut at least some of the bill's pork. President Clinton has since joined the chorus, saying he too deplores the parochial waste Shuster and his cronies added to the measure.

In the popular telling, episodes like these represent epic struggles of good versus evil—of principled fiscal discipline versus craven political self-interest—with the nation's economic health and public faith in government at stake. But this narrative, related time and again by purveyors of elite wisdom and then repeated mindlessly by everyday citizens, has it exactly backward. The pork-busters are more anti-government than anti-waste. As for pork-barrel spending, it's good for American citizens and American democracy as well. Instead of criticizing it, we should be celebrating it, in all of its gluttonous glory.

Nearly a week has passed since Shuster made his appearance before the Chamber of Commerce, and now it is the pork-busters' turn to be making headlines. In what has become an annual rite of the budget process, Citizens Against Government Waste is staging a press conference near Capitol Hill to release its compilation of pork in the 1997 federal budget—a 40-page, pink-covered booklet it calls the "Pig Book." (Actually, the pocket-sized, 40-page version is just a summary of the unabridged "Pig Book," which weighs in at a hefty 170 pages, in single-sided, legal-sized computer printouts.)

CAGW has been fighting this fight for more than a decade, and its steady stream of propaganda, reports, and testimony is in no small part responsible for pork-busting's Beltway resonance. Republican Representative Christopher Cox calls CAGW "the premier waste-fighting organization in America"; the 1995–1996 Congress sought CAGW testimony 20 times. The interest in today's press conference— attended by more than 60 reporters and a dozen television crews—is testimony to the group's high esteem among the Washington press corps, although it doesn't hurt that CAGW has also provided the TV crews with a good photo opportunity.

Like many press conferences in this city, this one features several members of Congress, including McCain and Democratic Senator Russell Feingold. Unlike many press conferences in this city, this one also features a man dressed in a bright pink pig's suit, rubber pig masks free for the media to take, plus a live, charcoal-gray potbellied pig named Porky. For the duration of the event, Porky does little except scarf down some vegetable shreds. But the beast's mere presence gets a few laughs, which is more than can be said for the puns that CAGW's president, Tom Schatz, makes as he rattles off the recipients of this year's "Oinker Awards."

Senator Daniel Inouye of Hawaii secured $127,000 in funding for research on edible seaweed; for this and other appropriations, Schatz says, Inouye (who is of Japanese ancestry) wins "The Sushi Slush Fund Award." Senator Ted Stevens of Alaska sponsored $100,000 for a project called Ship Creek, so he gets "The Up Ship's Creek Award." (Stevens is a double winner: for his other pork, totaling some $477 million since 1991, CAGW also presents him with "The Half Baked Alaska Award.") The Pentagon budget included $3 million for an observatory in South America: "It's supposed to peer back millions of years in time," Schatz says, his deadpan poker face now giving way to a smarmy, half-cocked smile. "Maybe they're looking for a balanced budget." This dubious-sounding project Schatz dubs "The Black Hole Award." And on. And on.

You might think cornball humor like this would earn CAGW the disdain of the famously cynical Washington press corps. But, when Schatz is done, and the question-and-answer period begins, the reporters display barely any skepticism.

Instead, that evening, and during the following days, they will heap gobs of attention on the group. They don't flatter or endorse the organization per se, but the coverage shares a common assumption that the group's findings are evidence of political malfeasance. CNN, for example, will use the "Pig Book" 's release as a peg for stories bemoaning the persistence of pork in the federal budget. A story out of Knight Ridder's Washington bureau, which will run in nearly a dozen of the chain's newspapers, basically recapitulates the report. And all this comes on the heels of a front-page *Wall Street Journal* feature—sparked by a similar report from the Tax Foundation—highlighting the profligate pork barreling of the Senate majority leader, Trent Lott of Mississippi. Its headline: "MISSISSIPPI'S SENATORS CONTINUE A TRADITION: GETTING FEDERAL MONEY."

This is typical. Normally jaded Washingtonians, journalists especially, tend to view pork-busters not as ideologues but as politically disinterested watchdogs. Television producers, in particular, regularly summon CAGW experts to validate stories for such waste-focused segments as NBC's "The Fleecing of America" and ABC's "Your Money, Your Choice." While this image has a basis in reality—CAGW truly goes after pork-barreling Republicans with the same fervor it pursues Democrats—it is also a product of the organization's concerted attempt to wrap itself in the flag of nonpartisanship. "No matter how you slice it, pork is always on the menu in the halls of Congress," Schatz said at the press conference. "Some members of Congress simply couldn't resist the lure of easy money and putting partisan political interests over the best interest of taxpayers."

But it's not as if the pork-busters have no partisan or ideological agenda of their own. Some, like the Cato Institute, are explicit about their anti-government predisposition. CAGW is a little more cagey, but it remains true to the spirit of its past chairman, perennial right-wing Republican candidate Alan Keyes, as well as its cofounder, J. Peter Grace, who headed President Reagan's 1984 commission on government waste and whose antipathy to government in general was widely known. "The government is the worst bunch of stupid jerks you've ever run into in your life," he said once at a CAGW fund-raising dinner. "These people just want to spend money, money, money all the time."

That is, of course, a forgivable overstatement of a plausible argument. But it is also an overtly ideological one, and it calls into question the group's reliability when it comes to making delicate distinctions about what is truly wasteful. After all, CAGW is not just against pork, but against much of what the mainstream conservative movement considers bad or overly intrusive public policy—which encompasses an awful lot. In 1995, CAGW was not bashful about embracing the Contract With America, whose expansive definition of waste included many regulatory programs Americans deem quite worthwhile. "Taxpayers . . . demonstrated in two consecutive elections of a Republican Congress that the Washington establishment at its peril ignores the taxpayers' voice," the group's annual report boasts. "CAGW stood shoulder to shoulder with the reformers and enjoyed a sense of accomplishment at this burst of energy from revitalized taxpayers." CAGW's contributor list, not surprisingly, reads like a who's who of conservative interests, from Philip Morris Companies Inc. to the Columbia/HCA Healthcare Foundation Inc.

To be sure, CAGW is not the only Beltway organization whose partisan allegiances belie its nonprofit, nonpartisan status. At least a dozen other groups on both the left and the right do the exact same thing. Anyway, the fact that an argument may be ideologically motivated hardly means it's wrong.

But that doesn't mean it's right, either. Listen closely the next time some smug good-government type starts criticizing pork: it's an awful lot of fuss over what is, in fact, a very small amount of money. In the "Pig Book," for example, CAGW claims last year's budget included pork worth about $13.2 billion—or, as a pork-buster would say, "$13.2 billion!" Yes, you could feed quite a few hungry people with that much money, or you could give a bigger tax cut. But it's less than one percent of the federal budget.

And it's not even clear that all of the $13.2 billion of waste is really, well, waste. A good chunk of CAGW's $13.2 billion in pork comes from a few dozen big-ticket items, costing tens of millions of dollars each, scattered through various appropriations measures, particularly the Pentagon's. Among the programs: research of a space-based laser ($90 million), transportation improvements in Utah ($14 million), and military construction in Montana ($32 million).

But it's hardly self-evident that these all constitute waste, as the pork-busters suggest. At least some national security experts believe the space-based laser is a necessary defense against rogue nations that might get their hands on nuclear missiles. A lot of that Utah money is to help Salt Lake City prepare for Olympic traffic. And, if you've ever been to Montana, you know that there are a lot of military bases scattered across that vast state—which means a lot of soldiers who need buildings in which to live, eat, and work. In other words, all of these serve some credible purpose.

The wastefulness of the smaller items is similarly open to interpretation. Remember Senator Inouye's "Sushi Slush Fund Award"—the $127,000 for research on edible seaweed in Hawaii? It turns out that aquaculture is an emerging industry in Hawaii and that edible seaweed—known locally as "limu," "ogo," or "sea sprouts"—is "rich in complex carbohydrates and protein and low in calories," according to the *Honolulu Advertiser*. "It's a good source of vitamin A, calcium, and potassium, too."

Yes, the federal government is paying $3 million for a telescope in South America. But it has to, because the telescope is part of a U.S. effort to explore the southern hemisphere sky—which, of course, is only visible from the southern hemisphere. Although the telescope will be located in Chile, it will be operated remotely from the University of North Carolina at Chapel Hill. "When completed, the telescope will hold tremendous promise for scientists and the federal government," the university chancellor said when Republican Senator Lauch Faircloth of North Carolina announced the appropriation. "We at the university also have high hopes for what the project will mean for the North Carolina economy as well as for students of all ages—on this campus, across our state, and beyond."

And Senator Stevens's "Up Ship's Creek Award"? The Ship Creek water project was part of a bill authorizing studies of environmental cleanup across the country. Some $100,000 went to the U.S. Army Corps of Engineers to assess the impact of development on Ship Creek, which is Anchorage's primary source of freshwater.

Ironically, according to the Corps of Engineers, the study is exploring not only what kind of environmental precautions are necessary, but whether the federal government really has to pay for them, and whether local private entities might be convinced to foot part of the bill. In other words, one objective of the Ship Creek appropriation was to reduce government waste.

You could argue, as pork-busters do, that, while projects like these may serve some positive function in society—perhaps even deserving of government money—they should not be on the federal dime. Let the Hawaiians pay for their own calcium-rich dinners! Let Alaskans foot the bill for their own water study! But there's a respectable argument that sometimes parochial needs are in fact a legitimate federal interest, particularly when it involves things like pollution and commerce that cross state lines.

Certainly, that's the way a lot of people outside of Washington understand it. Last month, while the national media was busy flogging unthrifty lawmakers, several local newspapers rose to their defense. "We elect people to Congress not only to see to the nation's defense and keep the currency sound but also to bring home some pork," editorialized *The Fort Worth Star-Telegram*. "Pork can mean local jobs, local beautification, local pride, etc." The *Dayton Daily News* defended one project, a museum on the history of flight, that appeared on CAGW's hit list: "It is at the heart of a community effort that has been painstakingly nurtured for years by all manner of Daytonians. It combines the legitimate national purpose of recognizing the history of flight with the top-priority local purpose of getting Dayton recognized as a center of the history of flight." Other papers were more critical: they wanted to know why their congressmen hadn't brought home *more* bacon. "Alaskans aren't going to sit still for being No. 2 for long," *Anchorage Daily News* columnist Mike Doogan wrote in a spirited defense of pork. "We need the money. And we have our pride."

This is not to say that all or even most of what gets called pork is defensible on its own terms. (Did Bedford County, Pennsylvania, which happens to be smack in the middle of Shuster's rural district, really need a new airport when there were two others nearby?) Nor is it to say that the local interest in getting federal money should always trump the national interest in balancing the budget and distributing the federal largesse fairly. (Couldn't the state of Pennsylvania have paid for the Bedford County airport instead?) Nor is it even to say that local interests defending pork aren't being incredibly hypocritical—no one thinks an appropriation is pork when it's his.

No, the point is simply that you can't call something waste just because it makes a clever pun. "From what we can tell," says John Raffetto, communications director for the Senate Transportation Committee, "CAGW does no research to determine what purpose the project serves other than to flip through the pages of the bill and find projects that sound funny. If it sounds funny, that's pork. I have not heard from any member's office that has told me they've received a call from CAGW to ask what purpose that project has served."

Pork-busters concede they lack the time or resources to investigate items thoroughly. "Some may be worthy of consideration," says CAGW media director Jim Campi. "Our concern is that, if the projects went through the process the way they were supposed to, there would be a [better] opportunity to judge them on their merits."

This is the same argument that most animates McCain, Feingold, and other pork-busting lawmakers. But what constitutes a fair appropriations process? CAGW would have everyone believe that a project is pork if it is "not requested by the president" or if it "greatly exceeds the president's budget request or the previous year's funding." Huh? The whole point of the appropriations process is to give Congress a chance to make independent judgments about spending priorities. Particularly when Republicans control one branch of government and Democrats the other—as is the case today—differences will exist. The Republican Congress used to routinely declare the president's budget "dead on arrival." Did this mean the entire congressional budget was pork?

Two other criteria for defining pork are equally shaky. Invoking the familiar pork-busting wisdom, CAGW says a program is pork if it was "not specifically authorized"—meaning it wasn't in the original budget which contains general spending limits, but rather added on as part of the subsequent appropriations process, in which money is specifically allocated to each item. But the rationale for a separate budget and appropriations process is to allow Congress (and, for that matter, the president) an opportunity to change their minds about smaller items, as long as they stay within the broad guidelines of the budget agreement. CAGW also damns any projects "requested by only one chamber of Congress." But, just as Congress can disagree with the president over a project's merit, so the House can disagree with the Senate—that's the reason the architects of the Constitution created two houses in the first place. (Also, keep in mind that one reason the Senate doesn't propose as much pork is that senators—wary of getting stung in the national press for lacking frugality—will often wait to see how much pork the House passes. That way, they end up with the best of both worlds: they can quietly tell supporters that they backed the measure without ever incurring the wrath of pork-busting watchdogs.)

Make no mistake, though: Many pork-barrellers are trying to evade the scrutiny bills get when they move through the normal appropriations process. They stick in small bits of pork after hearings end because they know that nobody is going to vote against a multibillion-dollar bill just because it has a few million dollars of pork tucked in. And they can do so safe in the knowledge that, because there's very little in the way of a paper trail, they will not suffer any public consequences—unless, of course, a watchdog group or enthusiastic reporter manages to find out.

Pork-busters call this strategy sleazy, and it is. But remember, the whole point of our Constitution is to harness mankind's corrupt tendencies and channel them in constructive directions. In an oft-quoted passage of *The Federalist Number 51*, James Madison wrote, "if men were angels, no government would be necessary," and "the private interest of every individual may be a sentinel over the public rights." The Founders believed that sometimes local interests should trump national interests because they recognized it was a way to keep federal power in check. It's true this process lends itself to a skewed distribution of benefits, with disproportionate shares going to powerful lawmakers. But, again, pork is such a small portion of the budget that "equalizing" its distribution would mean only modest funding changes here and there.

Which brings us to the final defense of pork, one Madison would certainly endorse. Even if every single pork-barrel project really were a complete waste of federal money, pork still represents a very cheap way to keep our sputtering legislative process from grinding to a halt. In effect, pork is like putting oil in your car engine: it lubricates the parts and keeps friction to a minimum. This is particularly true when you are talking about controversial measures. "Buying off potential coalition members with spending programs they favor is exactly what the Founders not only expected, but practiced," political scientist James Q. Wilson has argued. He has also written: "If you agree with Madison, you believe in pork."

Think of the NAFTA battle in 1993. Contentious to the bitter end, the fate of the agreement ultimately fell on the shoulders of a handful of congressmen, all of whom privately supported it but feared the political backlash if they voted for it. Clinton gave each of them a little pork—for example, a development bank in border states that ostensibly would provide start-up money for entrepreneurs who had lost jobs because of NAFTA. The bank was just another way to pump some federal money into these districts, but that was the whole point. Thanks to that money, NAFTA became politically viable; these lawmakers could tell their constituents, plausibly and truthfully, that there was something in it for their districts.

To take a more current example, just look at BESTEA. U.S. transportation infrastructure is famously inadequate; the Department of Transportation says unsafe roads cause 30 percent of all traffic fatalities. But, when fiscal conservatives questioned the pork in the original BESTEA last year, the measure failed, forcing Congress to pass an emergency extension. This year, a more permanent, six-year version will likely pass, largely because the appearance of a budget surplus has tipped the scales just enough so that the pork seems tolerable. As John W. Ellwood and Eric M. Patashnik wrote in *The Public Interest* several years ago (in what was the best defense of pork in recent memory): "Favoring legislators with small gifts for their districts in order to achieve great things for the nation is an act not of sin but of statesmanship."

Last week, of course, BESTEA's high pork content had fiscal conservatives downright apoplectic. "Frankly, this bill really is a hog," Kasich said. "It is way over the top." But, without the pork, there might be no highway bill at all. As one highway lobbyist told *National Journal* last year, "The projects are the glue that's going to hold the damn thing together." A former transportation official said: "I've always taken the point of view that every business has some overhead. If that's what it costs to get a significant or a good highway bill, it's worth the price." Kasich would surely be aghast at such logic, but someday he and other fiscal conservatives might find it useful for their own purposes. Remember, they are the ones who say that balancing the budget will likely be impossible without severe and politically risky reforms of entitlements like Medicare. When the time comes to make those tough choices—and they need to pry a few extra votes from the opposition—you can bet they will gladly trade a little pork for *their* greater cause. They might feel guilty about it, but they shouldn't. Pork is good. Pork is virtuous. Pork is the American way.

DISCUSSION QUESTIONS

1. *What would you do?* If you were a member of Congress how would you balance the desire of your constituents to have you deliver benefits to the district and the national needs of fiscal responsibility and the collective good? If you were a leader in Congress would you use pork as a tool of coalition building, or would you take a principled stand against it?

2. How would you define pork barrel projects? Are all pork projects contrary to the national interest? How could one distinguish between local projects that are in the national interest and those that are not?

3. Members of Congress face strong incentives to serve constituent needs and claim credit for delivering federal dollars. Pork barrel projects provide the means to do just that. What changes in Congres or the political process might be made to alter legislative behavior, or to change the incentives they face for securing re-election? Do we want members of Congress to be focused primarily on broad national issues rather than local priorities?

4. Assess Firestone's article about the pork-laden war-spending bill from the perspective of Paige and Cohn. Which aspects of the bill would they highlight to support their point of view?

7 An Imperial Presidency?

In 1973, Arthur Schlesinger Jr. published a landmark book arguing that the United States was in an era of an "Imperial Presidency," in which presidents were abusing the powers of their office to wield unchecked authority, especially in international affairs. In large part because of the Cold War, power had become concentrated in the presidency, to the point where the president could do anything—steamroll Congress into adopting an open-ended authorization for military action in Vietnam on the basis of a fabricated attack on U.S. forces; carry out a secret unauthorized war in Cambodia; spy on his domestic opponents; abuse law enforcement powers—without interference from the other coordinate branches of government.

Critics of the Bush Administration—Schlesinger included—made analogous arguments about the president's actions leading up to the Iraq war in 2003. The substance of these arguments is that Bush, having already decided to invade Iraq and remove Saddam Hussein from power, misled Congress and the public in arguing that Iraq posed an imminent threat to U.S. security. The implication is that we had returned—or were getting close—to an era of unchecked presidential power reminiscent of the Vietnam era.

In a June 2003 article, Schlesinger revisited his imperial presidency thesis. He argues that the Bush policy of preventive war—which the president set out in early 2002—gives the president the power to wage war anywhere and anytime he might like. Under the preventive war doctrine, the U.S. asserted the right to use military force against another country, even if that country did not pose an immediate or imminent threat to the U.S. Supporters of the policy argued that September 11, and the possibility that terrorists might use nuclear weapons, showed that we could not wait until we knew that an attack was an immediate threat, but had to respond proactively to prevent such threats from even developing. Schlesinger, however, argues that this will have the effect of making the president the sole arbiter of when the country will go to war. This is a clear violation of the Constitution, which grants Congress, and *only* Congress, the power to "declare war."

But in "Too Much History," Noemie Emery argues that Bush's actions toward Iraq were hardly unique, and in fact were part of a longstanding pattern of preventive action. Citing a number of precedents, as well as cases where preemption should have occurred but did not—Czechoslovakia in 1938, Pearl Harbor in 1941, the Truman Doctrine in 1946, The Cuban Missile Crisis in 1962—Emery makes a case that a decisive use of force can prevent (and, indeed, *has* prevented) catastrophe. Bush's policy must be viewed in the context of the broad foreign policy and national security challenges that all presidents face, and in the context of the specific and grave dangers posed by the post-September 11 world.

John Isaacs, writing in the *Bulletin of the Atomic Scientists*, places blame on Congress, which in his view has abdicated its responsibility over war powers. Rather than have a serious debate over the grave issue of war, Isaacs notes that Congress was preoccupied with other issues, such as a tax cut, abortion, judicial nominations, and trivial commemorations. And rather than declare war—or prevent it, by refusing to appropriate money for the war—Congress passed the buck by passing a law authorizing the use of force and leaving it up to the president to decide.

ARTHUR SCHLESINGER JR.

The Imperial Presidency Redux

The weapons-of-mass-destruction (WMD) issue—where are they?—will not subside and disappear, as the administration supposes (and hopes).

The issue will build because many Americans do not like to be manipulated and deceived.

It will build because elements in Congress and in the media will wish to regain their honor and demonstrate their liberation from Bush/Cheney/Rumsfeld.

It will build because of growing interest in the parallel British inquiries by committees of the House of Commons. Robin Cook, the former foreign secretary, formulated the charge with precision: "Instead of using intelligence as evidence on which to base a decision about policy, we used intelligence as the basis on which to justify a policy on which we had already settled."

And the WMD issue will build because hyped intelligence produces a credibility gap. The credibility gap is likely to undermine the Bush doctrine and block the radical transformation of U.S. strategy to which the Bush administration is dedicated.

The strategy that won us the Cold War was a combination of containment and deterrence carried out through multilateral agencies. The Bush doctrine reverses all that. The essence of the Bush doctrine is "anticipatory self-defense," a fancy name for preventive war. Our new policy is to strike an enemy, unilaterally if necessary, before it has a chance to strike us.

Whatever legitimacy preventive war may claim derives from intelligence reliable enough to persuade responsible people, including allies, that the supposed enemy is *really* about to strike the United States. If no WMD turn up in Iraq, President Bush will lose a lot of credibility. It seems doubtful that he would be able to lead the American people into wars against Iran or North Korea simply on his presidential say-so. The credibility gap may well nullify the preventive-war policy.

And if a cache of WMD is found buried somewhere in Iraq, that is not sufficient to rescue the president. The bottom-line question is: Why were the WMD not deployed? When Saddam Hussein was fighting for his regime, his power, and his life, why in the world did he not use his WMD against the U.S. invasion? Heaven knows, he had plenty of warning.

Unearthing buried WMD would not establish Iraq as a clear and present danger to the United States. Deployment of WMD would have come much closer to convincing people that Iraq was a mortal threat.

Retreat from the preventive-war policy is all to the good, because the Bush doctrine transfers excessive power to the president. Abraham Lincoln long ago foresaw the constitutional implications of the preventive-war policy. On Feb. 15, 1848, he denounced the proposition "that if it shall become *necessary to repel invasion,* the President may, without violation of the Constitution, cross the line, and *invade* the territory of another country; and that whether such *necessity* exists in given case, the President is to be the *sole* judge."

Lincoln continued: "Allow the President to invade a neighboring nation, whenever *he* shall deem it necessary to repel an invasion . . . and you allow him to make war at pleasure. . . . If to-day, he should choose to say he thinks it necessary to invade Canada, to prevent the British from invading us, how could you stop him? You may say to him, 'I see no probability of the British invading us' but he will say to you 'be silent; I see it, if you don't.' "

"The Founding Fathers," Lincoln said, "resolved to so frame the Constitution that *no one man* should hold the power of bringing this oppression upon us."

If the Bush doctrine prevails, the imperial presidency will sure be redux.

NOEMIE EMERY
Too Much History

All through the Clinton administration and into the 2000 election, some said we had run out of history. It had been tapped out, like an overused resource. It had run dry, like a well. Then came September 11, and history came flooding back with a vengeance, swamping us all in a torrent of crisis and incident. We have so much history now that we have nowhere to put it. We have a history glut. Elected in peace, George W. Bush has become a war president, fighting hot wars and covert wars on terror, while trying to rebuild the Atlantic alliance and bring peace and order to the Middle East. He is making history more than he ever imagined, but he is also reliving it, in an unusual fusion of incidents. We are reliving not one but four past crises. And the years our present situation resembles are these:

1938

In 1938, the League of Nations, having failed to check Japanese aggression in Manchuria in 1931, Italian aggression in Ethiopia in 1935, and German aggression in the Rhineland in 1936, lapsed at last into utter inconsequence when it failed to prevent the partition of Czechoslovakia, a sellout that Britain and France hailed as "peace in our time." Peace in our time lasted just one year, before pumped up German forces rolled into Poland, setting off a world war that raged on five continents, killed 40 million people, and lasted six years. In the end, aggression was rolled back and order restored by a military alliance led by the United States and Great Britain, with Russia acting at times as an out-and-out foe, and at times as a critical ally.

In 2003, the United Nations, having failed to stop numerous incursions and massacres from Bosnia to Rwanda, once more proved its futility when its Security Council split bitterly on the issue of whether or not to enforce its own resolutions against Saddam Hussein. Once again, France helped the aggressor, aided in this instance by Russia and Germany. As the U.N. tossed itself into the dustbin of history, it became clearer and clearer that aggression would be halted and order restored by a military alliance led by the United States and Great Britain (with Russia in an on-and-off supporting role). "History keeps coming back, sometimes like a bad dinner," wrote columnist Paul Greenberg. And so it did, what with hapless attempts to disarm an aggressor, and endless French pleas for more talk. "Among the 18 European countries that now have signed on with America's latest crusade . . . was the Czech Republic," noted Greenberg. "Of course. The Czechs remember. Specifically, they remember being sold out." For the Czechs, the events of the year 1938 led to 50 years of enslavement. For the United States (which was not a member of the League), they led to attack and disaster. Which brings us to year number two.

1941

On December 7, 1941, the American fleet at Pearl Harbor was attacked by the Japanese Empire. U.S. losses were 19 ships sunk, 265 airplanes struck, and 2,403 dead. It was the first attack on U.S. soil since the British burned the White House in 1814. On September 11, 2001, three jetliners hijacked by Islamic terrorists crashed into the World Trade Center in New York City and the Pentagon in suburban Virginia and killed over 3,000 people. A fourth plane, brought down by a heroic passenger uprising, was headed for either the White House or the Capitol. It was the first attack by a foreign power on the American mainland since the British burned the White House in 1814. President Franklin D. Roosevelt had to rally his countrymen, and prepare a hot war to be fought on five continents, against the armed forces of the three Axis powers. President George W. Bush had to rally the country and prepare for a hot war to be fought on five continents, against the world-wide terrorist network, as well as its supporters. Roosevelt's enemies were nation-states, with formidable armies and large stores of conventional weapons. Bush's enemy is an all-but-invisible shadowy being, with no land or army, but access to multiple weapons of terror. Roosevelt's aim was to liberate territory and force the surrender of enemies. Bush's aim is to surgically extract the terrorists from the nations where they nest, a different and new kind of war. Roosevelt's enemies claimed he had advance knowledge of the strike at Pearl Harbor and allowed it to happen to gratify his desire to make war on Hitler. Bush's enemies claimed he had advance knowledge of the attacks in New York and Virginia, and allowed them to happen to gratify his desire to make war on Saddam. Roosevelt and Bush were both accused of being pushed into war by Jews.

By all accounts, Roosevelt knew from the mid-1930s onward that he would one day have to take up arms against Hitler; and he longed to effect a regime change in Germany. But he was unable to sell his case to his own people, and was forced to wait for a tragic attack. Bush likewise had global support for his retaliatory war on the Taliban, but faced wide resistance outside his own country to a preemptive assault on Iraq. In 2003 as in 1940, preemptive war was a hot issue and a hard sell. Which leads us to year number three.

1962

On October 16, 1962, President John F. Kennedy was given a series of photos proving that the Soviet Union was installing in Cuba 16 ballastic missiles capable of delivering nuclear warheads to Atlanta, Miami, New Orleans, Houston, Mexico City, and all of Central America as well as Washington, D.C. Cuba had never attacked the United States (rather the opposite), there was no proof that it possessed nuclear weapons, and no direct threat to fire the missiles was ever made. Nonetheless, Kennedy decided that the mere *presence* of such missiles in the hands of a hostile tyrant was so great a threat to the national interest that he was willing to risk war to have them removed.

On September 11, 2001, the damage done to the American nation with weapons no more complex than three planes filled with jet fuel made President George W. Bush see Saddam Hussein's development of weapons of mass destruction in a new and more sinister light. Iraq had never invaded America, and there was no proof that these weapons would ever be turned on American interests. Nonetheless, Bush determined that the mere *presence* of such weapons in the hands of a tyrant with Saddam's record posed such a grave threat to the national interest that he was prepared to risk war to have them destroyed. Kennedy was never willing to accept a solution that left Soviet missiles in Cuba. Bush was never willing to accept a solution that left weapons of mass destruction in the hands of Saddam Hussein. Kennedy was prepared either to bomb Cuba or to launch an invasion, but he gave the Soviet Union a chance to back down by first instituting a blockade of the island. Bush was prepared to make war on Iraq, but he gave Saddam a chance to survive by first demanding that Iraq fully disarm. On October 26, 1962, three Russian vessels turned back from Cuba, and the parties were able to reach a peaceful solution. In 2003, neither Saddam nor the U.N. appeared to be serious. And the only course remaining was war.

Bush saw threatening preemptive war as simply his duty as president. So did Kennedy, who told his brother that if he had *not* laid down his ultimatum, he would have been soon, and quite rightly, impeached. Pacifist critics reviled both men as cowboys. But for Kennedy, preemption was a one-time thing, an aberration in the forty-year run of the Cold War, which quickly reverted to its containment modality. For Bush, preemption is becoming a weapon of choice and necessity, an indispensable check on a new world of terror, to be used in self-defense by a new concert of nations. Which leads us to year number four.

1946

In the course of the year 1946, President Harry S. Truman came to understand that the assumptions he'd held about the world when he'd become president one year before no longer applied to the world he was living in, and the alliances inherited from World War II would have to be wholly reconfigured. Between September 11, 2001, and March 2003, George W. Bush came to understand that the assumptions he had held about the world when he'd become president one year before no longer applied to the world he was leading, and that the world order would have to be reconstructed and remade. Truman found that the coalition that had won World War II was no longer stable; that Russia was an enemy and China becoming one; and that the Western nations would have to rebuild their defeated Axis enemies as part of the new non-Communist bloc. Bush came to see that the alliance that had won the Cold War was splintering; that France and Germany were now at odds with the United States and Britain, which went to find allies among their former opponents, the once-captive Communist satellites. Both were surprised by the bad faith of their one-time war partners. Both were accused by their liberal critics of having started the quarrels themselves.

Truman built NATO to do the job that the U.N. could not, of safeguarding the West through collective security. Bush is faced with the job of remaking NATO to counter the new terrorist threat or replacing it. The Truman Doctrine, as it was soon called, "enumerated a heavy precedent for un-thought-out commitments to unassessed regimes in ill-defined places," wrote Derek Leebaert in *The Fifty Year Wound*. "Right now, we look back at Communism as centralized and so easy to contain. But that's not how it looked at the time."

Truman and Bush both started from the simple desire to safeguard their country, and gradually moved to the final idea that the only way to fight communism and terror was to end the conditions that made them appealing. Truman understood that his postwar world would have no lasting security unless he turned Japan and Germany into stable democracies. Bush understands that his world can have no real security without bringing reform and order to the terror-spawning Middle East. The hardest job of the 20th century went to Franklin D. Roosevelt, but the toughest decisions belonged to Harry S. Truman, who had to name, frame, and contain a wholly new form of trouble. Truman's problems, along with those of FDR and John Kennedy, now have all come to President Bush.

Some liberal critics will maintain to this day that it was Harry S. Truman who started the Cold War, with his belligerence toward the peaceable Soviet Union. The same types will tell you today, with the same straight faces, that the trainwreck in the United Nations and the deepening split in the Atlantic alliance are due to George Bush and his errors and arrogance. What others will say, with somewhat more reason, is that it would have been easier to get Stalin to agree to his own containment than to have gotten France to agree to any measure whatever penalizing Iraq. France sold Iraq the nuclear reactor that Israel had the good sense to take out in 1981. France spent the decade of the '90s helping Iraq evade U.N. rules.

Along with this de facto Iraqi alliance went another French subplot: to lead a coalition of the resentful in an effort to thwart the United States. The goal was to lead a unified Europe in the project of checking American power. In the event, it split Europe in half, breaking off its friends (Belgium, Germany, and Russia) from a larger pro-U.S. bloc. To Truman, the division of Europe was the cause of the Cold

War, and its reason for being. To Bush, the more complex split within Europe is peripheral to the war on terror, but it is a distraction and a huge complication in the effort to place the war on terror in a multinational frame. Roosevelt conducted his hot war within a mostly stable web of alliances. Truman built his new world order after the hot war had ended. Kennedy introduced his preemption idea in the frame of the Cold War, and returned to deterrence once the crisis had passed. Bush has to reframe his alliances in the midst of a hot war, with preemption an ongoing policy. Iraq did not split the Western alliance; it highlighted splits that were already there.

But even if NATO had been staunchly united, Bush would have found his Iraqi incursion a hard act to sell. He was trying to get the world to sign on to a war against a country he believed would attack in the future (thought it had issued no direct threat), using weapons of mass destruction he assumed (but could not prove) it had. "The question of whether they had nuclear weapons on the island was irrelevant; Kennedy had to assume that they did," writes Richard Reeves in *Profile of Power*. "He had already decided as soon as Bundy had shown him the photos that the United States had to take the missiles out."

Iraq was believed to be developing sinister weapons; Iraq had invaded two neighboring states. To Bush, the question of whether terrorists already had Iraqi weapons was irrelevant. He had to assume they would get them. And he had to take out, before they were usable, weapons that could do devastating harm to the United States. Not everyone regarded this imperative as self-evident. "By what right have you done this?" Khrushchev railed at Kennedy at the height of the crisis. "You are trampling on the generally accepted rules of law." Sentiments of this sort have been hurled at George W. Bush by dissenters at home, diplomats at the United Nations, French politicians, and demagogues everywhere. Kennedy was spared large public protests because his crisis arose and was settled so quickly, and the only debate was among the president's counselors. Bush endured protests for months.

Prior to 2003, there had been two key Western examples of preemptive action: Israel's strike at Saddam's nuclear reactor, and President Kennedy's blockade of Cuba. Both of these, and Bush's overthrow of Saddam's regime, were undertaken to prevent an attack with megadeath weapons. Disagreements arose when the danger of megadeath weapons plus terrorist methods collided with established tradition about what was just in war. "The law has not yet evolved to cope with the world after September 11," writes Clifford Orwin in Canada's *National Post*. The next job for Bush (when he cleans up his old ones) is to try to make sure that it does.

After this war, Bush should sit down *with his allies* to draw up *together* the rules and restrictions governing acts of preemption. A good place to start would be the suggestions laid down in the April 13 *Washington Post* by Anne-Marie Slaughter, president of the American Society of International Law. Under her rules, the presence of three conditions in a state or nation could justify preemptive use of force: "(1) possession of weapons of mass destruction or clear and convincing evidence of attempts to gain such weapons; (2) grave and systemic human rights abuses sufficient to demonstrate the absence of any internal constraints on government behavior; and (3) evidence of aggressive intent with regard to other nations." This, as she says, "sets a very high threshold," while recognizing unacceptable levels of risk.

Bush should adopt this standard and make it the basis of his policy. He should explain yet again why preemptive acts are now needed, pledge that they will be undertaken neither often nor lightly, and that most threats can be resolved short of the use of force. He can note that neither Kennedy nor the Israelis followed their acts of preemption with more, and that both made the world safer. He can note that this latest Iraq war may make other wars less likely by deterring provocative acts. One of the chores Bush didn't know he'd signed up for in becoming president is redesigning the codes of international law to make room for certain acts of preventive deterrence. It's a strange assignment for a frat boy from Texas, but then who could know?

And who could know, too, that this one-term-plus governor would be the man charged with remaking the Western alliance for the needs of the post-postwar world? Bush and Tony Blair, when they get to it, will face the task of constructing multinational arrangements—whose shape is not yet wholly clear—to police the world's rogue states and their caches of weapons for perhaps the next 50 years. At the core of this effort will be the new Gulf War coalition, with the United States and Great Britain as enforcers.

Bush and Blair will be taking apart and remaking the world put together by Truman and Churchill, reconfiguring it to meet different threats, from different parts of the world. They will be facing a world in which the challenges arise not from mighty coalitions but from shadowy networks, not from superpowers but from failed states and rogue states, not just from weapons delivered by missiles and bombers, but also from bombs placed in knapsacks, germs placed in envelopes, and canisters filled with deadly chemical agents. They will be facing infiltration through airports, not cross-border invasions; suicide bombers, not tank battalions; not just dictators with large ambitions, but madmen with nothing to lose.

These are new times that require new tactics and agencies. Even before France blew up the U.N. (and perhaps did NATO some serious damage), it was becoming evident that organizations built to cut off the next Hitler or Stalin need changes to cope with Saddam and Osama bin Laden. "Instead of seeking to restore the status quo, we should reinvent it," urges Anne-Marie Slaughter. Necessity will foster its own new inventions, as it did almost 60 years ago, this time without a French veto.

Let us not play up the strains of the present by running down those of the past. No president had a worse job than Franklin Roosevelt, a worse week than John Kennedy, a worse set of choices than Harry S. Truman, so many of which could have gone wrong. But no president other than Bush ever faced so many conflicting cross-pressures and strains. FDR joined a coalition when Pearl Harbor was bombed; he did not have to create one. Truman faced his worst moments only after containment and NATO were safely in place. Kennedy had no hostile Hans Blix to contend with, and the weapons he confronted were large enough to be photographed, and too large to be easily hidden or carted away.

In the course of this past year, President Bush and his people made two major errors, each in the context of foreign relationships. They failed to sense the depth and the breadth of the French disaffection. And they failed to sense the wide-ranging panic the idea of preemption would arouse. Critics have said they were too dense and too insular to register these shadings of foreign opinion. More likely they were simply too busy to pick up every nuance in the swirl of events. Let us recall that Truman had time to sell his containment doctrine to an unhappy world before his trial by fire: It was more than two years from Churchill's Iron Curtain speech in Fulton, Missouri, to the Soviet blockade of Berlin and the American airlift; and another two years from that to the war in Korea. Let us recall, too, that Franklin D. Roosevelt—the greatest political talent of the 20th century, a tested leader elected four times, a man richly gifted in guile and eloquence—could not coax his country into war to save itself and Great Britain until it had been savagely assaulted at home.

Sworn in as president in early 2001, Bush took office believing that "in time of peace the stakes . . . appear small." He pledged to "do small things with great love." Instead, history gave him high stakes and great pressures. How little he knew.

JOHN ISAACS
Congress Goes AWOL

On March 17, President George W. Bush announced to the nation that the United States was going to war against Iraq. The next day's headline should have read "Congress Declares War on Iraq"—except that Congress did not declare war, despite its constitutionally delegated responsibility. In fact, Congress has not officially acted on the question of war and peace since its October 2002 vote authorizing the president to decide.

Despite U.S. military actions in Korea in the 1950s and in Vietnam in the 1960s and 1970s, and more recent smaller conflicts in Panama, Grenada, Bosnia, Kosovo, and Afghanistan, Congress has failed to declare war since Pearl Harbor.

As the nation moved toward war in March, debates raged in the U.N. Security Council. The British, Canadian, and Turkish parliaments engaged in major debates. Harsh exchanges were traded between Washington, Paris, London, Moscow, Berlin, and other capitals. Dueling opinion pieces appeared in the nation's editorial pages, and worldwide demonstrations against the war were organized, using the Internet as a major channel of communications.

But Congress was silent.

Congress could have used the power of the purse to curtail the drive toward war. Before the fighting started, the administration adamantly refused to provide any estimate of the costs of the impending war. Administration officials argued repeatedly that the costs of the war and its aftermath were unknowable. Some members of Congress—primarily Democrats—complained, but got nowhere. The Bush team preferred to change the subject by crusading for the centerpiece of its domestic agenda—a $1.6 trillion tax cut, including a $726 billion "economic growth package"—despite rising federal budget deficits and the war.

On March 6, Cong. David Obey, a Wisconsin Democrat, asked wryly: "Can you imagine President Teddy Roosevelt or President Woodrow Wilson or FDR or Harry Truman saying we are going to war and your country needs you to accept a tax cut?"

Congress could have used the appropriations or budget process to deal with the question of war. Independent estimates indicated that the cost—to be borne virtually exclusively by U.S. taxpayers—might top $100 billion. The estimated $60 billion price tag for the 1991 Gulf War, in contrast, was mostly paid for by other nations. Eric Shinseki, army chief of staff, estimated that in addition to immediate costs, the United States would need to maintain an occupying force in Iraq of as many as 200,000 soldiers, perhaps for as long as a decade. And the Council on Foreign Relations estimated that it would cost a minimum of $20 billion a year to rebuild the country. (Finally, on March 24, the Bush administration asked Congress for $74.7 billion for fiscal 2003.)

Earlier, even as U.S. and British troops headed for the Iraqi border, Republicans were trying to pass an annual budget resolution without allocating a dime for the war, for rebuilding Iraq, or even for the continued fighting and reconstruction effort in Afghanistan. The House of Representatives approved a budget resolution without any of these funds, but did endorse the Bush administration's entire tax cut.

In the Senate, the verdict was mixed. The Senate rejected 56–43 an amendment offered by Kent Conrad, North Dakota Democrat, prohibiting the tax cut until the president submitted a detailed estimate of the cost of the war. It then turned around and approved 52–47 an amendment offered by Russ Feingold, Wisconsin Democrat, to set aside a reserve fund of $100 billion to pay for the war. The administration's belated submission of its war funds request did help the success of Louisiana Democrat John Breaux's amendment to halve the centerpiece of the Bush tax cut. The fate of both the Feingold and Breaux amendments was to be determined by a House-Senate conference committee completed after this writing.

The Senate spent the week before the president's war announcement consumed with a debate over the controversial procedure called "late-term" or "partial-birth" abortion and the nomination of D.C. Circuit Court nominee Miguel Estrada. It also found time to deal with National Girl Scout Week and Greek Independence Day. The House adopted medical malpractice insurance legislation. Neither body debated the war.

The Senate leadership of the two parties agreed to set aside a few hours for discussion on a sparsely attended Friday session on March 7. As Virginia Republican John Warner put it, the discussion would be on "the international situation . . . relating to the war on terrorism, with emphasis on Iraq and North Korea." Seven senators participated.

There were a few heroes who tried to get Congress to reconsider the war in a serious manner. In the Senate, 85-year-old Robert Byrd, Democrat of West Virginia, has been eloquent and even strident in denouncing the administration's drive to war. In a widely disseminated speech delivered on the Senate floor on February 12, Byrd argued that the United States was "about to embark upon the first test of a revolutionary doctrine applied in an extraordinary way at an unfortunate time. The doctrine of preemption—the idea that the United States or any other nation can legitimately attack a nation that is not imminently threatening but may be threatening in the future—is a radical new twist of the traditional idea of self-defense."

Byrd castigated the Bush administration for "split[ting] traditional alliances, possibly crippling, for all time, international order-keeping entities like the United Nations and NATO." And yet the Senate, he sadly noted, is "ominously, dreadfully silent. There is no debate, no discussion, no attempt to lay out for the nation the pros and cons of this particular war. There is nothing."

Vermont Democrat Patrick Leahy agreed in a March 3 Senate floor speech: "What I hear from people is: Why is there not any discussion about a possible war against Iraq? The British Parliament has had a major debate on it. The Turkish Parliament had a major debate on it. The Canadian Parliament had a major debate on it. . . . The impression of the American people, both Republicans and Democrats, is that the Senate does not want to discuss a war with Iraq."

Massachusetts Democrat Edward Kennedy, a liberal workhorse who in past years had devoted much of his time to health care, education, and other domestic issues, turned his focus toward the impending war in a March 13 Senate speech. "I am concerned," he said, "that as we rush to war with Iraq, we are becoming more divided at home and more isolated in the world community. Instead of persuading the dissenters at home and abroad, the administration by its harsh rhetoric is driving the wedge deeper. Never before, even in the Vietnam War, has America taken such bold military action with so little international support."

Both Byrd and Kennedy—and in the House, Oregon's Peter DeFazio—introduced resolutions to force Congress to vote a second time on whether the country should go to war.

They got nowhere. The Republican Party was adamantly opposed to a new vote; so too were the Democrats. The Republican motivation was easy to understand. Congress had spoken in October, giving the president full authority to proceed as he desired. As House Appropriations Committee Chairman C. W. "Bill" Young told the March 15 *Congressional Quarterly*, "Congress should now be micromanaging a war. Congress should be in a support role."

For the Democrats, a new vote would only have demonstrated the division within the party. When the Senate voted 77–23 for the use-of-force resolution in October, 29 Democrats voted "yea" and 21 voted "nay." House Democrats were also split; in an overall vote of 296–133, 126 opposed the resolution and 81 voted for it. Even war critics acknowledged that a new vote would have produced a similar outcome.

Congress's failure to act is not new. Many in both parties were uneasy with, or opposed to, U.S. military involvement in Kosovo and Bosnia, but refused to force President Bill Clinton to call the troops home. Since World War II, Congress has willingly ceded the power to make war—letting the president take responsibility for success or failure. And if the war goes badly, as in Somalia in the 1990s, Congress is also willing to let the president take the fall.

As the Vietnam War wound down and President Richard Nixon became increasingly crippled by Watergate, in 1973 Congress adopted the War Powers Act over a presidential veto. That bill would have forced a president to bring U.S. troops home from any overseas engagement within 60 days if Congress has not in the meantime approved the fighting.

It was a bold action, but there has been no follow-through. For 30 years, Congress and presidents have ignored that law just as they have ignored the Constitution. As the war clouds gathered, Congress went AWOL—again. Senators and representatives decided they would rather talk about Iraq than vote, and better yet, change the subject.

DISCUSSION QUESTIONS

1. *What would you do?* You are an adviser to a member of Congress, and she is intrigued by Isaacs's idea that Congress could have stopped the Iraq war by refusing to appropriate money for that purpose. Provide an analysis of the Isaacs plan. Is his position realistic? Granting that Congress *could* have done this, what are the political obstacles to using the power of the purse to stop a war? How do you think the public might respond to such a step?

2. In terms of evaluating the appropriate use of presidential power, are there significant differences between a policy of preemptive war (using military action to stop a surprise attack known to be imminent) and a policy of preventive war (using military action to prevent a threat from emerging)?

3. How should we measure presidential power?

8   Evaluating Bureaucratic Performance: Can Government Be Run Like a Business?

Ask most people what they think of when they hear the term *government bureaucracy*, and you'll likely hear "red tape," "waste," "incompetence," or worse. It is telling that perhaps the worst charge made against President Bill Clinton's ill-fated 1994 Health Care Reform Act was that it would result in health care delivered with the courtesy of the Department of Motor Vehicles and the efficiency of the Post Office. It has become a common refrain that government needs to be run more like a business, with attention to the bottom line, a focus on "customer" needs, and a focus on mission overlap and efficiency.

In the public mind a government agency is the antithesis of an efficient, lean organization. Unlike nimble, well-run organizations (think Southwest Airlines or Dell Computer), government agencies plod along, providing poor service at high cost and choked by inefficient rules that prevent innovation.

Is this a fair picture? Political scientist James Q. Wilson argues that government agencies will *never* operate like a business, nor should they be expected to. His 1989 comparison of the Watertown, Massachusetts, Registry of Motor Vehicles (representative of any government agency) with a nearby McDonald's (representative of private, profit-seeking organizations) shows that the former will most likely never be able to service its clientele as well as the latter. The problem, though, is not bureaucratic laziness or bad employees, but rather the very characteristics of the two types of organizations. In order to understand "what government agencies do and why they do it," Wilson argues that we must first recognize that government bureaucracies operate in a political marketplace rather than an economic one. An agency's annual revenues, personnel resources, and management rules are determined by elected officials, not by the agency's ability to meet the demands of its customers in a cost-efficient manner. Agencies are not, as a rule, rewarded if they become more efficient, nor are they penalized for not performing their functions well. Private organizations, in contrast, have much more control over their own goals and structure, and they are rewarded with increased profits if they become more efficient. Perhaps most critically, a government agency's goals are often vague, difficult if not impossible to measure, and often even contradictory. In business, the goals and evaluation processes are much simpler: the goal of any business is to maximize profit, and it is relatively easy to look at performance to see whether this goal is being met.

Goals and performance are much harder to measure for public agencies. The second reading is an excerpt from a General Accounting Office report on the Department of State. In 1993, Congress enacted a law—The Government Performance and Results Act of 1993—designed to make federal agencies more efficient. Among other things, the law requires agencies to review their activities, with the goal of identifying how they achieve desired results. This process forces agencies to specify what, precisely, their goals are. In late 2001, the GAO issued its report on the State Department. What does the department do? According to the agency's own mission statement, "The Department of State is the lead institution for the conduct of American diplomacy, a mission based on the role of the Secretary of State as the President's principal foreign policy adviser."

As the GAO report makes clear, the outcomes the State Department set for itself are extraordinarily ambitious, very general, and nearly impossible to evaluate. The goals—eliminate the threat from weapons of mass destruction; expand foreign markets for U.S. goods and services; enhance the ability of Americans to travel and live abroad safely; reduce international crime and the availability of illegal drugs; reduce international terrorist attacks—seem to be well outside the ability of any one agency to control, and the GAO criticized many of the specific performance targets the department used to determine whether it was meeting the goals. In many cases, the GAO concluded, the department relied on quantifiable measures—the number of people trained, the number of academies established, the number of agreements reached—without explaining how those measures were related to specific goals.

JAMES Q. WILSON
What Government Agencies Do and Why They Do It, from *Bureaucracy*

By the time the office opens at 8:45 A.M., the line of people waiting to do business at the Registry of Motor Vehicles in Watertown, Massachusetts, often will be twenty-five deep. By midday, especially if it is near the end of the month, the line may extend clear around the building. Inside, motorists wait in slow-moving rows before poorly marked windows to get a driver's license or to register an automobile. When someone gets to the head of the line, he or she is often told by the clerk that it is the wrong line: "Get an application over there and then come back," or "This is only for people getting a new license; if you want to replace one you lost, you have to go to the next window." The customers grumble impatiently. The clerks act harried and sometimes speak brusquely, even rudely. What seems to be a simple transaction may take 45 minutes or even longer. By the time people are photographed for their driver's licenses, they are often scowling. The photographer valiantly tries to get people to smile, but only occasionally succeeds.

Not far away, people also wait in line at a McDonald's fast-food restaurant. There are several lines; each is short, each moves quickly. The menu is clearly displayed on attractive signs. The workers behind the counter are invariably polite. If someone's order cannot be filled immediately, he or she is asked to step aside for a moment while the food is prepared and then is brought back to the head of the line to receive the order. The atmosphere is friendly and good-natured. The room is immaculately clean.

Many people have noticed the difference between getting a driver's license and ordering a Big Mac. Most will explain it by saying that bureaucracies are different from businesses. "Bureaucracies" behave as they do because they are run by unqualified "bureaucrats" and are enmeshed in "rules" and "red tape."

But business firms are also bureaucracies, and McDonald's is a bureaucracy that regulates virtually every detail of its employees' behavior by a complex and all-encompassing set of rules. Its operations manual is six hundred pages long and weighs four pounds. In it one learns that french fries are to be nine-thirty-seconds of an inch thick and that grill workers are to place hamburger patties on the grill from left to right, six to a row for six rows. They are then to flip the third row first, followed by the fourth, fifth, and sixth rows, and finally the first and second. The amount of sauce placed on each bun is precisely specified. Every window must be washed every day. Workers must get down on their hands and knees and pick up litter as soon as it appears. These and countless other rules designed to reduce the workers to interchangeable automata were inculcated in franchise managers at Hamburger University located in a $40 million facility. There are plenty of rules governing the Registry, but they are only a small fraction of the rules that govern every detail of every operation at McDonald's. Indeed, if the DMV manager tried to impose on his employees as demanding a set of rules as those that govern the McDonald's staff, they would probably rebel and he would lose his job.

It is just as hard to explain the differences between the two organizations by reference to the quality or compensation of their employees. The Registry workers are all adults, most with at least a high school education; the McDonald's employees are mostly teenagers, many still in school. The Registry staff is well paid compared to the McDonald's workers, most of whom receive only the minimum wage. When labor shortages developed in Massachusetts during the mid-1980s, many McDonald's stores began hiring older people (typically housewives) of the same sort who had long worked for the Registry. They behaved just like the teenagers they replaced.

Not only are the differences between the two organizations not to be explained by reference to "rules" or "red tape" or "incompetent workers," the differences call into question many of the most frequently mentioned complaints about how government agencies are supposed to behave. For example: "Government agencies are big spenders." The Watertown office of the Registry is in a modest building that can barely handle its clientele. The teletype machine used to check information submitted by people requesting a replacement license was antiquated and prone to errors. Three or four clerks often had to wait in line to use equipment described by the office manager as "personally signed by Thomas Edison." No computers or word processors were available to handle the preparation of licenses and registrations; any error made by a clerk while manually typing a form meant starting over again on another form. [This article was written in 1989—*Editors*.]

Or: "Government agencies hire people regardless of whether they are really needed." Despite the fact that the citizens of Massachusetts probably have more contact with the Registry than with any other state agency, and despite the fact that these citizens complain more about Registry service than about that of any other bureau, the Watertown branch, like all Registry offices, was seriously understaffed.

In 1981, the agency lost 400 workers—about 25 percent of its work force—despite the fact that its workload was rising.

Or: "Government agencies are imperialistic, always grasping for new functions." But there is no record of the Registry doing much grasping, even though one could imagine a case being made that the state government could usefully create at Registry offices "one-stop" multi-service centers where people could not only get drivers' licenses but also pay taxes and parking fines, obtain information, and transact other official business. The Registry seemed content to provide one service.

In short, many of the popular stereotypes about government agencies and their members are either questionable or incomplete. To explain why government agencies behave as they do, it is not enough to know that they are "bureaucracies"—that is, it is not enough to know that they are big, or complex, or have rules. What is crucial is that they are *government* bureaucracies. As the preceding chapters should make clear, not all government bureaucracies behave the same way or suffer from the same problems. There may even be registries of motor vehicles in other states that do a better job than the one in Massachusetts. But all government agencies have in common certain characteristics that tend to make their management far more difficult than managing a McDonald's. These common characteristics are the constraints of public agencies.

The key constraints are three in number. To a much greater extent than is true of private bureaucracies, government agencies (1) cannot lawfully retain and devote to the private benefit of their members the earnings of the organization, (2) cannot allocate the factors of production in accordance with the preferences of the organization's administrators, and (3) must serve goals not of the organization's own choosing. Control over revenues, productive factors, and agency goals is all vested to an important degree in entities external to the organization—legislatures, courts, politicians, and interest groups. Given this, agency managers must attend to the demands of these external entities. As a result, government management tends to be driven by the *constraints* on the organization, not the *tasks* of the organization. To say the same thing in other words, whereas business management focuses on the "bottom line" (that is, profits), government management focuses on the "top line" (that is, constraints). Because government managers are not as strongly motivated as private ones to define the tasks of their subordinates, these tasks are often shaped by [other] factors.

* * *

REVENUES AND INCENTIVES

In the days leading up to September 30, the federal government is Cinderella, courted by legions of individuals and organizations eager to get grants and contracts from the unexpended funds still at the disposal of each agency. At midnight on September 30, the government's coach turns into a pumpkin. That is the moment—the end of the fiscal year—at which every agency, with a few exceptions, must return all unexpended funds to the Treasury Department.

Except for certain quasi-independent government corporations, such as the

Tennessee Valley Authority, no agency may keep any surplus revenues (that is, the difference between the funds it received from a congressional appropriation and those it needed to operate during the year). By the same token, any agency that runs out of money before the end of the fiscal year may ask Congress for more (a "supplemental appropriation") instead of being forced to deduct the deficit from any accumulated cash reserves. Because of these fiscal rules agencies do not have a material incentive to economize: Why scrimp and save if you cannot keep the results of your frugality?

Nor can individual bureaucrats lawfully capture for their personal use any revenue surpluses. When a private firm has a good year, many of its officers and workers may receive bonuses. Even if no bonus is paid, these employees may buy stock in the firm so that they can profit from any growth in earnings (and, if they sell the stock in a timely manner, profit from a drop in earnings). Should a public bureaucrat be discovered trying to do what private bureaucrats routinely do, he or she would be charged with corruption.

We take it for granted that bureaucrats should not profit from their offices and nod approvingly when a bureaucrat who has so benefited is indicted and put on trial. But why should we take this view? Once a very different view prevailed. In the seventeenth century, a French colonel would buy his commission from the king, take the king's money to run his regiment, and pocket the profit. At one time a European tax collector was paid by keeping a percentage of the taxes he collected. In this country, some prisons were once managed by giving the warden a sum of money based on how many prisoners were under his control and letting him keep the difference between what he received and what it cost him to feed the prisoners. Such behavior today would be grounds for criminal prosecution. Why? What has changed?

Mostly we the citizenry have changed. We are creatures of the Enlightenment: We believe that the nation ought not to be the property of the sovereign; that laws are intended to rationalize society and (if possible) perfect mankind; and that public service ought to be neutral and disinterested. We worry that a prison warden paid in the old way would have a strong incentive to starve his prisoners in order to maximize his income; that a regiment supported by a greedy colonel would not be properly equipped; and that a tax collector paid on a commission basis would extort excessive taxes from us. These changes reflect our desire to eliminate moral hazards—namely, creating incentives for people to act wrongly. But why should this desire rule out more carefully designed compensation plans that would pay government managers for achieving officially approved goals and would allow efficient agencies to keep any unspent part of their budget for use next year?

Part of the answer is obvious. Often we do not know whether a manager or an agency has achieved the goals we want because either the goals are vague or inconsistent, or their attainment cannot be observed, or both. Bureau chiefs in the Department of State would have to go on welfare if their pay depended on their ability to demonstrate convincingly that they had attained their bureaus' objectives.

But many government agencies have reasonably clear goals toward which progress can be measured. The Social Security Administration, the Postal Service, and the General Services Administration all come to mind. Why not let earnings depend importantly on performance? Why not let agencies keep excess revenues?

* * *

But in part it is because we know that even government agencies with clear goals and readily observable behavior only can be evaluated by making political (and thus conflict-ridden) judgments. If the Welfare Department delivers every benefit check within twenty-four hours after the application is received, Senator Smith may be pleased but Senator Jones will be irritated because this speedy delivery almost surely would require that the standards of eligibility be relaxed so that many ineligible clients would get money. There is no objective standard by which the tradeoff between speed and accuracy in the Welfare Department can be evaluated. Thus we have been unwilling to allow welfare employees to earn large bonuses for achieving either speed or accuracy.

The inability of public managers to capture surplus revenues for their own use alters the pattern of incentives at work in government agencies. Beyond a certain point additional effort does not produce additional earnings. (In this country, Congress from time to time has authorized higher salaries for senior bureaucrats but then put a cap on actual payments to them so that the pay increases were never received. This was done to insure that no bureaucrat would earn more than members of Congress at a time when those members were unwilling to accept the political costs of raising their own salaries. As a result, the pay differential between the top bureaucratic rank and those just below it nearly vanished.) If political constraints reduce the marginal effect of money incentives, then the relative importance of other, nonmonetary incentives will increase. * * *

That bureaucratic performance in most government agencies cannot be linked to monetary benefits is not the whole explanation for the difference between public and private management. There are many examples of private organizations whose members cannot appropriate money surpluses for their own benefit. Private schools ordinarily are run on a nonprofit basis. Neither the headmaster nor the teachers share in the profit of these schools; indeed, most such schools earn no profit at all and instead struggle to keep afloat by soliciting contributions from friends and alumni. Nevertheless, the evidence is quite clear that on the average, private schools, both secular and denominational, do a better job than public ones in educating children. Moreover, as political scientists John Chubb and Terry Moe have pointed out, they do a better job while employing fewer managers. Some other factors are at work. One is the freedom an organization has to acquire and use labor and capital.

ACQUIRING AND USING THE FACTORS OF PRODUCTION

A business firm acquires capital by retaining earnings, borrowing money, or selling shares of ownership; a government agency (with some exceptions) acquires capital by persuading a legislature to appropriate it. A business firm hires, promotes, demotes, and fires personnel with considerable though not perfect freedom; a federal government agency is told by Congress how many persons it can hire and at what rate of pay, by the Office of Personnel Management (OPM) what rules it must follow in selecting and assigning personnel, by the Office of Management and Budget (OMB) how many persons of each rank it may employ, by the Merit Systems Protection Board (MSPB) what procedures it must follow in demoting or discharging personnel, and by the courts whether it has faithfully followed the rules of Congress, OPM, OMB, and MSPB. A business firm purchases goods and services by internally defined procedures (including those that allow it to buy from someone other than the lowest bidder if a more expensive vendor seems more reliable), or to skip the bidding procedure altogether in favor of direct negotiations; a government agency must purchase much of what it uses by formally advertising for bids, accepting the lowest, and keeping the vendor at arm's length. When a business firm develops a good working relationship with a contractor, it often uses that vendor repeatedly without looking for a new one; when a government agency has a satisfactory relationship with a contractor, ordinarily it cannot use the vendor again without putting a new project out for a fresh set of bids. When a business firm finds that certain offices or factories are no longer economical it will close or combine them; when a government agency wishes to shut down a local office or military base often it must get the permission of the legislature (even when formal permission is not necessary, informal consultation is). When a business firm draws up its annual budget each expenditure item can be reviewed as a discretionary amount (except for legally mandated payments of taxes to government and interest to banks and bondholders); when a government agency makes up its budget many of the detailed expenditure items are mandated by the legislature.

All these complexities of doing business in or with the government are well-known to citizens and firms. These complexities in hiring, purchasing, contracting, and budgeting often are said to be the result of the "bureaucracy's love of red tape." But few, if any, of the rules producing this complexity would have been generated by the bureaucracy if left to its own devices, and many are as cordially disliked by the bureaucrats as by their clients. These rules have been imposed on the agencies by external actors, chiefly the legislature. They are not bureaucratic rules but *political* ones. In principle the legislature could allow the Social Security Administration, the Defense Department, or the New York City public school system to follow the same rules as IBM, General Electric, or Harvard University. In practice they could not. The reason is politics, or more precisely, democratic politics.

* * *

PUBLIC VERSUS PRIVATE MANAGEMENT

What distinguishes public from private organizations is neither their size nor their desire to "plan" (that is, control) their environments but rather the rules under which they acquire and use capital and labor. General Motors acquires capital by selling shares, issuing bonds, or retaining earnings; the Department of Defense acquires it from an annual appropriation by Congress. GM opens and closes plants, subject to certain government regulations, at its own discretion; DOD opens and closes military bases under the watchful guidance of Congress. GM pays its managers with salaries it sets and bonuses tied to its earnings; DOD pays its managers with salaries set by Congress and bonuses (if any) that have no connection with organizational performance. The number of workers in GM is determined by its level of production; the number in DOD by legislation and civil-service rules.

What all this means can be seen by returning to the Registry of Motor Vehicles and McDonald's. Suppose you were just appointed head of the Watertown office of the Registry and you wanted to improve service there so that it more nearly approximated the service at McDonald's. Better service might well require spending more money (on clerks, equipment, and buildings). Why should your political superiors give you that money? It is a cost to them if it requires either higher taxes or taking funds from another agency; offsetting these real and immediate costs are dubious and postponed benefits. If lines become shorter and clients become happier, no legislator will benefit. There may be fewer complaints, but complaints are episodic and have little effect on the career of any given legislator. By contrast, shorter lines and faster service at McDonald's means more customers can be served per hour and thus more money can be earned per hour. A McDonald's manager can estimate the marginal product of the last dollar he or she spends on improving service; the Registry manager can generate no tangible return on any expenditure he or she makes and thus cannot easily justify the expenditure.

Improving service at the Registry may require replacing slow or surly workers with quick and pleasant ones. But you, the manager, can neither hire nor fire them at will. You look enviously at the McDonald's manager who regularly and with little notice replaces poor workers with better ones. Alternatively, you may wish to mount an extensive training program (perhaps creating a Registration University to match McDonald's Hamburger University) that would imbue a culture of service in your employees. But unless the Registry were so large an agency that the legislature would neither notice nor care about funds spent for this purpose—and it is not that large—you would have a tough time convincing anybody that this was not a wasteful expenditure on a frill project.

If somehow your efforts succeed in making Registry clients happier, you can take vicarious pleasure in it; in the unlikely event a client seeks you out to thank you for those efforts, you can bask in a moment's worth of glory. Your colleague at McDonald's who manages to make customers happier may also derive some vicarious satisfaction from the improvement but in addition he or she will earn more money owing to an increase in sales.

In time it will dawn on you that if you improve service too much, clients will start coming to the Watertown office instead of going to the Boston office. As a result, the lines you succeeded in shortening will become longer again. If you wish to keep complaints down, you will have to spend even more on the Watertown office. But if it was hard to persuade the legislature to do that in the past, it is impossible now. Why should the taxpayer be asked to spend more on Watertown when the Boston office, fully staffed (naturally, no one was laid off when the clients disappeared), has no lines at all? From the legislature's point of view the correct level of expenditure is not that which makes one office better than another but that which produces an equal amount of discontent in all offices.

Finally, you remember that your clients have no choice: the Registry offers a monopoly service. It and only it supplies drivers' licenses. In the long run all that matters is that there are not "too many" complaints to the legislature about service. Unlike McDonald's, the Registry need not fear that its clients will take their business to Burger King or to Wendy's. Perhaps you should just relax.

If this were all there is to public management it would be an activity that quickly and inevitably produces cynicism among its practitioners. But this is not the whole story. For one thing, public agencies differ in the kinds of problems they face. For another, many public managers try hard to do a good job even though they face these difficult constraints.

GENERAL ACCOUNTING OFFICE

Department of State: Status of Achieving Key Outcomes and Addressing Major Management Challenges

Dear Senator Thompson:

As you requested, we reviewed the Department of State's (State) fiscal year 2000 performance report and fiscal year 2002 performance plan required by the Government Performance and Results Act of 1993 (GPRA) to assess the department's progress in achieving selected key outcomes that you identified as important mission areas. Our review includes a discussion of State's past performance and future performance targets for counterterrorism and other key foreign policy efforts, which were developed prior to the terrorist attacks on New York City and Washington, D.C., on September 11, 2001. We recognize the events of that day and subsequent days may greatly alter State's approach to its strategic goals and objectives in many of the areas we examined for this review, particularly those involving counterterrorism. We hope that this report provides the department and others with insights that will assist them when developing new efforts to counter terrorism and protect American citizens, assets, and interests, both at home and abroad. In this review, we focused on the same outcomes we addressed in our June 2000 review of the department's fiscal year 1999 performance report and fiscal year 2001 performance plan to provide a baseline by which to measure the department's performance from year to year. These selected key outcomes are as follows:

- eliminate the threat from weapons of mass destruction;
- expand foreign markets for U.S. products and services;
- enhance the ability of American citizens to travel and live abroad securely;
- reduce international crime and availability and/or use of illegal drugs; and

- reduce international terrorist attacks, especially against the United States and its citizens.

As agreed, using the selected key outcomes for State as a framework, we

(1) assessed the progress State has made in achieving these outcomes and the strategies the department has in place to achieve them and

(2) compared State's fiscal year 2000 performance report and fiscal year 2002 performance plan with the department's prior-year performance report and plan for these outcomes.

Additionally, we agreed to analyze how State addressed its major management challenges, including the government-wide high-risk areas of human capital and information security, that we and State's Inspector General identified. Appendix I provides detailed information on how State addressed these challenges. State reported little progress in eliminating the threat from weapons of mass destruction during fiscal year 2000; however, it reports substantial progress toward achieving the other four key outcomes by meeting many of its performance goals and targets. Based on our analysis, it is difficult to determine the level of progress on the five outcomes because the performance report does not always clearly describe what State sought to accomplish due to a lack of linkages between activity-based performance indicators and outcomes and a failure to report on many performance indicators prescribed in the performance plan for fiscal year 2000. The department provided little discussion on why certain indicators were not reported, why others did not meet expected performance, and what strategies would be used to achieve the unmet (and unreported) performance targets. Finally, the report discussed information technology as a strategy for achieving outcomes only for assisting Americans traveling and living abroad, and it did not address human capital issues in the context of achieving any outcome. State's performance plan for 2002 clearly linked the department's strategies and indicators to its key outcomes and discussed how it will address some of the unmet and unreported indicators in both 2001 and 2002. The plan's performance goals and indicators are objective and measurable, although many are activity rather than outcome oriented.

Planned Outcome: Eliminate the Threat from Weapons of Mass Destruction. State reported little progress in eliminating the threat from weapons of mass destruction, particularly reflected in its inability to achieve the targets for three performance indicators: (1) establishing nonproliferation export controls in the 12 countries formerly comprising the Soviet Union (the Newly Independent States), (2) ratifying the Strategic Arms Reduction Treaty III, and (3) reaching agreement with Russia on antiballistic missile defense and theater missile defense demarcation. The department presented strategies for meeting these indicators in the future. Progress toward achieving targets related to a third indicator—countries joining the Chemical Weapons Convention—was unclear because State did not demonstrate that the countries joining the convention during fiscal year 2000 were the actual targeted nations. Finally, the department reported no progress related to the Antiballistic Missile Defense and Theater Missile Defense treaties. Although State's performance plan for 2002 greatly reduced the number of performance goals and indicators, many of the performance targets lack valid measures of progress.

Planned Outcome: Expand Foreign Markets for U.S. Products and Services. State reported successes in expanding foreign markets for U.S. products and services, saying it fully or partially achieved performance targets for all seven indicators. However, we disagree with State's assessment on two of the seven indicators—the number of Newly Independent States joining the World Trade Organization and the number of countries maintaining a 90-day petroleum stock. In addition, it is difficult to see the relationship between the latter indicator and the goal of expanding foreign markets for U.S. products and services. State's 2002 performance goals and indicators for its two major efforts—opening new markets and expanding trade—are objective and measurable, and the department's strategies clearly link performance goals and indicators to outcomes; however, many of the measures are activity based rather than outcome oriented.

Planned Outcome: Enhance the Ability of American Citizens to Travel and Live Abroad Securely. State reported substantial progress in achieving this outcome; however, we found that only one of the two current performance targets was achieved. Furthermore, the department did not report on basic services it provides. State dropped two performance indicators prescribed in the 2000 performance plan—memoranda of understanding between State and commercial airlines and status of Year 2000 compliance—because neither remained applicable during 2000. The department achieved its primary targets associated with its indicator for disseminating information via the Internet. However, success in achieving the performance target for reducing the caseload of child abduction caseworkers was overstated because the department did not achieve the actual levels of cases per worker outlined in the performance plan for 2000. In addition, State did not report on two of its most prominent activities—the issuance of passports and the treatment of U.S. citizens in foreign prisons—although the performance plan for 2000 did not list either as specific indicators for these areas. The department stated it would address the partially met indicator related to child abduction caseloads by developing a new case-tracking system. In addition, in 2002, the department will continue using its consular Web site; implement computerized tracking systems for international adoptions and American citizens incarcerated abroad; and report on other prominent services, such as passport services.

Planned Outcome: Reduce International Crime and the Availability and/or Use of Illegal Drugs. State reported success in achieving performance targets; however, it is difficult to determine progress achieving the outcome because State's indicators were output rather than outcome oriented and presented no data related to stemming the flow of illegal drugs. State presented data on the number of people trained and the number of international law enforcement academies established, but it did not report how this training affected the levels of international crime and its impact on the United States and its citizens. In 2002, State is to focus on new anticrime and antismuggling operations; begin negotiating an anticorruption agreement; and take actions to make progress on investigating, prosecuting, and convicting major narcotics criminals. While some of the indicators associated with the international crime performance goals are not easily measurable, they are generally results oriented.

Planned Outcome: Reduce International Terrorist Attacks, Especially Against the United States and Its Citizens. State reported it successfully achieved its performance targets on all indicators; however, it is difficult to determine progress toward achieving the outcome because linkages between the outcome and its related activities and indicators were not clear. In addition, indicators were output based, generally reporting the number of people trained or training sessions held. Moreover, the department did not report on the two basic measures that define the outcome—the number and severity of terrorist attacks. In 2002, State's goals are to reduce the number of attacks, bring terrorists to justice, reduce or eliminate state-sponsored terrorist acts, delegitimize the use of terror as a political tool, enhance international response, and strengthen international cooperation and operational capabilities to counter terrorism. In addition, the department will report on the number of terrorist attacks and the number of human casualties, as it did for fiscal year 1999.

* * *

Despite efforts to improve the clarity and readability of its performance report, State's report for 2000 suffered from many of the same weaknesses of the 1999 report. Two major weaknesses are that (1) many indicators continue to be activity based rather than outcome oriented and (2) relationships between some key outcomes and strategies and indicators remain unclear. In addition, State changed some indicators, or the methodologies for measuring them, with little or no discussion on why it did so; and like 1999, the department failed to report on many of the performance indicators defined by its plan for 2000. Moreover, State did not discuss strategies for addressing unmet (and unreported) performance targets and did not provide assessments of how performance in fiscal year 2000 could affect estimated performance levels for 2001.

The 2000 performance report continues to rely on activity- or output-based indicators, rather than outcome-oriented indicators; and State did not establish connections between its actions and the success or failure of key outcomes. We recognize that the nature of State's mission and operating environment makes it difficult for the department to avoid either having very broad key outcomes that are then not addressed sufficiently by the indicators or broad indicators that make it difficult to assess State's role in the outcome. Given this difficulty, we find it commendable that most reported indicators are quantifiable and that all reported indicators have baselines and targets. Nevertheless, as we suggested in 1999, there are opportunities to better describe State's outputs and clarify how they affect outcomes.

For example, assessing whether terrorist attacks were reduced requires either a comparison of the relative number of terrorist attacks or a count of instances when specific attacks were prevented. In the 1999 report, one of the indicators for this issue was the "level of terrorist attacks against American citizens and interests." This indicator provided a direct measure of whether the goal was met (outcome), but it is unclear on what action the United States took (output) to influence the outcome. Rather than linking an action or strategy to the indicator, as noted above, in its 2000 report State did not report the number or severity of terrorist attacks.

The relationships between some strategies and key outcomes were not always apparent. For example, State does not clearly explain how some strategies, such as establishing law enforcement academies in southern Africa and New Mexico, related to the key outcome of minimizing the impact of international crime and stemming the flow of illegal drugs. State also reported on some indicators that were not clearly linked to key outcomes. For example, it is not clear how a nation maintaining a 90-day stock of petroleum reserves becomes a more open market for U.S. goods and services. In addition, reducing the caseload of overseas child abduction investigators appears more closely related to reducing the impact of international crime on American citizens than providing efficient, knowledgeable, and courteous services to Americans traveling and living abroad.

Furthermore, the relationship between performance indicators and strategies were not always clear. In particular, it is unclear whether each strategy is designed to pursue specific indicators under a performance goal or whether the strategies are part of a more general effort. For example, three of the five indicators for the key outcome, "opening foreign markets" to U.S. goods and services, related to a single strategy—"advancing civil aviation, transport, telecommunications, and energy initiatives"—while most of the remaining nine strategies had no readily associated indicators.

Some indicators to measure performance in 1999 were changed in 2000 without explanation, which makes it difficult to track performance from one year to the next. For some indicators used in 1999, measurement methodologies were altered with no discussion in either the performance plan or performance report for 2000, resulting in orders of magnitude differences. For the indicator "sales of U.S. telecommunications and information technology equipment," State's 1999 performance report showed a 1998 baseline of $18.9 billion in sales and a 1999 target of $20.6 billion, but it did not provide actual performance for 1999. For the same indicator in 2000, State reported a 1998 baseline of $111 billion in sales, a 1999 actual level of $123 billion, a 2000 target of $120 billion, and a 2000 actual level of $140 billion. It is apparent that State changed the methodology for assessing this indicator, but the department did not explain why it did so.

In addition, State changed past performance results for some indicators. For example, regarding expansion of markets for U.S. products and services, the actual level for the total exports of goods for 1999 cited in State's 1999 performance report was $693 billion. However, the 2000 performance report adjusted the 1999 actual level for the total exports of goods to $673 billion. State provided no explanation for this change. If the fiscal year 2000 report's actual level for 1999 is correct, then State did not reach its 1999 performance target of $685 billion that it reported it had successfully met in its 1999 performance report.

* * *

CONCLUSION

Weaknesses in State's fiscal year 2000 performance report made it difficult to determine the department's progress toward achieving the key outcomes. These weaknessses are rooted in performance goals and indicators established in its performance plan for 2000, which was prepared in 1998 and which we have criticized in a prior report. State acknowledged flaws in its previous GPRA products and sought to correct many of them in its performance plan for 2002. State has taken a major step toward implementing GPRA requirements by producing a fiscal year 2002 plan that is superior to earlier efforts. Although we identified several areas where improvements can be made, such as developing indicators that are focused on results instead of outputs, we believe that the improved plan lays the groundwork for State to provide a more clear assessment of its performance and progress next year. In its future performance report, State will need to focus its efforts on reporting on all indicators in the plan and, if targets are not achieved, providing clear explanations of the reasons why and what actions State plans to achieve the targets in the future.

DISCUSSION QUESTIONS

1. *What would you do?* Imagine that you are the head of a small federal agency, and an employee comes up with a plausible plan that would allow your agency to provide the same level of service with half the budget and half the staff that you currently have. What do you do? Do you present the plan to Congress? What sorts of conflicting pressures might you face?

2. How would you describe the goals and functions of the State Department? How would you, realistically, derive standards of performance that would tell you whether the department is achieving those goals? Is this task of goal definition and measurement easier for other agencies (perhaps the National Aeronautics and Space Administration, the Department of Agriculture, or the Drug Enforcement Administration)?

3. What incentives do legislators have to make bureaucracies more efficient? One school of thought holds that legislators, in fact, *prefer* that agencies be inefficient, so that legislators can step in and help constituents with problems that arise. That way, legislators get credit for problem solving. Do you find this reasoning plausible?

4. It is easy to criticize the State Department's evaluation process—after all, the agency has some of the most difficult and vague responsibilities of any federal agency. Is there an alternative? If the goals and outcomes mentioned in the report aren't the right ones, then what should they be?

9 The Judicial Nomination Process

Politicians, scholars, lawyers, and judges have long debated the role of the federal courts in a democratic system. Whereas Alexander Hamilton viewed the judiciary as the "least dangerous branch" of government, Thomas Jefferson and others worried about the potential for an imperial judiciary unencumbered by any institutional or electoral checks. The debate continues today, not only over the validity of different philosophies of judicial interpretation, but over the role of the Senate in confirming presidential nominations to the federal bench. Since many controversial and polarizing issues are (or are likely to be) fought over in the courts—abortion, affirmative action, gay rights, criminal law—these nomination battles have become more important. Democrats claim that Republican senators tried to block or stall confirmation of Clinton's judicial nominations; Republicans are now making the same argument about Democratic senators and Bush's picks. As of December 2003, Democrats had filibustered six of Bush's judicial nominations (including Miguel Estrada, Charles Pickering, and Priscilla Owens).

Jack Newfield asserts that President Bush is trying to stack the federal judiciary with extreme right-wing appointments who will bring overt partisan ideology to the federal bench. These judges, Newfield argues, would roll back decades of progress in civil rights, restrict abortion, and pursue a right-wing agenda. In his view, the Senate has a responsibility to reject these extremist nominees and insist that Bush send forward more moderate candidates. He agrees with Senator Charles Schumer (D-NY) that it is perfectly appropriate to consider a candidate's ideology, and the balance of ideological power in the federal courts, when evaluating judicial nominations. Republican complaints that the Democrats are obstructionist are hypocritical, since during the Clinton Administration these same Republicans blocked many qualified nominees because of the same sort of political objections.

In direct contrast to Newfield, Stephen B. Presser, a law professor at Northwestern University, expresses great concern over the use of ideology in the Senate conformation process. Presser is especially opposed to the use of the filibuster as a tactic to prevent nominations from coming to the Senate floor for a vote. In the case of Miguel Estrada, whom Bush nominated to the federal appellate court in D.C., there was no question about Estrada's qualifications (he is a graduate of Harvard Law School; clerked for Justice Anthony Kennedy; worked in the Solicitor General's Office; and was rated "well qualified" by the American Bar Association). The only objection that Senate Democrats raised to Estrada was to his ideology. Moreover, Estrada would have been approved if the full Senate were to vote on this nomination, but because a filibuster requires sixty votes to stop, there is now a de facto sixty-vote requirement for a judicial confirmation.

Presser argues that evaluating judicial nominees through the lens of ideology is inconsistent with the Senate's proper role in the confirmation process. Throughout U.S. history, judicial nominees have been accorded a "presumption of fitness," and an ideological litmus test intrudes upon the president's appointment power.

STEPHEN B. PRESSER

The Role of the Senate in Judicial Confirmation

For the last few weeks, a constitutional crisis has been brewing in the United States Senate. It is a constitutional crisis all but ignored by the public, but the resolution of this crisis is likely to determine the nature of federal jurisprudence for the next few decades. At one level, the struggle in the Senate is a struggle over one or two notable nominees to the lower federal courts, most particularly Miguel Estrada and Priscilla Owen, but, at a deeper level, the struggle is over what many of the Senate Democrats have called "judicial ideology," by which they mean a disposition to decide particular cases in a particular manner. For the first time in memory, in public, one political party, the Senate Democrats, has taken the position not only that judges should be picked based on their preference for designated outcomes in cases that might come before them, but also that the Senate ought to be an equal partner in picking judges and that nominees who come before the Senate have a burden of persuading sixty senators (the number necessary to cut off debate in the Senate), that they are worthy of ascension to the bench.

For those of us who still believe that judging ought to be impartial, that there actually is content to the rule of law, and that it ought not to be the task of judges to make policy from the bench, there is cause for great alarm over what is now happening in the Senate. It was that alarm, of course, even before the current imbroglio, that led candidate Bush to proclaim that he wanted to appoint judges who would interpret, not make law, and to point to Supreme Court Justices Antonin Scalia and Clarence Thomas as his models. Now that he has sought to do just that, those uncomfortable with the jurisprudence of Scalia and Thomas, those who would like to see constitutional interpretation as something other than fidelity to the original understanding of that document, have sought to deny Bush nominees confirmation. There is reason to be upset then, not only over the Senate's frustrating the constitutional task of the president, but also over the theory of judging that lies behind the Democrats' refusal to allow Senate votes on some of the Bush nominees.

Let's take the constitutionality of what Miguel Estrada's opponents have done as our first point of inquiry. Estrada served with distinction in the Solicitor General's office. In both private practice and in the government, he was a respected member of the bar of the United States Supreme Court. He had a splendid law school record at Harvard Law School, and he secured a prestigious clerkship with Supreme Court Justice Anthony Kennedy. He had hearings before the Senate Judiciary Committee. He was unanimously rated "well-qualified" by the American Bar Association body charged with passing on nominees, formerly the "gold-standard" of qualifications for the bench, by the very Senate Democrats who now oppose his nomination. These opponents know that if the Estrada nomination is ever brought to a vote on the Senate floor, he will be confirmed, but they have managed to avoid such a vote by filibustering and invoking Senate Rule XXII. That rule, the "cloture" provision, states that the only way to cut off debate on a nomination or a pending bill is by a motion for which sixty of the hundred senators vote "aye." Rule XXII and the other Senate

Rules can be changed only by the vote of two-thirds of the senators present, so that, as long as Estrada's opponents number more than forty, they can prevent a vote on his nomination. As this is written, the Estrada opponents have just begun employing the same tactic to prevent a vote on the nomination of Priscilla Owen, a Texas Supreme Court Justice with credentials as impressive as those of Estrada, and who also received the ABA's "well-qualified" ranking. Other Bush nominees are likely to be treated in an identical matter.

By invoking Senate Rule XXII, used now for the first time in connection with a nominee to the lower federal courts (there is one instance of the practice having been used against a Supreme Court nominee, the bipartisan move against Lyndon Johnson's nomination of Abe Fortas for chief justice, which nomination was eventually withdrawn), the Democrat minority in the Senate, has, in effect, raised the number of senators necessary to confirm a nominee from the mere majority previously regarded as sufficient to confirm, to the super-majority requirement of sixty. As John C. Armor, writing for UPI, recently observed, since other constitutional provisions, notably the clauses regarding treaties, impeachments, expelling members, overriding presidential vetoes and constitutional amendments expressly require two-thirds supermajorities, the clear implication is that the clause regarding confirmation of judicial nominees, which merely speaks of "Advice and Consent," should not. One could then argue that Senate Rule XXII, at least when used to defeat a judicial nominee by denying him a vote on the Senate floor, unconstitutionally raises the number of votes required for confirmation, and thus ought not to be permitted to frustrate the president's appointment power. Intriguingly enough, when the same problem was affecting matters during the term of President Clinton, one of his most distinguished counsel, Washington super-lawyer Lloyd Cutler, made just that argument in an op-ed piece published in the *Washington Post* on April 19, 1993, suggesting that the unconstitutional rule be abolished. This could be accomplished, Cutler wrote, if

> [t]he Senate Rules Committee, [which the Republicans now control], would approve an amendment of Rule XXII permitting a majority to cut off debate after some reasonable period. When the amendment comes before the Senate, the [Republicans] would need to muster only 51 favorable votes (or 50 plus the vice president's vote).

Cutler recommended that a senator

> would raise a point of order that this number is sufficient either to pass the amendment or to cut off debate against it, because the super-majority requirements of Rule XXII are unconstitutional. The vice president would support this view, backed up by an opinion of the attorney general. Following Senate custom on constitutional points, the vice president would refer the question to a vote of the entire Senate, where the same 51 or more votes, or 50 plus the vice president's vote, would sustain it.

At that point Rule XXII would be history and the problem of unconstitutionality would vanish, as the Senate would be able to cut off debate by a mere majority vote.

Cutler had recommended this course to Democrats, of course, but his strategy could be used by Republicans, as well. Unfortunately, there is great reluctance to overturn longstanding Senate practice, such as Rule XXII, but if there ever were an occasion for it, it might well be the first time in history that Rule XXII has been used to defeat a lower-court nominee.

Overturning Rule XXII at this time, or using some other means to stop the frustration of Estrada's and Owen's appointments would also be wise because the motivation behind the Democrat senators' frustrating tactics is a serious revision of the original understanding of the appointment powers and the Senate's role in the process. In two hearings on the judicial appointments process while the Democrats still controlled the Senate, in an effort to challenge the nomination philosophy candidate Bush had expressed on the campaign trail, Senator Charles Schumer of New York made clear his belief (buttressed by some academics friendly to the Democrats' point of view) that it ought to be the task of the Senate to achieve a "balance" of judicial ideologies on the bench, and that each nominee had a burden of satisfying the senators that he or she was qualified for the position. By "judicial ideology," Senator Schumer made clear at those hearings, he meant a belief that particular judicial decisions, including apparently many regarding race, religion, and abortion, were correctly decided and ought to be expansively applied and followed in the future. Senator Schumer (and some of his witnesses) strongly suggested that any Bush nominee with contrary views ought not to be permitted to be confirmed unless a nominee with a "judicial ideology" favored by Senator Schumer and those like him was also confirmed, in order to maintain "balance."

There is, of course, no constitutional requirement of "balance" on the bench, and, more importantly, Senator Schumer's concept of "judicial ideology," seems inconsistent with the Constitution's presumption with regard to judging. *Federalist No. 78*, and the writing of the founders tells us that the proper "judicial philosophy" (*not* "judicial ideology"), is to decide cases according to a neutral interpretation of the Constitution and laws. Judges are not to arrive on the bench with a preconceived set of responses or determined to implement a particular "ideology." Senator Schumer, pursuant to ascendant ideas in the legal academy about judges as forces for social change, has a different conception of judging, and wants a bench that will implement the policies he and many of his fellow Democrats favor. President Bush has made clear that he does not share that view, and his remarks about preferring judges who will not legislate from the bench (the views also of Scalia and Thomas) put him squarely at odds with Senator Schumer. If the President is forced (by the unconstitutional application of Rule XXII, or by other means) to give up half of his nominations to satisfy some Senators' ideological preferences, his constitutional appointment powers will have been severely compromised.

Those powers would be similarly compromised if Senator Schumer's notion that nominees have a burden of proof they must meet to satisfy ideologically driven Senators goes unchallenged. According to *The Federalist*, at least, and according also to the prevailing practice in more than two centuries of judicial appointments, a presumption of fitness has been generally accorded to presidential judicial nominees, and the Senate has properly opposed nominees only when they have been lacking in character or professional legal accomplishments. The authors of *The Federalist* made clear that the assignment of the "Advice and Consent" role to the Senate was to prevent the President from using the nomination process to reward unqualified or corrupt family members or cronies, and not to prevent him from actions taken in good faith to appoint qualified persons of high character. It is true that some nominees have been rejected or questioned on other grounds throughout our history (one thinks of the criticism leveled at Louis Brandeis, which did not prevent his confirmation, and that at Robert Bork, which did). It has been almost unheard of, however, for this kind of ideological litmus test to be applied to deny a confirmation vote to lower-court nominees.

If President Bush is made to give in to the tactics of the Senate Democrats on this point, he will not only have suffered an ignoble political defeat, but he will have failed in his oath to support the Constitution, because he will have compromised his powers and will have seriously undermined the rule of law on which the Constitution depends. One suggestion that has been made, for example, by Victor Williams, is to do an end run around the Senate Democrats, by making a series of recess appointments of his judicial nominees. As Mr. Williams recently pointed out in the *National Law Journal*,

> Clause 3 of Article II, Section 2, states: "The President shall have Power to fill up all Vacancies that may happen during the Recess of the Senate, by granting Commissions which shall expire at the End of their next Session." The recess-appointments clause protects the government from Senate inaction and guarantees the ceaseless functioning of the judiciary. More than 300 jurists have risen to the bench via a recess appointment: Earl Warren, William Brennan, Potter Stewart, Griffin Bell and Augustus Hand, to name a few.

Mr. Williams notes that John F. Kennedy "recess-appointed more than 20% of his judges, and each was subsequently confirmed for a tenured bench. . . . It was just such a Kennedy recess appointment that placed Thurgood Marshall, then a successful lawyer for the National Association for the Advancement of Colored People, on the 2d Circuit." President Clinton made similar use of the recess appointment power, and there is, thus, precedent for President Bush to go that route. Still, the Republicans criticized Clinton for his attempt to circumvent the confirmation process through recess appointments. Thus, recess appointments for President Bush's nominees, though they ought to be considered if there are not other alternatives, are still a dubious attempt to make two wrongs equal a right.

My casebook co-author, Catholic Law School's Dean Douglas Kmiec, recently wrote in the *Wall Street Journal* that what is being done to Miguel Estrada is a "national disgrace." He favors stopping the Democrat Senators' tactics by a frontal attack on "Senate Rule V, [which] provides that the rules of the Senate shall continue from one Congress to the next unless amended by two-thirds of those present and voting." Dean Kmiec notes that "[t]his violates fundamental law as old as Sir William Blackstone, who observed in the mid-18th century that 'Acts of Parliament derogatory from the power of subsequent parliaments bind not.'" Kmiec also observes that the Supreme Court has repeatedly held that the legislature does not have the power to bind itself in the future. As the Court stated in *Ohio Life Ins. and Trust Co. v. Debolt* (1853), for the political process to remain representative and accountable, 'every succeeding Legislature possesses the same jurisdiction and power . . . as its predecessors. The latter must have the same power of repeal and modification which the former had of enactment, neither more nor less.'

This is a good strategy for preventing the filibuster's use as a means of changing the constitutional requirements for nominees, and would solve the problem, but perhaps such drastic means would not be necessary if President Bush (now that the War in Iraq is coming to an end and rebuilding has begun) were to make a few prime-time speeches exposing the manner in which the Senate is frustrating his appointment power through tactics of dubious constitutionality and in complete derogation of the traditional conception of the role of judges, senators, and presidents.

JACK NEWFIELD
The Right's Judicial Juggernaut

On June 26, 2001, Senator Charles Schumer of New York published an astonishing Op-Ed column in the *New York Times* in which he argued that ideology should be considered as one factor in the confirmation of federal judges. The column was astonishing not for its sentiments, which had been expressed by others, but for its blunt frankness, and for the fact that it was coming from a member of the Senate Judiciary Committee, which was about to pass judgment on scores of the president's choices for the federal bench.

"The not-so-dirty little secret of the Senate," Schumer wrote, "is that we do consider ideology, but privately. . . . If the President uses ideology in deciding whom to nominate to the bench, the Senate, as part of its responsibility to advise and consent, should do the same in deciding whom to confirm. Pretending that ideology doesn't matter—or, even worse, doesn't exist—is exactly the opposite of what the Senate should do."

Schumer's thinking should not be misunderstood. He is not advocating that ideology be the sole standard for judging nominees—only that it be discussed openly and honestly. Schumer says that other factors are equally important to evaluate, including integrity, temperament, intellectual excellence, and "the racial, ethnic, gender and experiential diversity of the particular bench." Schumer is not proposing any litmus test, which is what he was falsely accused of by a *New York Post* editorial and by Paul Gigot in the *Wall Street Journal*. In his *Times* op-ed, Schumer wrote that one of the factors in confirmation decisions should be "the composition of the courts at the time of nomination"—a reference to the philosophical balance on each of the thirteen courts of appeal and the Supreme Court.

In the confirmation process, ideology should matter in direct proportion to how much it mattered in the president's thinking when he made the nomination. Since

Bush said during the campaign that Antonin Scalia and Clarence Thomas are his favorite judges, this sent a vivid message about just judicial role models, and how his mind works.

But the ambition of this article is larger than just Schumer's point about ideology. It is also about the president's determination to keep nominating extremists to pack the federal bench. It is about the Senate Judiciary Committee's constitutional responsibility to advise and consent on judges, and not be a rubber stamp. It is about the hypocrisy of Republican senators who blocked some superb nominees during the Clinton years because they didn't approve of their ideas—and who now cry foul when the same scrutiny is applied to their choices. And it is about the coming war over the nomination of Miguel Estrada to the U.S. Court of Appeals for the D.C. Circuit, and the emerging opposition—from former co-workers as well as Latinos—to this clone of Clarence Thomas.

Schumer's position was already shared by Judiciary Committee Democrats Ted Kennedy and Richard Durbin. Now the committee has rejected both Priscilla Owen and Charles Pickering for the Court of Appeals for the Fifth Circuit, suggesting that Schumer's premise that ideology matters has found enough converts to prevail—at least on some days.

Pickering of Mississippi was easy to oppose, since he was hostile to voting rights and civil rights, and was even troubled by the well-settled legal principle of "one person, one vote." But getting all ten Democrats, now [2001–02] in the majority on the Judiciary Committee, to be synchronized on a regular basis is a tricky and fragile thing. Dianne Feinstein is a loner who is a reliable liberal vote only when abortion is at issue. The quirky campaign finance reformer Russell Feingold cast the deciding vote to confirm John Ashcroft as Attorney General within the committee; his Democratic colleagues are now counting on the power of atonement. Joe Biden argued vigorously all through the 1990s that ideology should *not* matter in evaluating judicial nominees. The Judiciary Committee chair, Patrick Leahy, is well liked and a solid liberal vote. But he is sometimes a little gun-shy about partisan conflicts. He can overreact to attacks from President Bush or from Karl Rove, the Dr. Frankenstein in the judge-making laboratory, mixing test tubes of politics, polls, and demographics.

The problem now is that the Democrats have already approved all of Bush's moderate nominees—and more than seventy nominees in all, including fourteen appeals court judges. They did this trying to convince Bush to send them more moderates. But most of those who have not yet received a hearing are rigid zealots, without doubts.

Biden, Herbert Kohl, and presidential contender John Edwards did vote to confirm D. Brooks Smith for the Court of Appeals for the Third Circuit even though Smith is just as much of an absolutist as Pickering. Smith had been reversed more than fifty times by the circuit court he was joining, mostly because of his rulings against workers and consumers. The *Times* editorialized against his nomination, pointing out that Judge Smith "has taken an extremely narrow view of Congress's power to legislate under the Commerce Clause, which has often been used to pass laws protecting civil rights."

But Smith was sponsored by the only "moderate" Republican on the committee, Arlen Specter of Pennsylvania. And Specter persuaded his close friend Biden, from adjacent Delaware, to vote for Smith. At that point, with the fight lost, the other Democrats on the committee decided to let Kohl and Edwards off the hook. Edwards of North Carolina had voted against Pickering of Mississippi, and the right wing in his home state had been attacking him ever since. Since blocking Smith was a lost cause, because of Biden's defection, the other Democrats felt sympathy for Edwards, who was getting whipsawed between his national ambitions and his home-state politics.

By giving Edwards a pass on Smith, the Kennedy-Schumer-Durbin Democrats hope to save Edwards for the imminent confrontation over Miguel Estrada's nomination by Bush for the now-evenly-balanced D.C. Circuit Court of Appeals. Hearings begin on September 26 [2002].

A Democratic staffer on the Judiciary Committee told me, "Estrada is forty, and if he makes it to the circuit, then he will be Bush's first Supreme Court nominee. He could be on the Supreme Court for thirty years and do a lot of damage. We have to stop him now. It may come down to how Biden and Feinstein vote in the committee . . . Estrada is hard right in an emotional way. But because he is not a sitting judge, there is no paper trail on him, no published opinions. And because he is Hispanic [an immigrant from Honduras], Bush is counting on some liberals not to oppose him."

Conservatives acted shocked and outraged by Schumer's advocacy of openly making ideology one consideration to prevent judicial extremism from spreading. But all Schumer is trying to do is maintain some balance on the country's federal appeals courts, which Bush and Rove are trying to pack with Scalia echoes and Thomas clones.

Nan Aron, president of the Alliance for Justice, a liberal group that monitors judicial selections, told me, "The extreme right already controls seven of the thirteen circuit appeals courts. The D.C. Circuit is the crown jewel of the federal system, and it is now evenly balanced. This is the court that is often the final decision maker on labor, civil liberties, and environmental cases. This is the court that sent both Thomas and Scalia to the Supreme Court." She added, "Estrada is a very partisan Republican. We know he helped prepare the Bush briefs in the Florida recount Supreme Court case. Normally, appeals court nominees have real prestige and a history of influential writing and thinking. Estrada has none of this."

The Bush-Rove judicial strategy is the repayment of the huge political debt that Bush owes the Christian right for the way it slimed and savaged John McCain during the South Carolina primary in 2000. (Schumer told me that shortly after his *Times* op-ed was published, McCain took him aside and warned him, as a friend, that the fanatic fundamentalists would now be coming after him, because right-wing judges are what they expect from the Bush presidency.)

This South Carolina debt may illuminate why Bush has been so much more conservative as a President than he was as governor of Texas. It also explains why one of the heroes of the Christian right—John Ashcroft—got the surprise appointment to be Attorney General. Bush is satisfying social conservatives and fundamentalists like Gary Bauer, Jerry Falwell and Pat Robertson just by nominating rigid zealots like Pickering, the antichoice former oil and gas lawyer Priscilla Owen, former Strom Thurmond counsel Dennis Shedd, Jesse Helms protégé Terrence Boyle, Professor Michael McConnell, and Miguel Estrada. Even if some of them are denied confirmation, Bush is keeping the far right happy just by sending up their names. Bush has nothing to lose in Rove's way of thinking. Rove believes that every under-forty-five ideologue who does get through will write the future and tilt a circuit.

Schumer is essentially a moderate liberal playing defense, trying to slow down the ideological and generational packing of the circuit courts. He cares deeply about the courts, and he was an eyewitness to the Clarence Thomas impersonation of an open mind. And to *Bush v. Gore*. And to the Senate's mugging of Ronnie White.

Clarence Thomas swore on a Bible he would speak the truth. He then told the Senate Judiciary Committee during his 1991 confirmation hearing that he never once thought about abortion his entire adult life, that he never even discussed *Roe v. Wade* with another member of the human species. He assured the Senate that he had no preconceived ideas about abortion or the right of privacy. It did not alter Thomas's preposterous story that his own sister had had an abortion. Or that he had given a well-known speech to the Heritage Foundation condemning abortion rights. Or that he was a student at Yale Law School in 1973, when the *Roe v. Wade* decision was announced, and that ruling was debated all over the campus.

Thomas withheld the truth, concealed his ideology, and was narrowly confirmed, 52 to 48. Then, in 1992, Justice Thomas joined Rehnquist and Scalia's dissent in *Planned Parenthood of Southeastern Pennsylvania v. Casey*, in which they argued that *Roe v. Wade* should have been overturned in that case.

Some senators are still suffering from a malady I have diagnosed as Thomas Trauma. They still resent being lied to by a Supreme Court nominee who is under oath. They still resent being played for fools. These senators, now in recovery from Thomas Trauma, are determined to pin down all future nominees on whether they believe the Constitution protects the right of choice under the right of privacy. Freshman Senator Maria Cantwell of Washington did a spectacular cross-examination of the slithery Judge Pickering on this point, when Pickering claimed, "My personal view is immaterial and irrelevant."

Republican senators, who now whine about using ideology as one measure of a nominee, employed their own ideological jihad to block Peter Edelman and Ronnie White from district court judgeships during Clinton's presidency. Edelman is so judicious and fair-minded, he seems born to be a judge. Even Orrin Hatch eventually agreed not to oppose him. But when a few right-wing journalists and think tanks demonized Edelman, Clinton withdrew his nomination.

Ronnie White was the first black member of the Supreme Court of Missouri, and a first-rate jurist on the merits. But John Ashcroft, then the Republican senator from Missouri, launched a personal crusade to block White's confirmation. Ashcroft called White "pro-criminal" and soft on the death penalty, and labeled him an "activist judge."

The facts are that White had voted to affirm the death penalty in forty-one of fifty-eight cases. And Missouri's biggest law enforcement organization, the Fraternal Order of Police, had urged White's confirmation. But Ashcroft lined up all but one Republican in the Senate to vote against White, who was defeated on a 54-to-45 party-line vote. It was naked ideology—and perhaps racism.

During Clinton's second term, Senate Republicans, who were then in the majority, blocked the appointments of three highly qualified Hispanic judges. Enrique Moreno and Jorge Rangel were blocked from the Fifth Circuit, and Christine Arguello was blocked from the Tenth Circuit, by the denial of even a hearing. Republican senators said they opposed Moreno because he had no judicial experience—but neither does Estrada. Even though they killed the appointments of three excellent Hispanic nominees, Republican Senators Trent Lott, Rick Santorum, and Hatch have accused the Democrats of racism for not scheduling a hearing on Estrada fast enough.

Of course, the great spectacle of thinly disguised ideology remains the five Republicans on the Supreme Court who appointed Bush the president, in the way they decided *Bush v. Gore*. The cowardice of these five judges is now legendary.

Another factor lurking in the background here is that President Clinton's two Supreme Court appointments—Ruth Bader Ginsburg and Stephen Breyer—have not been effective counterweights to the ideological zeal of Scalia and Thomas. They have not been visionary liberals in the tradition of William Brennan, William Douglas, Thurgood Marshall, or Louis Brandeis. They have been less bold and lucid than John Paul Stevens, a Gerald Ford nominee. As Schumer put it to me in an interview, "I wouldn't object to one Scalia on the Court, *if there was also one Brennan*. It's about balance. All the extremists are on the right now."

Miguel Estrada, a partner in the Washington law firm of Gibson, Dunn & Crutcher, will turn forty-one on September 25. His mentors in Washington's clubby world of conservative lawyers have been Kenneth Starr and Theodore Olson; it was Olson who argued the Florida recount case for Bush in the Supreme Court, with Estrada helping him. Estrada has published no notable academic writing or books. Schumer told me, "Estrada is like a Stealth missile—with a nose cone—coming out of the right wing's deepest silo."

What should be alarming is that Bush picked Estrada over his own close friend and White House counsel Alberto Gonzales. Gonzales is a pragmatic moderate, close in thinking to Sandra Day O'Connor, though not necessarily Supreme Court material himself.

The fundamentalists and social conservatives did not trust Gonzales to oppose abortion. In two years on the Texas Supreme Court, Gonzales published twenty-one opinions. They reveal a respect for precedent and legislative intent, and reluctance to legislate from the bench. In one ruling, known as *Jane Doe 10*, Gonzales was part of the court's majority that reversed a lower court's ruling and permitted a 17-year-old to have an abortion without parental notification. The parents had told the court they did not believe in abortion. In a nasty dissent in this case, Priscilla Owen attacked the majority for "irresponsibility" and doubted their commitment to the rule of law. Gonzales wrote that Owen's dissent was "an unconscionable act of judicial activism."

This intended rebuke was apparently inspiring music to Bush. He then nominated Owen for the federal appeals court and passed over Gonzales for Estrada. Gonzales's views on parental notification convinced the Christian right and Karl Rove that he would never vote to repeal *Roe v. Wade* and that he would probably not participate in any nibbling away at abortion rights. So Estrada now has the inside track to become the first Hispanic on the Supreme Court.

In pushing Estrada, Bush seems to be using his father's formula with Clarence Thomas. He is willing to compromise on demographic diversity in order to avoid compromising on ideological diversity. Bush the Elder picked Thomas because he was an African American opposed to affirmative action, because he was willing to mask his thinking and because he was young enough to be a predictable right-wing vote on every legal issue for a generation. The risk to America is that Estrada might be another Thomas—an absolutist in the guise of an electoral wedge and demographic token.

From 1993 to 1996, Paul Bender was Principal Deputy Solicitor General of the United States and Estrada's direct supervisor in the office of Solicitor General. The two men worked together closely. Bender, a former law clerk to Justice Felix Frankfurter and Learned Hand and currently a professor at Arizona State Law School, was quoted in the *Los Angeles Times* this past spring as saying that Estrada is so "ideologically driven that he couldn't be trusted to state the law in a fair, neutral way. . . . Miguel is smart and charming, but he is a right-wing ideologue. He has an agenda that's similar to Clarence Thomas'." A year earlier Bender told the *Washington Post*, "I think [Estrada] lacks judgment and he is too much of an ideologue to be an appeals court judge."

In a telephone interview Bender, a registered Independent, told me, "I am not on any personal crusade against Miguel. But I still hold the same opinion about his lack of qualifications that I gave the *Washington Post* last year, when he was nominated. Miguel has no experience and extreme conservative views. He did not hide those views from me when I was his supervisor. But I don't want to go beyond that, or make this seem personal."

Perhaps the most damaging evidence against Estrada comes from two lawyers he interviewed for Supreme Court clerkships. Both were unwilling to be identified by name for fear of reprisals. The first told me: "Since I knew Miguel, I went to him to help me get a Supreme Court clerkship. I knew he was screening candidates for Justice Kennedy. Miguel told me, 'No way. You're way too liberal.' I felt he was definitely submitting me to an ideological litmus test, and I am a moderate Democrat. When I asked him why I was being ruled out without even an interview, Miguel told me his job was to prevent liberal clerks from being hired. He told me he was screening out liberals because a liberal clerk had influenced Justice Kennedy to side with the majority and write a pro-gay-rights decision in a case known as *Romer v. Evans*, which struck down a Colorado statue that discriminated against gays and lesbians."

I also interviewed a young law professor and former Justice Department attorney who told me a very similar story. "I was a clerk for an appeals court judge," the professor told me, "and my judge called Justice Kennedy recommending me for a clerkship with him. Justice Kennedy then called me and said I had made the first cut and would soon be called for an interview. I was then interviewed by Miguel Estrada and another lawyer. Estrada asked most of the questions. He asked me a lot of unfair, ideological questions, a lot about the death penalty, which I told him I thought was immoral. I felt I was being subjected to an ideological litmus test. Estrada was being obnoxious. He was acting like it was his job to weed out liberal influences on Justice Kennedy. I was never called back by anyone."

Attorney General Ashcroft has refused to give the Judiciary Committee any of Estrada's memorandums written while he worked in the SG's office—even though such material was released on Bork and Rehnquist. But one instructive brief has surfaced in *United Mine Workers of America v. Bagwell*. Estrada wrote an amicus brief arguing that $52 million in contempt fines against the union should stand—despite the fact that they were imposed without allowing the union a jury trial on the facts. The Supreme Court ultimately rejected Estrada's thinking, ruling that the imposition of fines without a jury trial violated the Constitution. Estrada misrepresented the legal precedents to fit his anti-union bias—exactly what Professor Bender says is his disqualifying attribute to be an appellate judge. Like the defeated Pickering and Owen, Estrada seems prone to ignore the text and intent of laws that contradict his closed mind.

The Bush political operation has been working overtime trying to generate at least some token Latino support for Estrada. In June the eighteen-member Hispanic Caucus of the Congress—all Democrats—had a closed meeting with Estrada to which the White House reluctantly agreed. "I asked him a very specific question about affirmative action and minority businesses," says Nydia Velázquez, the five-term Congresswoman from Brooklyn, "and he just would not say anything meaningful about it. And then he was quite insensitive about immigrant rights—and he is an immigrant himself! Estrada has no understanding of the needs and aspirations of the Latino community. He has no history of effort in trying to help other Hispanics." She adds, "I don't think he is going to make a good impression on the Senate. He does not answer questions. And if you ask him again, he becomes abrasive."

Seven-term Congressman José Serrano came away with an even harsher view. "Estrada seems baffled," Serrano told me, "about why we would even ask him questions about justice and empowerment. He wouldn't even acknowledge there has been discrimination against Hispanics in America. He seemed lost, like he had never been involved in any struggle to better the lives of Hispanics. He had no comprehension of Latino history and suffering."

As a result of this performance, Velázquez and Serrano say, the Hispanic Caucus is sending a letter to Senator Leahy opposing Estrada's confirmation. Perhaps even more significant, the Puerto Rican Legal Defense and Education Fund has also voted to formally oppose Estrada's confirmation. The fund's early decision may now influence other Latino civil rights organizations like the Mexican American Legal Defense and Education Fund, the National Council of La Raza and the National Puerto Rican Coalition.

All judicial selection contains an element of mystery, like a crapshoot. Nobody expected a Republican governor from California named Earl Warren to lead a unanimous Supreme Court to rule public school segregation unconstitutional. Nobody expected Hugo Black to rise above his origins in the Klan to become a liberal on race. Who knew that David Souter would turn out to be a fair and balanced jurist? (Ted Kennedy says his vote against confirming Souter is one of his biggest regrets in forty years in the Senate.)

Perhaps Miguel Estrada is not a clone of Clarence Thomas. But by choosing to wear a mask, by keeping his memos secret, by choosing to hide his views from the Hispanic Caucus, he feeds suspicion and apprehension. The burden is on Estrada—since he has never been a judge—to explain himself before the Judiciary Committee. He can answer questions honestly, without saying how he might rule in particular cases.

The modern benchmark for challenging judicial nominees based on their ideology is the speech Ted Kennedy delivered on the Senate floor just a few hours after Ronald Reagan nominated Robert Bork for the Supreme Court in July 1987. "Robert Bork's America," Kennedy warned, "is a land in which women would be forced into back-alley abortions, blacks would sit at segregated lunch counters, rogue police could break down citizens' doors in midnight raids, schoolchildren could not be taught about evolution, writers and artists could be censored at the whim of government, and the doors of the federal courts would be shut on the fingers of millions of citizens for whom the judiciary is—and is often the only—protector of the individual rights that are at the heart of our democracy."

Kennedy was criticized by those who would like Supreme Court nominations to be polite, academic debates about original intent and states' rights. But it required honest passion to mobilize the civil rights and women's organizations, the AFL-CIO and the black mayors and clergy. Bork was rejected by the Senate 58 to 42, and this saved legal abortion in America when it was in jeopardy. President Reagan picked Anthony Kennedy to take Bork's place, and Justice Kennedy has accepted *Roe v. Wade* as settled law.

The right wing now claims that Bork's defeat was the beginning of "the politics of personal destruction," as Bork himself put it. But the struggle over Bork's nomination was totally about ideas, not personal flaws. The hearings turned on Bork's ideology about free speech, race, equal protection, due process, abortion, privacy, and the role of judicial precedent. Bork shot himself in the head when he said, in response to a question from Senator Specter, that under his theory of the Constitution there was no sound basis for the 1954 Court decision ordering school desegregation in the District of Columbia.

Republicans are now accusing Senate Democrats of "obstructionism" for rejecting several nominees and carefully researching the views of others. They are trying to make it seem un-American to oppose, or investigate, a President's nomination to the federal bench—even though they have done it with vicious regularity themselves, to Ronnie White, Peter Edelman, Jorge Rangel, Enrique Moreno and many others. But public confrontations over judicial nominations go back to the birth of the Republic. In 1795 the Senate defeated George Washington's nominee to be Chief Justice, John Rutledge, over his criticism of the Jay treaty. During America's first century, one of every four Supreme Court nominees was rejected by the Senate. The Founding Fathers gave the Senate the power of advise and consent for judicial nominees for sound reasons involving checks and balances among the branches of government that are elected and appointed.

Applying Herman Melville's "No! in thunder" to the extremist nominees for lifetime appointments is as American as baseball, the blues, and the Constitution itself.

DISCUSSION QUESTIONS

1. *What would you do?* You are a member of Congress on the Senate Judiciary Committee. Your Republican colleagues have introduced a bill to prohibit filibusters on judicial nominations. Should senators be permitted to filibuster judicial nominees? Critics of the filibuster note that it is used more and more, to the point where nearly any controversial action is filibustered. Under the rules, this means that forty-one senators can block congressional action. Supporters note that the filibuster is necessary to prevent political majorities from controlling every last portion of American government. And because judges may remain in their positions for decades, it is particularly important for the minority party to have some say in who those judges will be. Would you support the effort to eliminate the filibuster on judicial nominations? Why or why not?

2. Would Presser's argument against Senate consideration of a nominee's ideology be weakened if presidents were known to choose nominees because of their ideology? Is it plausible to suggest that all presidents choose the best person without regard to his or her ideology?

3. Do you agree or disagree with the following statement: "The debate over 'ideology' is actually nothing more than a debate over a nominee's view of abortion rights."

4. Do you think that federal judges—who serve for life unless they are impeached—should be subjected to removal if they issue a long string of unpopular opinions (note that this would require a Constitutional amendment)? Do you think that judges should serve ten or fifteen years rather than for life? What would be the consequences of these changes? How, if at all, do you think they might change the politics of nominations?

10 Ballot Initiatives: Voice of the People or the Powerful?

One of the central threads running through American political culture and political history is a fear of concentrated political power. For the founders, this fear dictated the necessity of a federal system of checks and balances and separation of powers. For citizens, this fear has led to periodic attempts to reform the political system to "give government back to the people." The most recent of these efforts on the national scale were Ross Perot's surprisingly strong presidential candidacies in 1992 and 1996 and the rise of political movements to, among other things, limit the number of terms held by elected officials and reform campaign finance laws. Although the term limits movement appears to have stalled, significant campaign finance reform was passed in the form of the Bipartisan Campaign Reform Act, signed into law in 2002, and a number of states have passed or are investigating so-called clean elections laws.

Early in the twentieth century, progressive reformers introduced some of the most significant efforts to allow citizens to challenge concentrated power, the recall (allowing citizens to remove an elected official from office), the initiative (allowing citizens to propose legislation on the ballot), and the referendum (allowing citizens to approve or reject decisions of the legislature and executive). Recall elections are more rare than initiatives or referenda, but in 2003 the state of California held a recall election to decide the fate of Governor Gray Davis. Initiatives and referenda have been used to pass or defeat legislation concerning major issues such as the use of race as a factor in college admissions, the level of state or local tax revenues, which services would be provided to immigrants, and the use of bilingual education in public schools, among many others.

David Broder argues that the initiative might have started with the intention of preventing the concentration of political power, but the reality has been quite different. To Broder, rather than challenging concentrated power, initiatives are a tool of powerful interests. Organized interests with substantial financial resources are especially advantaged. Initiative campaigns, he writes, often mask the economic interests of those advocates on either side of the issue. Well-funded scare campaigns lead voters to support, frequent unknowingly, the position of large, wealthy, special interests. Broder is concerned that citizens so often assume legislatures, elected by the public, are corrupt, but seem to accept at face value that initiatives are a tool of the people. That may have been the original intention, he asserts, but they are now a tool of the powerful.

Despite Broder's critique, ballot initiatives do have their defenders. Lino Graglia argues that government tends to be overwhelmingly dominated by a liberal mindset, and the initiative is one of the key tools available to conservatives to keep government in check. The effect of the initiative in recent years, he suggests, has been largely to allow the conservative views held by a majority of Americans to influence public policy directly. Listing a long string of successes in California, including the termination of school busing for racial balance, the abolition of compulsory bilingual education, and ending the use of racial preferences in higher education admissions, Graglia notes that "it is hardly possible to ask more from any political device." Indeed, Graglia would like to see the ballot initiative extended to national elections.

Conservatives' success with the initiative has not gone unnoticed by liberals. While some liberals might complain about ballot initiatives, David Sarasohn reports that other liberals are determined to challenge conservatives and use the initiative to push progressive causes. He discusses the plan of the Economic Opportunity Institute in Washington state to use the state's initiative process in an aggressive manner to achieve liberal victories, such as mandating that the state's minimum wage be adjusted annually to compensate for rising prices. Although the two authors disagree on whether government is currently controlled by liberals or conservatives, both Graglia and Sarasohn suggest that the initiative can be used to challenge concentrated power, just as it was intended to do.

DAVID S. BRODER

Dangerous Initiatives: A Snake in the Grass Roots

An alternative form of government—the ballot initiative—is spreading in the United States. Despite its popular appeal and reformist roots, this method of law-making is alien to the spirit of the Constitution and its carefully crafted set of checks and balances. Left unchecked, the initiative could challenge or even subvert the system that has served the nation so well for more than two hundred years.

Though derived from a century-old idea favored by the Populist and Progressive movements as a weapon against special-interest influence, the initiative has become a favored tool of interest groups and millionaires with their own political and personal agendas. These players—often not even residents of the states whose laws and constitutions they seek to rewrite—have learned that the initiative is a more efficient way of achieving their ends than the cumbersome and often time-consuming process of supporting candidates for public office and then lobbying them to pass legislation. In hundreds of municipalities and half the states—particularly in the West—the initiative has become a rival force to City Hall and the State House. (The District of Columbia allows voters to enact laws by initiative, but the states of Maryland and Virginia do not.) In a single year, 1998, voters across the country bypassed their elected representatives to end affirmative action, raise the minimum wage, ban billboards, permit patients to obtain prescriptions for marijuana, restrict campaign spending and contributions, expand casino gambling, outlaw many forms of hunting, prohibit some abortions and allow adopted children to obtain the names of their biological parents. Of 66 statewide initiatives that year, 39 became law. Simply put, the initiative's growing popularity has given us something that once seemed unthinkable—not a government of laws, but laws without government.

This new fondness for the initiative—at least in the portion of the country where it has become part of the political fabric—is itself evidence of the increasing alienation of Americans from our system of representative government. Americans have always had a healthy skepticism about the people in public office: The writers of the Constitution began with the assumption that power is a dangerous intoxicant and that those who wield it must be checked by clear delineation of their authority.

But what we have today goes well beyond skepticism. In nearly every state I visited while researching this phenomenon, the initiative was viewed as sacrosanct, and the legislature was held in disrepute. One expression of that disdain is the term-limits movement, which swept the country in the past two decades, usually by the mechanism of initiative campaigns. It is the clearest expression of the revolt against representative government. In effect, it is a command: "Clear out of there, you bums. None of you is worth saving. We'll take over the job of writing the laws ourselves."

But who is the "we"? Based on my reporting, it is clear that the initiative process has largely discarded its grass-roots origins. It is no longer merely the province of idealistic volunteers who gather signatures to place legislation of their own devising on the ballot. Billionaire Paul Allen, co-founder of Microsoft, spent more than $8 million in support of a referendum on a new football stadium for the Seattle Seahawks. Allen, who was negotiating to buy the team, even paid the $4 million cost of running the June 1997 special election—in which Washington state voters narrowly agreed to provide public financing for part of the $425 million stadium bill.

Like so many other aspects of American politics, the initiative process has become big business. Lawyers, campaign consultants, and signature-gathering firms see each election cycle as an opportunity to make money on initiatives that, in many cases, only a handful of people are pushing. Records from the 1998 election cycle—not even one of the busiest in recent years—show that more than $250 million was raised and spent in this largely uncontrolled and unexamined arena of politics.

This is a far cry from the dream of direct democracy cherished by the nineteenth-century reformers who imported the initiative concept from Switzerland in the hope that it might cleanse the corrupt politics of their day. They would be the first to throw up their hands in disgust at what their noble experiment has produced.

The founders of the American republic were almost as distrustful of pure democracy as they were resentful of royal decrees. Direct democracy might work in a small, compact society, they argued, but it would be impractical in a nation the size of the United States. At the Constitutional Convention in 1787, no voice was raised in support of direct democracy.

A century later, with the rise of industrial America and rampant corruption in the nation's legislatures, political reformers began to question the work of the founders. Largely rural protest groups from the Midwest, South, and West came together at the first convention of the Populist Party, in Omaha in 1892. The Populists denounced both Republicans and Democrats as corrupt accomplices of the railroad barons, the banks that set ruinous interest rates, and the industrial magnates and monopolists who profited from the labor of others while paying meager wages.

Both the Populists and Progressives—a middle-class reform movement bent on rooting out dishonesty in government—saw the initiative process as a salve for the body politic's wounds. An influential pamphlet, "Direct Legislation by the Citizenship through the Initiative and Referendum," appeared in 1893. In it, J. W. Sullivan argued that as citizens took on the responsibility of writing the laws themselves, "each would consequently acquire education in his role and develop a lively interest in the public affairs in part under his own management."

Into this feisty mix of reformers came William Simon U'Ren, a central figure in the history of the American initiative process. In the 1880s, U'Ren apprenticed himself to a lawyer in Denver and became active in politics. He later told Lincoln Steffens, the muckraking journalist, that he was appalled when the Republican bosses of Denver gave him what we would now call "street money" to buy votes.

In the 1890s, having moved to Oregon in search of a healthier climate, U'Ren helped form the Direct Legislation League. He launched a propaganda campaign, distributing almost half a million pamphlets and hundreds of copies of Sullivan's book in support of a constitutional convention that would enshrine initiative and referendum in Oregon's charter. The proposal failed narrowly in the 1895 session of the legislature, in part because the Portland Oregonian labeled it "one of the craziest of all the crazy fads of Populism" and "a theory of fiddlesticks borrowed from a petty foreign state."

Eventually, U'Ren lined up enough support for a constitutional amendment to pass easily in 1899. It received the required second endorsement from the legislature two years later, with only one dissenting vote. The voters overwhelmingly ratified the amendment in 1902 and it withstood a legal challenge that went all the way to the Supreme Court.

U'Ren's handiwork is evident today in his adopted state. The official voters' pamphlet for the 1996 Oregon ballot—containing explanations for sixteen citizen-sponsored initiatives and six others referred by the legislature—ran 248 pages.

It also included paid ads from supporters and opponents.

Money does not always prevail in modern-day initiative fights, but it is almost always a major—even a dominant—factor. In the fall of 1997, more than two hundred petitions were circulating for statewide initiatives that sponsors hoped to place on ballots the following year. The vast majority did not make it. The single obstacle that eliminated most of them was the ready cash needed to hire the companies that wage initiative campaigns.

In 1998, the most expensive initiative campaign was the battle over a measure legalizing casino-style gambling on Indian lands in California. The Nevada casinos, fearful of the competition, shelled out $25,756,828 trying to defeat the proposition. The tribes outdid them, spending $66,257,088 to win. The $92 million total was a new record for California.

But of all the ventures into initiative politics that year, perhaps the most successful was engineered by three wealthy men who shared the conviction that the federal "war on drugs" was a dreadful mistake. They banded together to support medical marijuana initiatives in five Western states. The best known of them was billionaire financier George Soros of New York, who had made his fortune in currency trading. He and his political partners—Phoenix businessman John Sperling and Cleveland businessman Peter B. Lewis—personally contributed more than

75 percent of the $1.5 million spent on behalf of a successful medical marijuana initiative in just one of the states, Arizona.

The issue isn't whether medical marijuana laws are good or bad. As Arizona state Rep. Mike Gardner complained to me, "The initiative was part of our constitution when we became a state, because it was supposed to offer people a way of overriding special interest groups. But it's turned 180 degrees, and now the special interest groups use the initiative for their own purposes. Why should a New York millionaire be writing the laws of Arizona?"

When I relayed Gardner's question to Soros, he replied: "I live in one place, but I consider myself a citizen of the world. I have foundations in thirty countries, and I believe certain universal principles apply everywhere—including Arizona."

It won't be long before the twin forces of technology and public opinion coalesce in a political movement for a national initiative—allowing the public to substitute the simplicity of majority rule for what must seem to many Americans the arcane, out-of-date model of the Constitution. In fact, such a debate is already underway, based on what I heard at a May 1999 forum sponsored by the Initiative and Referendum Institute here in Washington.

M. Dane Waters, the institute's president, cut his political teeth on the term-limits movement, and the group's membership includes firms in the initiative industry. But Waters strove to keep the forum intellectually honest, inviting critics as well as supporters of the initiative process.

There was no doubt about the leanings of most of those in attendance. The keynote speaker was Kirk Fordice, then governor of Mississippi, who was cheered when he saluted the audience as "the greatest collection of mavericks in the world. The goal that unites us is to return a portion of the considerable power of government to individual citizens . . . and take control from the hands of professional politicians and bureaucrats."

Fordice, a Republican, noted that his state was the most recent to adopt the initiative, in 1992. Since then, he lamented, "only one initiative has made it onto the ballot," a term-limits measure that voters rejected. "Thank God for California and those raggedy-looking California kids who came in and gathered the signatures," he said. "Now the [Mississippi] legislature is trying to say we can't have them come in, and we're taking it to court."

Then came Mike Gravel, former Democratic senator from Alaska and head of an organization called Philadelphia II, which calls for essentially creating a new Constitution based on direct democracy. Gravel's plan—simplicity itself—is to take a national poll, and if 50 percent of the people want to vote on an issue, it goes on the next general election ballot. Then Congress would have to hold hearings on the issue and mark up a bill for submission to the voters. Once an issue gets on the ballot, only individuals could contribute to the campaign for passing or defeating it.

When I began researching the initiative process, I was agnostic about it. But now that I've heard the arguments and seen the initiative industry in action, the choice is easy. I would choose James Madison and the Constitution's checks and balances over the seductive simplicity of Gravel's up-or-down initiative vote. We should be able to learn from experience, and our experience with direct democracy during the last two decades is that wealthy individuals and special interests—the very targets of the Populists and Progressives a century ago—have learned all too well how to subvert the initiative process to their own purposes. Admittedly, representative government has acquired a dubious reputation today. But as citizens, the remedy isn't to avoid our elected representatives. The best weapon against the ineffective, the weak, and the corrupt is in our hands each Election Day.

LINO A. GRAGLIA
Revitalizing Democracy

Government—organized, legitimized coercion—presents a dilemma. On the one hand, government is necessary to obtain certain benefits, such as the creation and enforcement of property rights that are essential to the efficient use of resources. On the other hand, giving some individuals organized power over others is very dangerous. Power, the ability to command and enforce obedience, is not good for the soul; it seems inevitably to lead to an exaggerated appraisal of one's wisdom and goodness as compared to those qualities in others. Power expands ego, and ego yearns for more power, with the result that government tends inexorably to grow far beyond what justifies its existence and therefore to limit human freedom unnecessarily.

Because government is dangerous, we should have no more of it than necessary and strive to make what we must have as little dangerous as possible. The only way this can be done is by making it effectively democratic, that is, subjecting it in a fairly direct and immediate way to popular control. One way in which the American system as it now operates can be made more democratic is the adoption of measures of direct democracy.* * *

* * *

Almost half the states now provide for some form of direct democracy on important issues by allowing initiatives and referenda. It would greatly revitalize and enhance democracy in this country if such measures were adopted by all of the states, if they were made easier to implement in the states that already have them, and perhaps most important, if they were adopted by the national government.

The initiative and referendum were promoted at the turn of the century by so-called progressives who saw direct democracy as a way of overcoming the conservative political influence of corporate and financial interests. Today, however, the dominant influences on government are not conservative, and direct democracy therefore serves primarily to protect conservative and traditional interests. Whatever may have been the case earlier, it now seems that the leaders of any political organization in the United States, from the local school board to the United States Senate, will be substantially to the left of its membership or constituents. It is apparently an inherent property of democratic government that it will inevitably fall into the hands of liberals, who are inherently distrustful of their fellow citizens, and thus become less and less democratic. Liberals are by definition (in the modern American context) unhappy the world is not better, while conservatives are grateful it is not worse. Liberals, therefore, are up and doing, seeking new ways to improve the world, which always results in more government, law, coercion, and, inevitably, more power to liberals. Conservatives, convinced that most changes would be for the worse, are largely content to leave the world alone and hope it reciprocates the favor.

The unfortunate tendency of democratic governments to fall into the hands of liberals has greatly increased in recent times as current leaders tend to be more highly educated than leaders in the past. Studies indicate that people tend to become more conservative, that is, more skeptical of innovation as they become better educated, but only through college. The over-educated, those with post-graduate degrees, tend to become more liberal. Perhaps they become disoriented from living too long in a world of words or perhaps it is only the already disoriented who stay too long in academia. The respect that was once given to business leaders for worldly success is today more typically given to our more educated leaders for their intellectual attainment. The Supreme Court Justices all have post-graduate degrees—albeit only from law schools—and usually from the most liberal of institutions. Like other government officials, they seek the commendation of academics and others of our intellectual elite, and this requires that they give evidence of their intellectual growth by moving to the left.

Whatever the reason, it seems clear that the influence of academics and other intellectuals on policymaking has greatly increased since the New Deal, which was openly founded and implemented by a "brain trust." The nightmare of the American intellectual, overwhelmingly on the far left of the American political spectrum, is that policymaking should fall into the hands of the American people. The American people, after all, favor such things as neighborhood schools, capital punishment, prayer in schools, restrictions on pornography, and the prohibition of flag burning, all anathema to the enlightened academic and certainly to the typical law professor. For them, direct democracy is a realization of their nightmare.

The effect of direct democracy in recent years has been, in almost every case, to reject liberal policy measures adopted by political leaders and substitute more conservative measures favored by a majority of the people. It is hardly too much to say that every socially beneficial policy choice in recent years to come out of California, the bellwether of the nation, has been the result of a referendum. Referenda have enabled Californians to impose limits on taxation, reinstitute capital punishment, terminate school busing for racial balance, abolish compulsory bilingual education, and prohibit the use of racial preferences in higher education, employment, and contracting. It is hardly possible to ask more from any political device. Racial preferences were also ended by referendum in the state of Washington. In Colorado, it was used to reinstitute the right of property owners to make individual choices on the basis of sexual orientation. The latter result, of course, was overturned by the Supreme Court, illustrating that the results of referenda, no less than ordinary legislation, are subject to the basic rule of our peculiar system that elections are fine as long as Supreme Court Justices get the last vote.

George Orwell is supposed to have remarked that there are some ideas so preposterous that only the highly educated can believe them. William Buckley expressed the same idea with the observation that he would rather be governed by the first 2,000 names in the Boston phone book than by the Harvard faculty. The ordinary Boston citizen is much less educated than a typical Harvard faculty member and therefore much less likely to devise a grand scheme of social improvement that would probably leave us worse off and surely make us less free. The source of many of our current problems is that we *are* to a large extent being ruled by the Harvard faculty and their academic counterparts, with the Supreme Court functioning essentially as their mirror, mouthpiece, and enacting arm. Initiatives and referenda are means of escaping or modifying this rule, of counteracting the socially destructive schemes of deep thinkers with the native realism and inherent good sense of the average citizen.

* * *

DAVID SARASOHN
Taking (Back) the Initiative

The Economic Opportunity Institute sounds like a typical think tank—of any political persuasion. Each of the name's three interchangeable words evokes Dupont Circle, position papers, and regression analysis.

But the institute, from the small building it shares with an architect a few blocks from the University of Washington—about as far from the other Washington as you can get without the Pacific lapping over your fax machines—sees itself differently.

Progressive policy institutes, explains the group's statement of philosophy, come in three flavors. There's "think-tank hands-off research," as in universities. There's "more populist analyses that are picked up by local and national media"—still not quite the institute's style. The third category, in which policy development meets real-world advocacy, "is the niche that we want to exploit," says EOI. "Our job is to develop populist majoritarian policy and push that policy forward into the public eye." In other words: less think, more tank.

Because of that attitude, Washington is now the first state in the country with a minimum wage adjusted for inflation. From another EOI innovation, the state has a program to develop a childcare career ladder, to provide some professional respect and better pay for a generally minimum-wage work force that has major responsibilities and huge turnover and gets treated like a Play-Doh proletariat.

A bill EOI supported in the 2000 state legislative session that would use surpluses in the unemployment fund to create a paid-family-leave program—standard in Europe, unimaginable in the United States—made it through a State Senate committee, then died. Now, EOI's founder and executive director, John Burbank, is working on the idea with Washington's U.S. Senator Patty Murray, who is interested in proposing it as a federal pilot program.

And this spring, the institute announced that it would push its second statewide ballot initiative, this one allying with Washington health providers for a measure that would add a 60-cent tax to a pack of cigarettes, using the proceeds for health care for 50,000 working-poor Washingtonians. EOI developed the measure, did preliminary polling, and helped assemble the coalition. In the campaign this fall, the institute will run statewide media tours, meet with editorial boards and reporters, develop one-page issue blurbs on different parts of the measure, and boldly go to places where progressive activists have rarely gone before—like talk radio.

Over many years as a community organizer, Democratic staff member, political director of the Washington State Labor Council and graduate student, John Burbank concluded that progressive forces weren't just losing the struggle, they weren't fighting the right one. While progressives talked social theory, the right turned to the ballot box and the airwaves. And it was winning.

"The right has understood the power of the initiative, shaping debate, forcing debate onto their part of the field," says Burbank, sitting in one of Seattle's many espresso shops, as central to the local culture as Microsoft. "Some people say they're an abominable way to make law, but [initiatives] are there, and if you dismiss them, you're turning them over to the right wing." In Washington—as in many other states—there are well-funded, well-connected conservative advocacy institutes eager to seize any opportunity to set the terms of discussion.

The Economic Opportunity Institute—starting out three years ago in a few cubicles in what the *Seattle Times* calls the "funky, ultraliberal Fremont neighborhood"—wasn't born on the barricades, or out of a single inspired and overstuffed checkbook. It came out of Burbank's 1997 master's thesis at the University of Washington's school of public administration (several of his fellow students would later become EOI staff members). His thesis designed—in precise detail, including a budget and proposed board—an Economic Security Institute to take on Washington State's four conservative think tanks. Burbank also intended to challenge forces on the progressive side, which he saw as focusing too heavily on foreign policy and social issues, losing some of the bread-and-butter focus that appealed to both poorer and middle-class voters.

That's why EOI—which works on the slogan "New Tools for Building the Middle Class"—likes to focus on gritty, practical issues like health care for the working poor and childcare development. It also works to present the issues in a media-savvy way that appeals to middle-class voters: For example, treating quality childcare not as a question of equity, but as a way to promote parental employment.

"Work has an enormous resonance with the middle class," Burbank says. "One of the sieves that we put issue development through is, 'Can it distribute benefits up and down the income ladder?' Some issues may disproportionately benefit lower-income people but resonate with middle-income people."

EOI's childcare campaign is a case in point. Not only did the institute's efforts lead Washington Governor Gary Locke to set up the childcare career ladder, but when a fiscal crunch threatened the program during the current legislative session, EOI's positioning as a public advocacy force helped produce 1,200 personal messages to the governor's office. Partly as a result, Burbank expects Locke to back not just maintaining but expanding the program.

And Burbank's playing with another idea: a city initiative in Seattle to raise

$10 million a year for childcare with a tax on espresso drinks. This is a little like taxing wine in Bordeaux, and he remarks musingly, "Everybody laughs at that." But it could solidify local childcare funding and quality, would have to carry only the solidly liberal Seattle electorate and with success might spread to other cities. At least, Burbank argues, the effort would "build a database and catalyze discussion."

Burbank, a thin, intense man who tends to explain things at loving length, argues that some activists insist on portraying themselves as advocates for the poor, which leads to a double trap: They can't draw enough mainstream, middle-class support to win anything, and they "tend to isolate the lower-income constituency."

To some of those advocates, EOI's strategies seem indirect—and insufficiently relevant. "While I appreciate the work that they do, most of it doesn't really help the work that we do," says Jean Colman, director of the Welfare Rights Organizing Coalition in Seattle. "If the institute would help us do linking with middle-income folks to explain why there's a safety net and why it helps everybody, that would be a wonderful thing for them to do. I haven't seen them do that."

Still, EOI seeks to represent the interests of a diverse set of players in progressive politics. The board of EOI—in the move from thesis to practice, "Security" was replaced by "Opportunity"—reflects both Burbank's philosophy and his strategy. It includes union representatives, academics, a pollster and state legislators (including one who has since become co-speaker of the State House). A policy adviser to Governor Locke is a former board president, and still a member. They're not the figures swimming in the standard think tank; they show why Burbank prefers the term "activist public policy institute."

To Kim Cook, an EOI board member and regional director of the Service Employees International Union, the institute reflects the kind of approach—and alliance—needed to challenge an atmosphere that's proving toxic to progressive ideas. "There's been a lot of talk on the board about broadening the public debate and [changing] the antitax attitude," says Cook. The goal is "to bring more progressive initiatives to the electorate."

EOI's successful minimum-wage campaign, launched in early 1998 as the institute was just getting off the ground, confirmed Burbank's feeling that the initiative could be an effective liberal tool. The vote gave the state not just a minimum wage among the nation's highest, but the only one in the country indexed to inflation to rise automatically. Running initiatives, admits Spokane Democratic State Senator Lisa Brown, another EOI board member and an economics professor at Eastern Washington University, "can be risky. If you run a progressive initiative and lose, it can set you back. But with the chances of something happening legislatively so low, you work on other ways."

This is, of course, what the original progressives realized at the beginning of the past century when they created the initiative, and what right-wingers understood at the end of it when they seized on the tactic. Burbank wants liberals to reclaim the initiative at the start of the new one. To him, the initiative is not only a tool but an opportunity. A campaign to collect the 225,000 signatures to put something on the state ballot, he notes, is a chance for "building a terrific database from signatures and donors." Which, at least potentially, can help in building a real grassroots movement.

To compete at the ballot box, progressive activists need tight connections to the sympathetic institutions on their side. "The right-wing institutes are powerful not just in how they define the terms of the debate, but how they're linked to their financial power," Brown points out. Practically, that means progressives need unions in the room. And, as Brown's prominence on the board suggests, it means reaching around the state, expanding progressive efforts beyond their permanent bridgehead in Seattle and Puget Sound.

From the outset, EOI has focused on the role and use of media, of making connections in a world of quick-hit consciousness. "We can pursue all the policy development we want, but if we correspond only with the policy elites, we have failed in our mission," explains an early "Tool Kit" for the group. "We must develop and implement a comprehensive media plan that brings our policy issues to the public and engages them."

It's a matter of both whom the institute wants to reach, and whom it wants to help. The poor, and people who have dropped out, aren't "easily organizable politically, but they do listen to and are influenced by the media," argues Burbank. "To me that's very important stuff, talk-radio. We shouldn't shy away from it."

So Burbank, as part of the media theme that he calls "organically part of what we do," goes on any talk-radio show that will have him, even if that means talking to lots of people complaining that Hillary Clinton keeps breaking into their houses to steal their guns. The goal is to battle on every front—including the ones that progressives have generally evacuated. And the group, in listing its accomplishments, lists its press clippings along with its policy advances.

Increasingly, the EOI is in a position to move on multiple issues at once. Its staff, which started with Burbank and a press aide, is now up to ten and growing. Its budget is rising, with 80 percent of its funding coming from foundations.

And the foundations are encouraged. "One of the exciting things about EOI," says Michael Caudell-Feagan, a board member of the Stern Family Fund, "is that it's trying to change the terms of the debate with proposals that have broad appeal but deal with economic justice." Around the country, the foundation has been trying to seed similar institutes, such as the Center for Economic Justice in Texas, Good Jobs First in Washington, D.C., and the Oregon Center for Public Policy. Caudell-Feagan thinks EOI is setting out a direction and a pattern that liberals haven't been following, but which is gaining ground politically. "Slowly but surely," he says, "a number of foundations have begun to encourage groups that deal with bread-and-butter issues."

In dealing with those issues—and in focusing on media strategies, broad alliances and the initiative process—EOI has begun to turn around a battle progressives have been losing. "They seem to be doing a better job than anyone I can think of in our region, in a way that seems to have legs, at building a program for economic security for working-class and middle-class people," says Jeff Malachowsky, founder of the Portland, Oregon-based Western States Center.

Burbank's approach may be more mundane than some progressive strategies, and his vision of the middle class as the new liberal constituency—and the media as the new barricades—may lack a certain work-shirt romance. But he insists, and he's beginning to pile up some evidence, that on issues such as minimum-wage increases, health care coverage and childcare subsidies, progressives can build successes and alliances. The first step is to retake the initiative—the one on the ballot.

DISCUSSION QUESTIONS

1. *What would you do?* Assume that Broder's concerns about ballot initiatives are well founded. Assume also that you work for a governor in a state where initiatives are considered an important part of the democratic process. There is no chance of eliminating ballot initiatives in this state, but your boss would like to reform the process. Describe at least two reforms that the governor could propose that address issues raised by Broder.

2. Do the articles by Graglia and Sarasohn leave you less concerned about the complaints leveled by Broder, or do they intensify your concerns? If both conservative and liberal "special interests" can use the initiative as a means to political ends, are Broder's criticisms of ballot initiatives really all that damning?

3. As the articles indicate, the initiative process exists at the state level but not the national level. Would you favor expanding the ballot initiative process to national politics? Why or why not? Would the initiative reject the governing principles favored by the Founders? If so, is that alone enough reason to reject the idea?

11 The Electoral College: Reform It or Leave It Alone?

The 2000 presidential election raised a new series of questions about the place of the Electoral College within our political system. Al Gore won the popular vote by more than a half million votes, yet lost the presidency to George W. Bush in an Electoral College squeaker (271–267). This is the fourth time (or third, depending on how one counts the 1824 election) in which the popular vote winner did not become president. There have also been other close calls in which the shift of several thousand votes in a couple of states could have produced other popular vote losers (Woodrow Wilson, Harry Truman, John F. Kennedy, and Gerald Ford).

The authors in this chapter have a range of views about the wisdom of reforming the Electoral College. Arthur Schlesinger Jr., the eminent historian, makes a strong argument for change. He describes the compromise between the confederalists and federalists at the Constitutional Convention that produced the Electoral College. Conventional wisdom holds that this nod to the advocates of state power now serves as the largest impediment to reform: the small states that benefit from the Electoral College are unlikely to ratify any Constitutional amendment changing the system. However, Schlesinger argues that the Electoral College actually benefits the larger states. While the direct popular election of the president is appealing for its simplicity and fairness, Schlesinger recognizes the problems associated with the proposal, especially its impact on the party system. Instead, he advocates a creative solution of giving a bonus of 102 electoral votes to the popular vote winner. This would guarantee that the popular vote winner would become president, while preserving some of the virtues of the Electoral College system.

Norman Ornstein argues for preserving the Electoral College. All reforms, he warns, have unintended consequences. For example, if we elect presidents by popular vote one nightmare scenario is a national recount in which the problems faced in Florida would be multiplied by fifty as presidential candidates would scrounge for every vote out of the more than 105 million cast. Instead of reforming the Electoral College, Ornstein favors electoral reforms that would improve the technology of voting and the registration process.

More than one thousand proposals to change the Electoral College have been introduced in Congress in our history, including many that are less drastic than abolishing the institution and replacing it with the popular vote. Such proposals include getting rid of the two-seat bonus for each state (a reform, incidentally, that would have given Gore the presidency in 2000), making the Electoral College automatic (to get rid of the "faithless electors" problem), or dividing the vote proportionally within each state, either by congressional district or by popular vote within the state. The congressional district plan, which is currently practiced in Maine and Nebraska, is the approach favored by the author of our last selection. This approach would not require a constitutional amendment and would introduce more competition into the system by getting rid of the winner-take-all characteristic of the Electoral College.

ARTHUR M. SCHLESINGER JR.

Not the People's Choice

The true significance of the disputed 2000 election has thus far escaped public attention. This was an election that made the loser of the popular vote the president of the United States. But that astounding fact has been obscured: first by the flood of electoral complaints about deceptive ballots, hanging chads, and so on in Florida; then by the political astuteness of the court-appointed president in behaving as if he had won the White House by a landslide; and now by the effect of September 11 in presidentializing George W. Bush and giving him commanding popularity in the polls.

"The fundamental maxim of republican government," observed Alexander Hamilton in the 22d Federalist, "requires that the sense of the majority should prevail." A reasonable deduction from Hamilton's premise is that the presidential candidate who wins the most votes in an election should also win the election. That quite the opposite can happen is surely the great anomaly in the American democratic order.

Yet the National Commission on Federal Election Reform, a body appointed in the wake of the 2000 election and co-chaired (honorarily) by former Presidents Gerald Ford and Jimmy Carter, virtually ignored it. Last August, in a report optimistically entitled *To Assure Pride and Confidence in the Electoral Process*, the commission concluded that it had satisfactorily addressed "most of the problems that came into national view" in 2000. But nothing in the ponderous eighty-page document addressed the most fundamental problem that came into national view: the constitutional anomaly that permits the people's choice to be refused the presidency.

Little consumed more time during our nation's Constitutional Convention than debate over the mode of choosing the chief executive. The Framers, determined to ensure the separation of powers, rejected the proposal that Congress elect the president. Both James Madison and James Wilson, the "fathers" of the Constitution, argued for direct election by the people, but the convention, fearing the parochialism of uninformed voters, also rejected that plan. In the end, the Framers agreed on the novel device of an electoral college. Each state would appoint electors equal in number to its representation in Congress. The electors would then vote for two persons. The one receiving a majority of electoral votes would then become president; the runner-up, vice president. And in a key sentence, the Constitution stipulated that of these two persons at least one should not be from the same state as the electors.

The convention expected the electors to be cosmopolitans who would know, or know of, eminences in other states. But this does not mean that they were created as free agents authorized to routinely ignore or invalidate the choice of the voters. The electors, said John Clopton, a Virginia congressman, are the "organs . . . acting from a certain and unquestioned knowledge of the choice of the people, by whom they themselves were appointed, and under immediate responsibility to them."

Madison summed it up when the convention finally adopted the electoral college: "The president is now to be elected by the people." The president, he assured the Virginia ratifying convention, would be "the choice of the people at large." In the First Congress, he described the president as appointed "by the suffrage of three million people."

"It was desirable," Alexander Hamilton wrote in the 68th Federalist, "that the sense of the people should operate in the choice of the person to whom so important a trust was to be confided." As Lucius Wilmerding Jr. concluded in his magisterial study of the electoral college: "The Electors were never meant to choose the President but only to pronounce the votes of the people."

Even with such a limited function, however, the electoral college has shaped the contours of American politics and thus captured the attention of politicians. With the ratification of the Twelfth Amendment in 1804, electors were required to vote separately for president and vice president, a change that virtually guaranteed that both would be of the same party. Though unknown to the Constitution and deplored by the Framers, political parties were remolding presidential elections. By 1836 every state except South Carolina had decided to cast its votes as a unit-winner take all, no matter how narrow the margin. This decision minimized the power of third parties and created a solid foundation for a two-party system.

"The mode of appointment of the Chief Magistrate [President] of the United States," wrote Hamilton in the 68th Federalist, "is almost the only part of the system, of any consequence, which has escaped without severe censure." This may have been true when Hamilton wrote in 1788; it was definitely not true thereafter. According to the Congressional Research Service, legislators since the First Congress have offered more than a thousand proposals to alter the mode of choosing presidents.

No legislator has advocated the election of the president by Congress. Some have advocated modifications in the electoral college—to change the electoral units from states to congressional districts, for example, or to require a proportional division of electoral votes. In the 1950s, the latter approach received considerable congressional favor in a plan proposed by Senator Henry Cabot Lodge Jr. and Representative Ed Gossett. The Lodge-Gossett amendment would have ended the winner—take-all electoral system and divided each state's electoral vote according to the popular vote. In 1950 the Senate endorsed the amendment, but the House turned it down. Five years later, Senator Estes Kefauver revived the Lodge-Gossett plan and won the backing of the Senate Judiciary Committee. A thoughtful debate ensued, with Senators John F. Kennedy and Paul H. Douglas leading the opposition and defeating the amendment.

Neither the district plan nor the proportionate plan would prevent a popular-vote loser from winning the White House. To correct this great anomaly of the Constitution, many have advocated the abolition of the electoral college and its replacement by direct popular elections.

The first "minority" president was John Quincy Adams. In the 1824 election, Andrew Jackson led in both popular and electoral votes; but with four candidates dividing the electoral vote, he failed to win an electoral-college majority. The Constitution provides that if no candidate has a majority, the House of Representatives must choose among the top three. Speaker of the House Henry Clay, who came in fourth, threw his support to Adams, thereby making him president. When Adams then made Clay his secretary of state, Jacksonian cries of "corrupt bargain" filled the air for the next four years and helped Jackson win the electoral majority in 1828.

"To the people belongs the right of electing their Chief Magistrate," Jackson told Congress in 1829. "The first principle of our system," he said, is "that the majority is to govern." He asked for the removal of all "intermediate" agencies preventing a "fair expression of the will of the majority." And in a tacit verdict on Adams's failed administration, Jackson added: "A President elected by a minority can not enjoy the confidence necessary to the successful discharge of his duties."

History bears out Jackson's point. The next two minority presidents—Rutherford B. Hayes in 1877 and Benjamin Harrison in 1889—had, like Adams, ineffectual administrations. All suffered setbacks in their midterm congressional elections. None won a second term in the White House.

The most recent president to propose a direct-election amendment was Jimmy Carter in 1997. The amendment, he said, would "ensure that the candidate chosen by the votes actually becomes President. Under the Electoral College, it is always possible that the winner of the popular vote will not be elected." This had already happened, Carter said, in 1824, 1876, and 1888.

Actually, Carter placed too much blame on the electoral system. Neither J. Q. Adams in 1824 nor Hayes in 1876 owed his elevation to the electoral college. The House of Representatives, as noted, elected Adams. Hayes's election was more complicated.

In 1876, Samuel J. Tilden, the Democratic candidate, won the popular vote, and it appeared that he had won the electoral vote too. But the Confederate states were still under military occupation, and electoral boards in Florida, Louisiana, and South Carolina disqualified enough Democratic ballots to give Hayes, the Republican candidate, the electoral majority.

The Republicans controlled the Senate; the Democrats, the House. Which body would count the electoral votes? To resolve the deadlock, Congress appointed an electoral commission. By an 8–7 party-line vote, the commission gave all the disputed votes to Hayes. This was a supreme election swindle. But it was the rigged electoral commission, not the electoral college, that denied the popular-vote winner the presidency.

In 1888 the electoral college did deprive the popular-vote winner, Democrat Grover Cleveland, of victory. But 1888 was a clouded election. Neither candidate received a majority, and Cleveland's margin was only 100,000 votes. Moreover, the claim was made, and was widely accepted at the time and by scholars since, that white election officials in the South banned perhaps 300,000 black Republicans from the polls. The installation of a minority president in 1889 took place without serious protest.

The Republic later went through several other elections in which a small shift of votes would have given the popular-vote loser an electoral-college victory. In 1916, if Charles Evans Hughes had gained 4,000 votes in California, he would have won the electoral-college majority, though he lost the popular vote to Woodrow Wilson by more than half a million. In 1948, a shift of fewer than 30,000 votes in three states would have given Thomas E. Dewey the electoral-college majority, though he ran more than two million votes behind Harry Truman. In 1976, a shift of 8,000 votes in two states would have kept President Gerald Ford in office, though he ran more than a million and a half votes behind Jimmy Carter.

Over the last half-century, many other eminent politicos and organizations have also advocated direct popular elections: Presidents Richard Nixon and Gerald Ford; Vice Presidents Alben Barkley and Hubert Humphrey; Senators Robert A. Taft, Mike Mansfield, Edward Kennedy, Henry Jackson, Robert Dole, Howard Baker, and Everett Dirksen; the American Bar Association, the League of Women Voters, the AFL-CIO, and the U.S. Chamber of Commerce. Polls have shown overwhelming public support for direct elections.

In the late 1960s, the drive for a direct-election amendment achieved a certain momentum. Led by Senator Birch Bayh of Indiana, an inveterate and persuasive constitutional reformer, the campaign was fueled by the fear that Governor George Wallace of Alabama might win enough electoral votes in 1968 to throw the election into the House of Representatives. In May 1968, a Gallup poll recorded 66 percent of the U.S. public in favor of direct election—and in November of that year, an astonishing 80 percent. But Wallace's 46 electoral votes in 1968 were not enough to deny Nixon a majority, and complacency soon took over. "The decline in one-party states," a Brookings Institution study concluded in 1970, "has made it far less likely today that the runner-up in popular votes will be elected President."

Because the danger of electoral-college misfire seemed academic, abolition of the electoral college again became a low-priority issue. Each state retained the constitutional right to appoint its electors "in such manner as the legislature thereof directs." And all but two states, Maine and Nebraska, kept the unit rule.

Then came the election of 2000. For the fourth time in American history, the winner of the popular vote was refused the presidency. And Albert Gore Jr. had won the popular vote not by Grover Cleveland's dubious 100,000 but by more than half a million. Another nearly three million votes had gone to the third-party candidate Ralph Nader, making the victor, George W. Bush, more than ever a minority president.

Nor was Bush's victory in the electoral college unclouded by doubt. The electoral vote turned on a single state, Florida. Five members of the Supreme Court, forsaking their usual deference to state sovereignty, stopped the Florida recount and thereby made Bush president. Critics wondered: If the facts had been the same but the candidates reversed, with Bush winning the popular vote (as indeed observers had rather expected) and Gore hoping to win the electoral vote, would the gang of five have found the same legal arguments to elect Gore that they used to elect Bush?

I expected an explosion of public outrage over the rejection of the people's choice. But there was surprisingly little in the way of outcry. It is hard to imagine such acquiescence in a popular-vote-loser presidency if the popular-vote winner had been, say, Adlai Stevenson or John F. Kennedy or Ronald Reagan. Such leaders attracted do-or-die supporters, voters who cared intensely about them and who not only would have questioned the result but would have been ardent in pursuit of fundamental reform. After a disappointing campaign, Vice President Gore simply did not excite the same impassioned commitment.

Yet surely the 2000 election put the Republic in an intolerable predicament— intolerable because the result contravened the theory of democracy. Many expected that the election would resurrect the movement for direct election of presidents. Since direct elections have obvious democratic plausibility and since few Americans understand the electoral college anyway, its abolition seems a logical remedy.

The resurrection has not taken place. Constitutional reformers seem intimidated by the argument that a direct-election amendment would antagonize small-population states and therefore could not be ratified. It would necessarily eliminate the special advantage conferred on small states by the two electoral votes handed to all states regardless of population. Small-state opposition, it is claimed, would make it impossible to collect the two-thirds of Congress and the three-fourths of the states required for ratification.

This is an odd argument, because most political analysts are convinced that the electoral college in fact benefits large states, not small ones. Far from being hurt by direct elections, small states, they say, would benefit from them. The idea that "the present electoral-college preserves the power of the small states," write Lawrence D. Longley and Alan G. Braun in *The Politics of Electoral Reform*, ". . . simply is not the case." The electoral college system "benefits large states, urban interests, white minorities, and/or black voters." So, too, a Brookings Institution report: "For several decades liberal, urban Democrats and progressive, urban-suburban Republicans have tended to dominate presidential politics; they would lose influence under the direct-vote plan."

Racial minorities holding the balance of power in large states agree. "Take away the electoral college," said Vernon Jordan as president of the Urban League, "and the importance of being black melts away. Blacks, instead of being crucial to victory in major states, simply become 10 percent of the electorate, with reduced impact."

The debate over whom direct elections would benefit has been long, wearisome, contradictory, and inconclusive. Even computer calculations are of limited use, since they assume a static political culture. They do not take into account, nor can they predict, the changes wrought in voter dynamics by candidates, issues, and events.

As Senator John Kennedy said during the Lodge-Gossett debate: "It is not only the unit vote for the Presidency we are talking about, but a whole solar system of governmental power. If it is proposed to change the balance of power of one of the elements of the solar system," Kennedy observed, "it is necessary to consider all the others. . . . What the effects of these various changes will be on the Federal system, the two-party system, the popular plurality system and the large-State–small-State checks and balances system, no one knows."

Direct elections do, however, have the merit of correcting the great anomaly of the Constitution and providing an escape from the intolerable predicament. "The electoral college method of electing a President of the United States," said the American Bar Association when an amendment was last seriously considered, "is archaic, undemocratic, complex, ambiguous, indirect, and dangerous." In contrast, as

Birch Bayh put it, "direct popular election of the president is the only system that is truly democratic, truly equitable, and can truly reflect the will of the people."

The direct-election plan meets the moral criteria of a democracy. It would elect the people's choice. It would ensure equal treatment of all votes. It would reduce the power of sectionalism in politics. It would reinvigorate party competition and combat voter apathy by giving parties the incentive to get out their votes in states that they have no hope of carrying.

The arguments for abolishing the electoral college are indeed powerful. But direct elections raise troubling problems of their own—especially their impact on the two-party system and on JFK's "solar system of governmental power."

In the nineteenth century, American parties inspired visiting Europeans with awe. Alexis de Tocqueville, in the 1830s, thought politics "the only pleasure which an American knows." James Bryce, half a century later, was impressed by the "military discipline" of the parties. Voting statistics justified transatlantic admiration. In no presidential election between the Civil War and the end of the century did turnout fall below 70 percent of eligible voters.

The dutiful citizens of these high-turnout years did not rush to the polls out of uncontrollable excitement over the choices they were about to make. The dreary procession of presidential candidates moved Bryce to write his famous chapter in *The American Commonwealth* titled "Why Great Men Are Not Chosen Presidents." But the party was supremely effective as an agency of voter mobilization. Party loyalty was intense. People were as likely to switch parties as they were to switch churches. The great difference between then and now is the decay of the party as the organizing unit of American politics.

The modern history of parties has been the steady loss of the functions that gave them their classical role. Civil-service reform largely dried up the reservoir of patronage. Social legislation reduced the need for parties to succor the poor and helpless. Mass entertainment gave people more agreeable diversions than listening to political harangues. Party loyalty became tenuous; party identification, casual. Franklin D. Roosevelt observed in 1940: "The growing independence of voters, after all, has been proved by the votes in every presidential election since my childhood—and the tendency, frankly, is on the increase."

Since FDR's day, a fundamental transformation in the political environment has further undermined the shaky structure of American politics. Two electronic technologies—television and computerized polling—have had a devastating impact on the party system. The old system had three tiers: the politician at one end, the voter at the other, and the party in between. The party's function was to negotiate between the politician and the voter, interpreting each to the other and providing the links that held the political process together.

The electronic revolution has substantially abolished this mediating role. Television presents politicians directly to the voters, who judge candidates far more on what the box shows them than on what the party organization tells them. Computerized polls present voters directly to the politicians, who judge the electorate far more on what the polls show them than on what the party organization tells them. The political party is left to wither on the vine.

The last half-century has been notable for the decrease in party identification, for the increase in independent voting, and for the number of independent presidential candidacies by fugitives from the major parties: Henry Wallace and Strom Thurmond in 1948, George Wallace in 1968, Eugene McCarthy in 1976, John Anderson in 1980, Ross Perot in 1992 and 1996, and Ralph Nader and Pat Buchanan in 2000.

The two-party system has been a source of stability; FDR called it "one of the greatest methods of unification and of teaching people to think in common terms." The alternative is a slow, agonized descent into an era of what Walter Dean Burnham has termed "politics without parties." Political adventurers might roam the countryside like Chinese warlords, building personal armies equipped with electronic technologies, conducting hostilities against various rival warlords, forming alliances with others, and, if they win elections, striving to govern through ad hoc coalitions. Accountability would fade away. Without the stabilizing influences of parties, American politics would grow angrier, wilder, and more irresponsible.

There are compelling reasons to believe that the abolition of state-by-state, winner-take-all electoral votes would hasten the disintegration of the party system. Minor parties have a dim future in the electoral college. Unless third parties have a solid regional base, like the Populists of 1892 or the Dixiecrats of 1948, they cannot hope to win electoral votes. Millard Fillmore, the Know-Nothing candidate in 1856, won 21.6 percent of the popular vote and only 2 percent of the electoral vote. In 1912, when Theodore Roosevelt's candidacy turned the Republicans into a third party, William Howard Taft carried 23 percent of the popular vote and only 1.5 percent of the electoral votes.

But direct elections, by enabling minor parties to accumulate votes from state to state—impossible in the electoral-college system—would give them a new role and a new influence. Direct-election advocates recognize that the proliferation of minor candidates and parties would drain votes away from the major parties. Most direct-election amendments therefore provide that if no candidate receives 40 percent of the vote the two top candidates would fight it out in a runoff election.

This procedure would offer potent incentives for radical zealots (Ralph Nader, for example), freelance media adventurers (Pat Buchanan), eccentric billionaires (Ross Perot), and flamboyant characters (Jesse Ventura) to jump into presidential contests; incentives, too, to "green" parties, senior-citizen parties, nativist parties, right-to-life parties, pro-choice parties, anti-gun-control parties, homosexual parties, prohibition parties, and so on down the single-issue line.

Splinter parties would multiply not because they expected to win elections but because their accumulated vote would increase their bargaining power in the runoff. Their multiplication might well make runoffs the rule rather than the exception. And think of the finagling that would take place between the first and second rounds of a presidential election! Like J. Q. Adams in 1824, the victors would very likely find that they are a new target for "corrupt bargains."

Direct election would very likely bring to the White House candidates who do not get anywhere near a majority of the popular votes. The prospect would be a succession of 41 percent presidents or else a succession of double national elections.

Moreover, the winner in the first round might often be beaten in the second round, depending on the deals the runoff candidates made with the splinter parties. This result would hardly strengthen the sense of legitimacy that the presidential election is supposed to provide. And I have yet to mention the problem, in close elections, of organizing a nationwide recount.

In short, direct elections promise a murky political future. They would further weaken the party system and further destabilize American politics. They would cure the intolerable predicament—but the cure might be worse than the disease.

Are we therefore stuck with the great anomaly of the Constitution? Is no remedy possible?

There is a simple and effective way to avoid the troubles promised by the direct-election plan and at the same time to prevent the popular-vote loser from being the electoral-vote winner: Keep the electoral college but award the popular-vote winner a bonus of electoral votes. This is the "national bonus" plan proposed in 1978 by the Twentieth Century Fund Task Force on Reform of the Presidential Election Process. The task force included, among others, Richard Rovere and Jeanne Kirkpatrick. (And I must declare an interest: I was a member, too, and first proposed the bonus plan in the *Wall Street Journal* in 1977.)

Under the bonus plan, a national pool of 102 new electoral votes—two for each state and the District of Columbia—would be awarded to the winner of the popular vote. This national bonus would balance the existing state bonus—the two electoral votes already conferred by the Constitution on each state regardless of population. This reform would virtually guarantee that the popular-vote winner would also be the electoral—vote winner.

At the same time, by retaining state electoral votes and the unit rule, the plan would preserve both the constitutional and the practical role of the states in presidential elections. By insulating recounts, it would simplify the consequences of close elections. By discouraging multiplication of parties and candidates, the plan would protect the two-party system. By encouraging parties to maximize their vote in states that they have no chance of winning, it would reinvigorate state parties, stimulate turnout, and enhance voter equality. The national-bonus plan combines the advantages in the historic system with the assurance that the winner of the popular vote will win the election, and it would thus contribute to the vitality of federalism.

The national-bonus plan is a basic but contained reform. It would fit comfortably into the historic structure. It would vindicate "the fundamental maxim of republican government . . . that the sense of the majority should prevail." It would make the American democracy live up to its democratic pretensions.

How many popular-vote losers will we have to send to the White House before we finally democratize American democracy?

NORMAN ORNSTEIN

No Need to Repeal the Electoral College

Until this November, the Electoral College was a vague remembrance from high school civics classes, a subject to master for SATs (and then forget immediately afterward) or an occasional final Jeopardy category. Not anymore.

The election controversy of 2000, the first of any major magnitude since 1876, has put the Electoral College right in front of Americans' faces, on their television screens, and in daily conversations in barber shops, coffee houses, at office water coolers, and the dinner table.

Of course, if the Electoral College was civics trivia for most citizens, it has been a matter of great disagreement and concern to lawmakers and other opinion leaders since its inception. It was, after all, a compromise born of a struggle at the Constitutional Convention between small states and large states, or more accurately, between confederalists, who wanted to incorporate most of the Articles of Confederation, and those who wanted a large, national republic. As the late political theorist Martin Diamond has written, the confederalists wanted the president to be chosen directly by state legislatures. James Madison, James Wilson, and Governor Morris preferred a direct popular vote. That option was vehemently rejected by the confederalists. So Madison and his allies hit upon the Electoral College as a way to keep the states involved, but retain a role for the people. The state legislatures would choose electors, but they would be guided by the popular vote.

Their compromise did not stop the controversy. Actually, nothing has. The EC was changed early on (in 1804) via the Twelfth Amendment to the Constitution, creating separate votes by electors for president and vice president to avoid the problem of a president elected from one party and a vice president from the other. (Until then, the candidate with the most electoral votes became president and the runner up became vice president). The EC was changed again via legislation in states in the nineteenth century, as they responded to the democracy movement and went to having the electors selected via direct popular vote within the states (almost always on a winner-take-all basis).

1,028 PROPOSALS TO CHANGE THE SYSTEM

But those adjustments have not erased the broader debate. The Congressional Research Service has uncovered 1,028 legislative proposals for changing the system since the First Congress. Between 1889 and 1946, 109 constitutional amendments to reform the Electoral College were introduced in Congress, with another 265 between 1947 and 1968. In 1967, an American Bar Association commission recommended that the Electoral College be scrapped and replaced by direct popular vote for the president, with a provision for a runoff if no candidate achieved the threshold of 40 percent of the votes. The ABA plan, introduced by Indiana Senator Birch Bayh and endorsed by the Nixon White House, passed the House 338–70, but died on a filibuster in the Senate led by North Carolina Senator Sam Ervin.

Since 1969, there have been at least 113 reform proposals introduced in Congress—with many more certain to come next year. Most of the proposals call directly for abolition of the EC, and its replacement by direct popular vote. Others call for retaining the EC, but mandating that states divide their electoral votes by congressional district (as is now done voluntarily in Nebraska and Maine), or by proportion of popular votes cast in each state. A small number calls simply for the elimination of electors—the real-live, flesh-and-blood people who go to their state capitols in mid-December to cast the electoral votes—and their replacement by an automatic system.

WHY REFORM?

Why the insistent calls for reform, mostly via elimination? The main reason is the broader cultural and societal impetus for more and more "democracy"—the same impetus that has extended the vote to women, minorities, and young people, and that has generated the movement to direct democracy via initiatives and referendums.

Another reason is the trend toward nationalization of politics in America—the sense that an emphasis on states is archaic for a modern national government. A third reason is the fear of an election outcome that would be viewed as illegitimate—especially one where a presidential candidate wins a majority of the national popular vote but still loses the presidency to a candidate who prevails in the Electoral College.

America has certainly had its electoral crises related to the Electoral College: in 1800, when an EC tie between Thomas Jefferson and Aaron Burr required the House to select the president, taking 36 ballots and ending up with Jefferson winning and his foe Burr serving as vice president; in 1824, when a four-way race left no candidate with a majority of electoral votes, and House maneuvering made John Quincy Adams, who led neither in popular nor electoral votes, the winner; in 1876, when disputed electoral slates in three states (including Florida) had to be sorted out by an electoral commission. In addition, in 1888, we had the dreaded result of a president (Grover Cleveland) elected without a popular vote majority or plurality (albeit with little evident national controversy or disagreement).

But three (or four) crises out of more than fifty presidential elections is remarkably small. And the drive for reform, based on the actual crises or the threat of another precipitated by the Electoral College, tends to ignore the crises that could be generated by direct national popular vote for the president.

The calls for reform accelerated with the 2000 presidential vote count, which started as a bad dream and ended up as a recurring nightmare—kind of like the movies *Groundhog Day* and *Friday the 13th* combined. The subsequent calls for repeal of the Electoral College were led by Senator-elect Hillary Rodham Clinton.

IRON LAW OF UNINTENDED CONSEQUENCES

It is only natural, of course, when a problem emerges, to seek a way to solve that problem. But the impulse to do so also brings with it what many have called "The

Iron Law of Unintended Consequences." This election snarl provides a perfect example. As an exercise, let's look at this election through the lens of Frank Capra's *It's a Wonderful Life*: What would have happened if there were no Electoral College?

For one thing, we would have had no quick and clean resolution of the election. On the morning after the election, Al Gore led George W. Bush by around 200,000 votes, or about 0.2 percent. That on the surface might seem substantial enough. But there were approximately 3 million absentee and vote-by-mail ballots yet to be counted, including well over one million in California, and several hundred thousand each in Oregon and Washington. It took more than three full weeks for all those absentee and vote-by-mail ballots to be tallied, with doubt remaining over the final leader for nearly all that period.

The almost-final difference between the candidates was 333,576 votes, roughly 0.3 percent [Editors' note: The official vote tally shows Gore winning 543,895 more votes than Bush, or .516 percent; see http://www.fec.gov/pubrec/fe2000/prespop.htm]. That is well below the number that triggers an automatic recount in Florida and many other states (some use 0.5 percent, some 0.33 percent, and so on.) Can anyone doubt that a hard-fought presidential campaign ending with a cloud over the counts in a number of counties and precincts around the country would call for a recount?

But that would not be a recount like Florida—confined to sixty-seven counties, each with its own clear-cut partisan power structure and administration. Instead we would have a nationwide recount, taking place in thousands of election units, some counties, some cities, some precincts, depending on individual states. All the ballot boxes in the country would have to be impounded. Instead of the squadron of lawyers who have descended on Florida to oversee, sue, and kibitz about the recounts, we would have armies of lawyers, exceeding the troops massed for the D-Day invasion, fanning out across the country to argue, bicker, and litigate.

This horrific nightmare would not likely be a one-time thing if the Electoral College were abolished. There has been a sharp trend in the country toward absentee ballots and vote-by-mail. The parties have encouraged it, because it is easier and cheaper to get out the vote by targeting voters and getting commitments in advance, fulfilled just by filling out a ballot and mailing it in. The states have moved in that direction because it can increase turnout and reduce their costs of keeping polling places open and filled with workers. California has up to a third of its voters going absentee, Washington about 60 percent, and Oregon went to a total vote-by-mail system this time. In 1996, the Census Bureau calculated that 20 percent of voters nationwide voted absentee; the number from this election will approach 30 percent.

PROBLEMS WITH ABSENTEES

But there are huge problems with absentee voting, starting with the fact that more and more people are voting weeks before the campaign ends, before they know what happens or how the candidates react under the intense pressure of the final days of the process.

Imagine if a fifteen-round heavyweight championship fight had the judges vote on a winner after the twelfth round. The staggered voting has sharply increased the costs of campaigning, and has actually increased the amount of negative campaign advertising; instead of saving their firepower until the final two weeks, when most voters begin to pay attention, candidates and parties in heavy absentee states have been forced to advertise much sooner for the early voters, and then spend more to target the later ones.

More significant for the purposes of evaluating the Electoral College, absentee votes and vote-by-mail have other important characteristics: one, they are more laborious to count—envelopes have to be opened individually, signatures checked, ballots certified, and searches done to be sure citizens vote only once, and counts taken. Oregon's self-vaunted all vote-by-mail system was a national embarrassment; the state only included ballots that arrived by the close-of-business Election Day, but it couldn't come up with any counts for days thereafter.

Of course, in most states, a large share of the absentee ballots don't arrive by Election Day. Many states are like Florida, allowing ten days after an election for overseas and other ballots postmarked by Election Day to come in and be counted. In Washington, any ballot postmarked Election Day is counted no matter when it arrives, adding to potential delays. So brace yourselves: Eliminate the Electoral College, and it will be a rare presidential election where we know the outcome even a week after!

Proponents of the repeal of the Electoral College might argue that this scenario is not a great brief in favor of it. If both the EC and direct popular vote have even equal potential built in for nightmares, why not opt for the more directly democratic process?

The answer is that there are many other powerful arguments in favor of the Electoral College. The EC tends to produce larger and more decisive margins for wins when the popular vote is very close, leading to a more definitive judgment of victory, and giving presidents some greater sense of legitimacy and mandate—a necessity in a system of checks and balances where a president relies heavily on intangibles like credibility.

John F. Kennedy's 1960 popular-vote margin over Richard Nixon was 118,000 votes, or just over 0.1 percent, one vote per precinct. But Kennedy won 303 electoral votes, 56 percent of them, a cushion large enough to discourage a challenge from Nixon and enough to give him some running room as president.

This factor is even more important when there is a three-way race for president and the winner ends up well below 50 percent of the popular vote. In 1968, with George Wallace running as an independent, Richard Nixon received only 43.4 percent of the popular vote, a precarious margin overall and with only a slender popular advantage over Democrat Hubert Humphrey. But even though Wallace siphoned off 46 electoral votes that year, Nixon still received 301 electoral votes, 31 over the majority necessary, 120 more than Humphrey and enough to give him some sense of mandate in a difficult, divisive, and bitter year.

In 1992, with H. Ross Perot running as an independent, Bill Clinton received just over 43 percent of the popular votes—but won with a near-landslide 370 electoral votes, 69 percent of the total.

CLOUT FOR SMALL STATES

The EC was designed originally to give states both large and small some role in presidential contests. It has done just that, while also encouraging candidates to campaign in small states and sparsely populated regions and to do retail, face-to-face campaigning instead of just television air wars targeting the large cities and other populous areas.

Large states, partly because they have all retained their winner-take-all electoral vote formula, have remained important, although the importance of one-party dominant large states would clearly increase with direct popular vote (hence Senator-elect Clinton's position.) But smaller states have clearly greater importance than they would have without the EC; indeed, in most elections, small states would be largely irrelevant without their electoral votes as lures.

Because of the obvious clout the EC gives to small states, the chances of Electoral College repeal remain small. They are smaller yet because of the public reaction to the November (or should we say December) 2000 results—the clear prospect after this election that a George W. Bush presidency would come with Al Gore having won the national popular vote caused not the slightest hint of public outrage.

So what will happen—and what should happen—in the aftermath of this election? One constitutional amendment would make some sense: the elimination of electors themselves and their replacement with automatic votes. Any concept of electors as actual deliberators disappeared in the early nineteenth century. Even though real examples of "faithless" electors are rare, the prospect is always there of rogue or faithless electors changing their votes, reneging on their pledges or being swayed by inducements, and especially with a very close election.

It also makes sense to remind states that they do not need a constitutional amendment to change the distribution of their electoral votes, perhaps joining Maine and Nebraska and dividing them by congressional district. In small one-party states, especially, this can give them more clout by dangling for the opposite party the prospect of winning one or two electoral votes out of the four or five because of a congressional district or two with different political leanings than the overall state. (In large states, on the other hand, division by congressional district could dilute their power and add to the confusion and close results in a tight election.) Remember too, that if large states like California allocated their electors by congressional district, it would create opportunities for more third- and fourth-party candidates like Ralph Nader to run for president, pick off a handful of districts (and electors), and perhaps throw the election into the House of Representatives.

But there is more that should happen now than direct reform or change in the Electoral College itself. This November, Americans learned as vividly as one can imagine that in our elections, every vote counts. Unfortunately, they have also learned, just as vividly, that not every vote is counted—not even close. For all except a handful of election aficionados, the messy, sloppy, underfunded, undermanned, sometimes incompetent and occasionally corrupt administration of our elections, in a process more decentralized than any area other than garbage collection, has come as a shock.

ELECTION REFORM

It demands reform—major, swift, and comprehensive—in the way Americans run our elections. Elections are woefully underfunded, resulting in outdated equipment, misaligned machines, poorly trained and inadequate personnel, out-of-date voter registration information at the polling places, poorly designed ballots, and huge voter errors.

The first step to reform is more money. And the money—probably $250 million, a small sum in the context of a nearly $2 trillion federal budget, but huge for local officials—becomes the key to substantive reform. States should consider their own reform programs, providing grants to election districts. And Congress should pass a bill providing the money in the form of matching grants (like the Highway Trust Fund, with a 90 percent to 10 percent ratio) to localities that agree to implement the following substantive reforms:

Uniform ballots for federal elections. No more "butterfly" ballots or other comparable monstrosities; all voters should confront the same, simple, and easy-to-use ballot, with clearly defined and directed choices.

Uniform use of modern "touch-screen" technology. In many jurisdictions in the country, including Baltimore city for example, voting is done by touch screens similar to ATM machines that most Americans are familiar with. The capital investment in new equipment is significant, but because of the costs of printing paper ballots, maintaining the old machines, and hiring the personnel to count the paper ballots, the long-term costs of using modern technology are actually lower.

Updating and upgrading voter registration data. Many legally registered voters went to the polls on November 7 only to be told that their names were not on the registration printout lists. Some lists had not been updated or synchronized; some had not been transferred from motor vehicle offices. It is an affront to democracy to prevent people who want to vote and have complied with the rules from doing so. Money and effort can fix the problem.

Use of local area networks (LANs) so that voters can cast their ballots either near their homes or their workplaces. Voting by Internet would exacerbate the problems listed below with absentee balloting. But information technology can make it easier for people with difficult work schedules to vote, and have the vote count in their home precincts.

Weekend, twenty-four-hour voting, with uniform poll-closing times. It is time to move the system from elections on the first Tuesday following the first Monday in November to elections that run from, say, 8:00 A.M. Saturday morning to 8:00 A.M. Sunday morning. Opening and closing times should be staggered across the time zones so that all the polls close at the same time. This might make election eve less dramatic for viewers and for networks, but it would enhance turnout, and make for fewer media muffs.

Discouragement of runaway absentee voting. Absentee ballots used to be for military personnel and those unavoidably away from home. Now voting by mail has become an easy tool of convenience—convenience for election officials who can ease the burden and cost at polls on Election Day; for parties, who can more easily target voters in their get-out-the-vote drives; and for voters who can avoid the hassle of voting at the polls. But those voters also lose the protection of privacy of the closed curtain in the polling place, and the importance of the collective act of gathering to exercise the sacred franchise. Absentee voting also raises the prospect of widespread corruption, a fact in many areas, with widespread use of absentee voting. Absentee voting should be for absentees—period. Make voting at the polls easier, but stop the trend of voting by mail.

The Electoral College will always remain controversial. The controversy may grow in the Information Age, with individual empowerment and the drive for direct democracy ascendant. But this "archaic" device is not anti-democratic—any more than a World Series that picks a winner by best-of-seven games, instead of by the overall number of runs scored, is wrong or illegitimate. As the data and arguments above suggest, the EC has legs—it continues to provide major benefits to American democracy. We need reform, and we need it now—in election administration and campaign finance. We do not need repeal of the Electoral College.

JAMES GLASSMAN
Reform the Electoral College, Don't Toss It

The five-week post-election contest between Al Gore and George W. Bush has utterly demystified the Electoral College in the minds of Americans. Most of them tell pollsters they want to get rid of it.

So do lots of politicians, including Hillary Rodham Clinton, the most famous Senator-elect, who announced that she would sponsor legislation "to do away with the Electoral College and move to the popular election of our Presidents." Senator Arlen Specter (R-Penn.) concurred.

Both Senators later admitted that passing a constitutional amendment to switch to a popular vote was a long shot. The reason, of course, is that the Electoral College gives disproportionate power to small states—that was one of the main reasons the Framers invented it—making those states unlikely ratifiers of any amendment.

It is true we don't elect our president by direct democracy, but that's precisely the point. The Constitution is a blueprint for protecting citizens, either as individuals or as members of minority groups, from the passions of majority rule. In fact, until 1832, electors were chosen almost exclusively by state legislators. The Framers wanted a system that preserved federalism. They considered giving each state an equal vote, then compromised. In the Electoral College, a state has an elector per congressional district plus an elector for each of its two Senators.

The Electoral College has three practical effects. First, candidates have to pay attention to smaller states, as both Gore and Bush did this year, battling over the five votes of West Virginia and even Delaware's three. Second, the system usually magnifies small differences in popular votes, providing the winner with a more substantial mandate. For example, in 1960, John F. Kennedy beat Richard Nixon by just a few tenths of a percentage point in the popular vote but won, 303–219, in the Electoral College.

Third, the Electoral College nearly eliminates the power of third parties and regional candidates. In the vast majority of elections, someone wins a majority. Rarely is a second round, with corrupt deal-making (as in 1824), required in the House of Representatives.

Still, the system has drawbacks. While candidates often pay great attention to smaller states, they sometimes completely ignore larger ones. In 2000, for instance, New York was written off by the GOP from the start, as was Texas by the Democrats. In a state like Massachusetts, which almost always goes Democratic, dispirited Republicans believe their votes never count; ditto, Democrats in Wyoming. Finally, as we saw in Florida, an excruciatingly tight race within a state can hold a bundle of electoral votes in the balance.

But there is a practical way to improve the system, and it doesn't require amending the Constitution. States, which have broad powers in choosing their electors, could change their state election statutes and adopt the system used in Maine since 1972 and in Nebraska since 1992: each state gives one electoral vote to the candidate who wins the most votes within each congressional district, and the state's other two electoral votes go to the candidate with the most votes statewide.

This year, both of Maine's congressional districts went to Gore, all three of Nebraska's went to Bush. But imagine the consequences of such a system for other states. In Virginia, for example, Democrats have strength in the D.C. suburbs and in the urban areas of Norfolk and Richmond. Bush swept the state easily, winning all thirteen electoral votes, as has every Republican since 1968.

But under proportional voting, Gore would have taken three congressional districts—and thus three electoral votes. So Bush's margin (with the two Senate votes) would have been 10–3. Meanwhile, in Maryland, all of whose ten votes went to Gore this time, a proportional system would have given two votes to Bush.

Which party would gain with this reform? It's hard to say. Republicans would be able to take seats in New York and Florida, while Democrats would score in states where they are now shut out, such as Georgia and Colorado. Key industrial states, such as Illinois, Ohio, and Pennsylvania, which are usually close, would award some of their votes to each candidate, which seems more fair.

A month after the election, *USA Today* analyzed the 2000 vote as though every state were using the Maine–Nebraska system. The final margin: Bush 271, Gore

267—the exact finish under the current scheme. That's a freak; in most cases, results would differ.

Since the election, bills have been introduced in the legislatures of Texas, California, and Indiana to change to proportional voting. It's a good idea. The campaign will be broader, more voters will feel they were recognized, and the risk of dozens of electoral votes hanging on a single county will be eliminated.

The two-party system will still dominate, even though it will be slightly easier for smaller parties to win a few electoral votes by concentrating on individual districts. Federalism—at least in presidential elections—will survive, and the Electoral College will keep providing its mystical benediction on each president.

DISCUSSION QUESTIONS

1. *What would you do?* You are a House member from a small state that voted for Al Gore. Many of your constituents are angry that he won the popular vote but lost the election, and they want you to introduce a constitutional amendment to abolish the Electoral College.

2. If the politics of getting approval for a proposal was not relevant, which reform would you support? How would taking politics into account change your position?

3. What do you think Norman Ornstein would say about Arthur Schlesinger's proposal to reform the Electoral College? Are there any unintended consequences to this proposal? Do you think Ornstein would be more supportive of James Glassman's proposal?

12 Political Parties: Which Way for the Democrats?

When a major party suffers a landslide defeat—the Republicans in 1964, the Democrats in 1984—commentators often mull over the possibility that the losing party is going extinct. In 2003, some are making the same sort of argument about the Democrats, but not because of any huge electoral defeat (recall that, despite losing in the Electoral College, Democratic candidate Al Gore actually received more popular votes than George Bush). Rather, the Democrats, some argue, are having some difficulty finding their collective voice, and do not seem to be able to articulate any coherent agenda other than reflexive opposition to anything the Bush Administration does. In July 2003, the Democratic Leadership Council, a group of centrist Democrats who urge the party to make more moderate positions, cautioned the presidential contenders against taking the party to the extreme left, and urged party leaders to rethink their opposition to tax cuts and the war in Iraq. More aggressive partisans countered that the Democrats would hardly benefit from adopting a "Bush-lite" agenda. Remembering Democratic president Harry Truman's famous quip, they note that when a voter has a choice between a Republican and a pretend-Republican, they'll choose the real thing every time.

The leaders of either major party would like to think of theirs as "a party for all the people," but this sentiment quickly runs up against the reality that not all the people agree on what the party should do. This basic conundrum faces not only party leaders and candidates but also citizens and observers of the parties. Some citizens believe that the way to success is for a party to forge a middle ground in public policy and try to make advocates on all sides of an issue feel that, although they may not get everything they want, they get a little something from the party's position. Other citizens believe that a party should take strong stands, stick to its principles, and fight the good fight. Even if the party loses, it is better to lose while upholding one's principles than to win while compromising one's principles. To this group, half a loaf is worse than none. Many voters who supported Ralph Nader, the Green Party presidential candidate in 2000, felt this way even though Nader's strength in the race arguably cost Gore the election. This same debate occurs among scholars, with some arguing for parties to be unified and follow a clear direction in public policy (the "responsible parties" school), while others argue that it is a job of presidents and parties to increase social cohesion and integration through political compromise (the "functional parties" school).

These issues are always difficult for party leaders and candidates to sort out, but they might be particularly difficult in the early twenty-first century. At the same time as political elites have become more ideologically polarized, election results have become increasingly split down the middle, with the 2000 presidential election perhaps the perfect example. Even with this relatively even split however, the balance overall has lately tended to favor the Republicans. For the first time in over seventy years, they have won majorities in five consecutive congressional elections. They regained the presidency following two terms of a relatively popular Democratic president. They hold most of the governorships around the country and control more state legislatures than the Democrats (twenty-one to the Democrats' seventeen, with eleven split between the two parties; Nebraska's legislature is excluded because it is nonpartisan). Is there any hope for the Democrats?

To David Brooks, Democrats (and the left more generally) have lost their bearings altogether, and are now reduced to hyperbolic over-the-top criticism of the Bush Administration. While it is common for political opponents to caricature each other to obtain a rhetorical advantage, the Democrats have gotten out of hand: party leaders and prominent liberals describe the Bush Administration as "dictatorial," engaged in the "deliberate, intentional destruction" of the country. Harold Myerson, editor of the self-identified liberal journal *The American Prospect*, claimed that Bush was the most dangerous president in U.S. history, and likened Bush to Jefferson Davis. This criticism is fueled by rage, according to Brooks, and will not make it easy for the party to appeal to centrist, swing voters who will hold the key to the 2004 election.

Ruy Teixeira, co-author of the book *The Emerging Democratic Majority*, is less pessimistic (although he notes that his book, which forecast a resurgence of the Democratic party, was published just before the 2002 midterm elections in which the Republicans did far better than they were expected to). He argues that Republican successes in 2000 and 2002 are exaggerated, and notes that Republicans are not likely to keep their electoral advantages in the long run. Republicans win, in his view, largely by "demagoguing" Democrats on national security, appealing to a shrinking base of white voters, and support for increasingly unpopular tax cuts. Concerns over the economy, efforts to mobilize Democratic voters, and the "hawkishness" of the Democratic presidential contenders all point to good prospects for a Democratic victory in 2004.

RUY TEIXEIRA
Deciphering the Democrats' Debacle

Last year, John Judis and I published a book entitled *The Emerging Democratic Majority*, which argued that a series of economic, demographic, and ideological changes was laying the basis for a new Democratic majority that would materialize by decade's end—not certainly, we argued, but very probably as long as the Democratic Party put forth decent political leadership to challenge the dominant, but dwindling, current Republican majority.

Our book arrived in stores last September. Two months later, in the midterm elections, the Republicans surprised nearly everyone by winning control of the Senate and further solidifying their majority in the House, unifying Republican control of the federal government for only the second time in half a century. Needless to say, this wasn't my ideal outcome. In the annals of publishing, this wasn't quite so unfortunate as, say, James Glassman's prediction of a 36,000 point Dow just before the 2000 stock market crash, but it still evoked a fair amount of understandable ribbing and forced me to think hard about our thesis. So after the election, I pored over survey data, county-by-county voting returns, and a great deal of underlying demographic data and thought long and hard about what the data showed. And as a result, I've decided that . . . we're still right!

THE MYTH OF A 9/11 MAJORITY

First, despite the Republican tsunami described by many media outlets, the actual electoral shift was quite mild. Though politically the election was a landmark, the underlying numbers suggest a continuing partisan balance. Democrats lost two seats in the Senate, six in the House, and gained three governorships. As nonpartisan analyst Charlie Cook has pointed out, "A swing of 94,000 votes out of 75,723,756 cast nationally would have resulted in the Democrats capturing control of the House and retaining a majority in the Senate on November 5. If that had occurred, obituaries would have been written—inevitably and prematurely—about the presidency of George W. Bush. Instead, we are entertained by predictions that the Democratic Party, as we know it, may cease to exist."

Given the very evenness of partisan division in this country, even minor fluctuations in public sentiment can cause sudden lurches in political power. Indeed, the last election differed markedly from 1994, when huge Republican gains (fifty-two House and nine Senate seats, ten governorships) really did change the partisan balance dramatically.

Nevertheless, the shock of 2002 initially devastated Democratic morale. Many in the party seemed helpless before the Republican success, ready to concede the 2004 election. For their part, Republicans were riding high, canonizing Karl Rove, and mentally fitting Bush for a spot on Mount Rushmore. Conservatives like Fred Barnes even spoke fondly of an "emerging 9/11 majority."

But that's begun to change. Democratic Senator Mary Landrieu's December runoff victory in Louisiana put Republican triumphalism in perspective. Subsequent events have revived Democratic hopes, as Bush's approval ratings, especially on the economy, have fallen and his diplomatic failures leading up to the Iraq war have been exposed. That's not the only encouraging news. A careful reading of the election and its aftermath suggests the GOP position has serious underlying weaknesses. In fact, the Republican victory depended on a series of unsustainable advantages that a tough, smart Democratic effort should be able to counter, forcing a competitive 2004 election and the likely—though not certain—ascendancy that Judis and I predicted by the end of the decade.

THE WHITE STUFF

The GOP's midterm wins depended heavily on their advantages in five areas that are either unlikely to persist or were overrated to begin with: a reliance on white voters, the growth of exurban voters, heavy GOP turnout, the tax-cut issue, and war. I'll tackle these in order.

Last November was all about the white vote. For all the talk of Republican minority outreach, the voters who showed up for the GOP on election day were, with few exceptions, white. In the 2000 election, 54 percent of whites voted for Bush and 56 percent for congressional Republicans; in 2002 that figure rose to 58 percent, which, coupled with higher turnout of whites, especially conservative whites, was enough for victory. Viewed one way, that's good news for Republicans, since whites comprise the overwhelming majority of U.S. voters. Trouble is, that majority is steadily diminishing. What's more, Republicans' core constituencies among white voters—those in rural areas, married men, married homemakers, and so forth—are also shrinking relative to other voter groups, which makes the demographic challenge of maintaining a majority even tougher.

As Matthew Dowd, polling director at the Republican National Committee, has pointed out, if minorities and whites vote in 2004 as they did in the 2000 election, Democrats will win by 3 million votes, for just that reason. In the long term, unless the GOP can make inroads among minority voters, they'll lose. In 2002, they made essentially no inroads at all. Recall that in the 2000 election, Al Gore got 90 percent of the black vote; in 2002, blacks appear to have voted at similar rates—if not slightly higher—for Democratic congressional and gubernatorial candidates. Hispanic support for Democrats was similarly rock solid, despite strenuous GOP outreach efforts. For example, California governor Gray Davis beat his Republican challenger Bill Simon by 65 to 24 percent among Hispanics—figures essentially identical to those by which Davis beat his 1998 challenger, Dan Lundgren. Nationally, a Greenberg-Quinlan-Rosner poll taken after the 2002 election indicated that Hispanics supported Democrats by 62 to 38 percent, figures nearly identical to 1998 numbers.

Research by political scientist James Gimpel confirms that Hispanic voting patterns haven't shifted. He found that Hispanics in ten states polled by Fox News supported Democrats over Republicans in Senate races by more than two to one (67 percent to 33 percent). Democrats didn't fare quite so well among Hispanics in governors' races in these states (54 percent to 46 percent), but that result probably had a great deal to do with the inclusion of Florida and the noncompetitive Colorado election in their sample. Gimpel found little evidence that Latinos are moving toward the Republican Party, despite all the talk of Hispanics as swing voters.

What limited data there are on Asian voters indicate that they, too, haven't wavered in their support of Democrats. In California, Asians voted for Davis over Simon by 54 to 37 percent, similar to their preference for Al Gore over George Bush in 2000. In other words, practically all the available data indicates that minority support for Democrats didn't budge in this election. For the GOP, that's a very bad sign.

COUNTY LINE

Republicans naturally want to make the case that their strong showing wasn't simply a result of demagoguing craven Democrats on national security. Surely, they'll tell you, there were deeper trends at work. One of the most fashionable of the theories put forward is that Republican gains reflected the rise of "exurbs"—those fast-growing edge counties on the fringes of large metropolitan areas that tend to vote

Republican. Since these areas are booming, argue conservatives like David Brooks, who wrote an influential post-election article in the *New York Times*, the future belongs to the GOP.

But while Brooks is correct that exurbs contributed to the 2002 Republican victories, his assertion that they were central to these victories is much shakier. Consider his two main examples, Colorado and Maryland. Colorado's quintessential exurb, Douglas County, just outside Denver, did vote overwhelmingly Republican in the state's Senate race, choosing Wayne Allard over Democrat Tom Strickland, 66 to 32 percent. That's about the same margin by which Bush beat Gore in Douglas County in 2000. But pull back a bit and the picture changes: The Denver-Boulder area as a whole voted for Democrat Strickland by a 6-point margin; that's larger than the 3-point victory Gore won in 2000, which in turn improved on Michael Dukakis's 1-point loss in 1988.

How can this be? Partly it's the influence of vote-rich Denver County, which is strongly Democratic and becoming more so. But another part of it is suburban Arapahoe and Jefferson counties around Denver that, as they've grown bigger, denser, and more diverse—less "exurban," if you will—have also become much less Republican. Arapahoe voted for Reagan in 1980 by 39 points, for Bush I in 1988 by 22 points, and for W. in 2000 by only 8 points. In the same period, Jefferson favored Reagan by 34 points, Bush by 15, and his son by just 8. These swings have contributed to a pro-Democratic trend in the Denver-Boulder area—a trend that buoyed Strickland's candidacy, rather than hurt it. The real story in Colorado was Strickland's poor showing elsewhere in the state, especially in small towns and rural areas.

Maryland's gubernatorial election is an even stronger refutation of the exurban thesis. To begin with, Democrats picked up two House seats in the 2002 election, and Gore beat Bush by 17 points in the last presidential election. While Republican gubernatorial candidate Robert Ehrlich did very well in exurban counties like Frederick (north of Washington, D.C.) and Harford (north of Baltimore), both of which already tend to vote Republican, Ehrlich's real coup was carrying counties Brooks doesn't mention—closer-in counties like Baltimore (the state's third-largest) and Howard (the state's fastest-growing county with more than 100,000 in population), both of which traditionally vote Democratic and have become more so over time. In other words, the real story is that Ehrlich's opponent, Kathleen Kennedy Townsend, ran a lousy race and lost many counties she should have won, and lost badly where she should have at least come close. Consequently, Ehrlich's victory hardly suggests an impending era of Republican exurban dominance in the very Democratic state of Maryland.

Elsewhere, examples of the exurban phenomenon run into the same problem: They are usually examples of—not the reasons for—pro-Republican voting. Take Northern Virginia's Loudon County, the sixth-fastest-growing county nationwide, cited by Brooks in another article. As Loudon has grown, it has grown more Democratic, moving from a 66–33 Republican advantage in 1988 to a much more modest 56–41 advantage in 2000. And, critically, the northern Virginia suburbs as a whole have shifted from a 20-point Republican edge to a mere 2-point edge over that same period. Evidently, Loudon's booming growth isn't enough to stop a political trend toward voting Democratic, much less start one toward voting Republican.

In fact, Loudon County illustrates an important, and—for Democrats—positive trend: Many of these fast-growing, Republican-leaning exurban counties are part of larger metropolitan areas that are actually trending in the opposite direction. That's because exurban counties are generally too small to outweigh pro-Democratic developments elsewhere in large metropolitan areas, and also because as exurban counties become bigger, denser, and more diverse, they generally become less—not more—Republican. So, in a sense, today's right-leaning exurb is tomorrow's left-leaning suburb. This makes a strategy based on exurbs as they appear today—nearly all white and low density—a tenuous one. If the GOP expects long-term political dominance from the growth of these same counties, it's likely to be disappointed.

TURN ON, TUNE IN, TURNOUT

The 2002 election was also an aberration from the perspective of voter turnout. Usually, it's the Democrats who fire up their base and deliver a bravura performance of getting voters to the polls. Last year, however, Democrats dragged their feet, while Republicans did an outstanding job. The GOP's "72-Hour Project" did particularly well, boosting white turnout. But Democrats didn't match this effort among their base; while minorities supported them at typically high rates, fewer showed up at the polls. In California, a *Los Angeles Times* exit poll—the only functioning exit poll in the nation—indicated that only 4 percent of voters in 2002 were black, compared to 13 percent in 1998. That's almost certainly an underestimate, but it does suggest a substantial falloff. The same poll indicated that just 10 percent of California voters in 2002 were Hispanic, down from 13 percent in 1998. And Gimpel's study of Fox News polls in 10 states indicates that Hispanics of low to middle income and education were much less likely to vote last year than those of high income and education, meaning that not only was Hispanic turnout likely lower in 2002, but those who did show up were unusually unrepresentative of the Hispanic community in a way that hurt Democrats and helped Republicans. (Turnout was especially low among independent Latinos with middling levels of education, who tend to vote heavily Democratic.)

More broadly, county-level voting returns suggest that turnout in Democratic-leaning large cities and inner suburbs, even where it did not decline, did not keep pace with increases in Republican-leaning exurbs and rural areas, which, on the whole, were highly mobilized. In Missouri, for example, the increase in votes cast over the 1998 election was much more moderate in heavily Democratic St. Louis city and Democratic-leaning St. Louis County than in the heavily Republican suburb of St. Charles County and especially in rural and extremely Republican Cape Girardeau County. The same pattern was true in Minnesota, where many Republican-leaning rural counties seemed to show exceptionally high turnouts, while Democratic-leaning urban ones lagged behind.

Of course, the relatively low turnout among minorities and in Democratic areas probably didn't matter much in states like California, where the Democrats prevailed by a large margin, or Florida, where they were so far behind that no reasonable increment of minority turnout could conceivably have saved them. But in close races like Missouri's, it may have cost the Democrats victory—and perhaps nationwide also, since it only took a swing of two seats for Republicans to take the Senate.

So the GOP was clearly the turnout party in 2002. But it's unlikely to be able to repeat this. To begin with, Democrats won't be caught napping again. They've launched their own version of the "72-Hour Project" called "Project 5104"—shorthand for winning 51 percent of the vote in 2004. The labor movement will match this expanded turnout initiative with its "Partnership for Working Families," which will target not just union voters, but also non-union liberals and Democratic-leaning voters in the party's 158 million-voter database.

Of course, better mechanics alone can't make up for low motivation, which was clearly one of the reasons Democratic voters didn't turn out in 2002. But three things will be different next time around. First, the 9/11 effect will have dissipated, and far fewer voters will be patriotically inclined to give President Bush the benefit of the doubt. Second, the Democrats are learning that "No ideas don't beat bad ideas." In 2002, they had no agreed upon economic policy, no plausible alternative foreign policy, and a handful of domestic program proposals like prescription drug benefits for seniors that Republicans neutralized with vague proposals of their own. Leading Democrats now know they need a broader agenda to give Democratic-leaning voters reason to show up. Finally, nothing drives voters to the polls like anger—the desire to strike a blow against the opponent. That desire was absent in 2002 due to a short-term confusion among many Democratic voters and lawmakers about whether and how to oppose Bush. But the president's virulent partisanship has erased such concerns among Democratic-leaning voters. In a recent *Los Angeles Times* poll, for example, 95 percent of Republicans approved of Bush's job performance, compared to just 28 percent of Democrats. This extraordinarily high point spread shows that non-Republican voters have become alienated by the administration's hard-right policies on everything from tax cuts and Medicare to Iraq. Bush may indeed be mobilizing his own base—but in the process he's mobilizing the other side's, too.

TITHES THAT BIND

It is an article of faith in the GOP these days that there is no such thing as a bad tax cut. Indeed, this extraordinary concept has overshadowed the "compassionate conservatism" Bush touted in his 2000 campaign. So the Republicans are betting, at least domestically, on the political appeal of tax cuts. They had an easy time of it in 2001, and now they're proposing a new round, including the complete elimination of the dividend tax. The Democrats didn't dare run against tax cuts last November, they reason, so why should the future be any different?

But early reaction to Bush's new tax-cut plan is remarkably tepid considering that the public's initial reaction to any new economic proposal (if no potential drawbacks are cited) tends to be positive. In this case, the lack of enthusiasm has a great deal to do with the fact that just 22 percent of the public paid any direct dividend tax at all last year. And a closer examination of the general apathy toward Bush's latest cuts reveals a remarkable fact: More people now think the amount of federal income tax they pay is "about right" (50 percent) than think it is "too high" (47 percent). Someone resuscitate Grover Norquist! According to Gallup, the last time the public felt this good about paying their taxes was March 1949. Perhaps this wasn't the ideal time to propose a large, deficit-ballooning tax cut for the rich after all.

Sure enough, survey data from a Greenberg-Quinlan-Rosner poll shows that Bush's new plan is sparking much less interest than his first tax cut did in January 2001. Back then, 49 percent thought Bush's proposal was good for the middle class, while 42 percent disagreed; this time just 37 percent think it's good for the middle class, compared to 48 percent who don't.

Other recent survey questions reveal that the public may have had its fill of tax cuts. By more than two to one, people would prefer more spending on education, health care, and Social Security to Bush's proposed tax cut (ABC); 61 percent believe the Bush plan will be "just somewhat" or "not very" effective in stimulating the economy (NBC); almost twice as many think the Bush economic plan would benefit the wealthy over Americans as a whole (NBC); 56 percent believe that if the Bush plan mostly benefits the wealthy, it will be an ineffective way to stimulate the economy (NBC). The public also expresses a preference for a stimulus program focused on infrastructure spending (roads, bridges, schools) rather than tax cuts, and by a whopping margin is nervous about the prospect of Social Security funds helping to fund the government if Bush's tax cut goes through. In other words, it's a considerably less friendly world for tax cuts in 2003 than it was in 2001 and—partly reflecting this fact—this time Democrats are lining up to oppose them.

Polling data suggests that this is a doubly smart move. Not only are tax cuts unpopular, but voters believe them to be an ineffective remedy for the public's real area of concern: the lousy economy. A recent Pew poll revealed that more people disapprove of Bush's performance on tax policy (44 percent) than approve of it (42 percent). On the economy, the president fares even worse. Before the invasion of Iraq, he was regularly drawing approval ratings in this area in the low 40s (and only in the high 30s among political independents, the best simple proxy for swing voters), with disapproval ratings in the low 50s. He received a slight bump from the war (rallying around the president on one issue commonly bleeds into unrelated areas), but is heading right back down. Should that continue into 2004, being identified with tax cuts is likely to be a liability, even in the short term. Over the long term, the fiscal damage wrought by tax cuts drains the economy, generates huge deficits, and ensures that voters' priorities can't be met: hardly a recipe for political dominance.

THE SPOILER OF WAR

That brings us to the GOP's biggest advantage in the last election and the one they're clearly relying on to carry them through the next: war and national security. Right now, the Bush administration's war in Iraq enjoys the support of about 70 percent of the American public. But even this advantage is unlikely to last. The war is temporarily suppressing Americans' genuine skepticism about the administration's approach to foreign policy, and the underlying softness of their support means that they could quickly tire of a lengthy occupation and the ancillary foreign and security problems.

For example, before the invasion, polls slowed that Americans opposed invading Iraq without U.N. support and strongly supported giving weapons inspectors more time, reflecting the public's overwhelming view that Iraq was a long-range, not an immediate, threat. And while general, no-conditions-specified questions about military action against Saddam Hussein always elicited support, this ebbed once stipulations were raised about U.S., and even Iraqi, casualties or about the possibility of a long-term occupation—now a certainty. Moreover, moderates and independents held these viewpoints more strongly than the broader public, indicating that this was the true center of U.S. public opinion.

In other words, the public held a very different view of Iraq than the president did. The administration espoused an evolving ideology that essentially relies on asserting unilateral American power, while the public preferred a more nuanced and pragmatic aproach of working through allies—more Wesley Clark, if you will, than Donald Rumsfeld. And, like Clark, they were inclined to see Iraq as more of an "elective war" than one waged out of necessity.

Of course, after the troops hit the ground, these doubts and nuances gave way to patriotic support. But they remain, evident even in post-invasion polls—such as Gallup's—that consistently find just 59 percent supporting the war as "the right thing to do," while the remaining 11–13 percent who favor it do so out of a desire "to support the troops" (25–27 percent oppose the war outright). There is more doubt and even opposition than during the first Gulf War or the attack against the Taliban regime in Afghanistan. Consequently, the public is less likely to cut Bush slack if the Middle East situation worsens than it was immediately following 9/11.

Besides, to truly benefit from being hawkish, it helps if your opponent is a softie whose party is implicated in a major foreign policy debacle. Today's Democratic Party is not handicapped by this and seems more intent on channeling the spirit of John F. Kennedy than George McGovern or Jimmy Carter. Four of the five leading candidates for the Democratic nomination voted for the resolution supporting Bush on Iraq. And the voguish term for today's Democratic frontrunner, decorated Vietnam veteran John Kerry isn't "pinko," but "tough dove."

THE ROAD AHEAD

Despite all the evidence that Republicans are not assured of winning in 2004, Democrats are hardly certain to knock off a sitting president. What the 2002 election and its aftermath reveal is that the underlying trends identified in *The Emerging Democratic Majority* have not been negated; they've been temporarily overwhelmed by Republican successes. The country is still changing in ways congenial to Democrats. A Democratic Party that practices smart, tough politics and fields viable candidates faces no fundamental obstacle to achieving political dominance by decade's end.

But let's get serious—can we really expect that from the Democrats? That's what Republicans ask—and even many Democrats, who see the weaknesses in the current GOP position, but can't quite bring themselves to subscribe to the message of my book. The truth is that many intelligent members of both parties believe the Republicans to be the only true practitioners of effective politics.

Perhaps this is why my party is currently out of power, but I believe differently. Take the Democrats' minority vote. Skeptics will point out that that devious Karl Rove has access to the same numbers I've laid out above and will certainly devise a plan to snare minority voters for Republicans in 2004 and beyond. True as far as it goes, but it doesn't mean he'll succeed. The 2002 elections showed just how little success Republicans have enjoyed so far. The fact of the matter is that the partisan affiliations, policy priorities, and views on the role of government of blacks and Hispanics skew dramatically toward the Democrats. It's going to be difficult for Republicans to change their own priorities and approach to government enough to appeal to these groups and break down their Democratic affiliations.

So what about the gender gap? Isn't the GOP making headway there as smart, tough Republican operatives take advantage of women's sensitivity to public safety issues to move them away from the Democrats? Not really. Survey data from the 2002 election indicates that the gender gap favored Democrats about as much as it ever has. Gallup, whose pre-election poll nailed the result almost perfectly, had the gender gap slightly larger last year than in 2000. And Gallup data indicate that what really drove the surge toward Republicans just before the election was not security-conscious women, but those reliable Republican stand-bys: white men.

Now, it is true that women are substantially more likely than men to fear being the victim of a terrorist attack (see "Homeland Security is for Girls," *The Washington Monthly*, April 2003). So, even though it wasn't much of a factor in 2002, perhaps those worried women will gravitate toward the GOP's national security toughness over the longer haul? Not likely. On virtually every poll question one might care to look at, women are less likely than men to trust and support Bush administration policies on Iraq and related issues, the main vehicle through which the president is supposedly fighting terrorist attacks. Before the war started, a *Los Angeles Times* poll showed that more women opposed a U.S. invasion of Iraq without Security Council blessing than supported it; and even after war began, far fewer women than men approve of the way Bush is handling the situation.

Beyond that, look at the record Bush has amassed on his 2000 campaign promises. "Compassionate conservatism" flummoxed hapless Democrats the first time around, but by now the administration has several years of not-so-compassionate baggage to explain away. And its hard-right policies on the environment, Medicare, Social Security, tax cuts, and Iraq have polarized Democrats against them (so much for being "a uniter not a divider") and alienated moderates and independents—the principal targets of compassionate conservatism in the first place. In other words, a party's policies and track record set real limits to what smartness and toughness can accomplish. The idea that Karl Rove can negate all this simply by waving his magic wand should not be taken seriously by Democrats or anyone else. What the Democrats should take seriously is the need to fight back and fight back hard, so they can exploit the underlying trends that are moving the country in a Democratic direction.

But these are trends, not guarantees. They're meaningless unless Democrats can find the right combination of politics and ideas to fire up their base while appealing to independents and other swing voters. Can they do it?

There are encouraging signs. From Sen. Landrieu's hard-fought special election to congressional Democrats' relentless campaign against the latest Bush tax cut to the hawkish position of most Democratic frontrunners, the party is in the process of refashioning itself to take advantage of Republican weaknesses and—just as important—avoid dumb mistakes. They need to build on this in 2004 and beyond by articulating an agenda that goes beyond reining in Republican excess and defending Social Security. Again, the signs are encouraging. The Democratic frontrunners, who set the tone for the party, have advanced serious proposals in areas like education, health care, pension reform, and international relations that could give voters a reason to back the Democrats.

John Judis and I argued that a Democratic majority was likely by the decade's end. That's still where I'd place my bet. But all the evidence I've laid out here suggests that Bush and the Republicans are vulnerable sooner, if Democrats can exploit those weaknesses. That would mean new ideas and compelling candidates. But, if they pull it off, that majority could come much sooner than you think—maybe even in 2004. You can say you read it here first.

DAVID BROOKS
Democrats Go Off the Cliff

Across the country Republicans and conservatives are asking each other the same basic question: Has the other side gone crazy? Have the Democrats totally flipped their lids? Because every day some Democrat seems to make a manic or totally over-the-top statement about George Bush, the Republican party, and the state of the nation today.

"This republic is at its greatest danger in its history because of this administration," says Democratic senator Robert Byrd.

"I think this is deliberate, intentional destruction of the United States of America," says liberal commentator Bill Moyers.

George Bush's economic policy is the "most radical and dangerous economic theory to hit our shores since socialism," says Senator John Edwards.

"The Most Dangerous President Ever" is the title of an essay in the *American Prospect* by Harold Meyerson, in which it is argued that the president Bush most closely resembles is Jefferson Davis.

Tom Daschle condemns the "dictatorial approach" of this administration. John Kerry says Bush "deliberately misled" America into the Iraq war. Asked what Democrats can do about the Republicans, Janet Reno recalls her visit to the Dachau concentration camp, and points out that the Holocaust happened because many Germans just stood by. "And don't you just stand by," she exhorts her Democratic audience.

When conservatives look at the newspapers, they see liberal columnists who pick out every tiny piece of evidence or pseudo-evidence of Republican vileness, and then dwell on it and obsess over it until they have lost all perspective and succumbed to fevers of incoherent rage. They see Democratic primary voters who are so filled with hatred at George Bush and John Ashcroft and Dick Cheney that they are pulling their party far from the mainstream of American life. They see candidates who, instead of trying to quell the self-destructive fury, are playing to it. "I am furious at [Bush] and I am furious at the Republicans," says Dick Gephardt, trying to sound like John Kerry who is trying to sound like Howard Dean.

It's mystifying. Fury rarely wins elections. Rage rarely appeals to suburban moderates. And there is a mountain of evidence that the Democrats are now racing away from swing voters, who do not hate George Bush, and who, despite their qualms about the economy and certain policies, do not feel that the republic is being raped by vile and illegitimate marauders. The Democrats, indeed, look like they're turning into a domestic version of the Palestinians—a group so enraged at their perceived oppressors, and so caught up in their own victimization, that they behave in ways that are patently not in their self-interest, and that are almost guaranteed to perpetuate their suffering.

When you talk to Democratic strategists, you find they do have rationalizations for the current aggressive thrust. In 2003, it's necessary to soften Bush up with harsh atacks, some say. In 2004, we'll put on a happier face. Others argue that Democrats tried to appeal to moderate voters in 2002 and it didn't work. The key to victory in 2004 is riling up the liberal base. Still others say that with all the advantages Bush has—incumbency, victory in Iraq, the huge fundraising lead—Democrats simply have to roll the dice and behave radically.

But all of these explanations have a post-facto ring. Democratic strategists are trying to put a rational gloss on what is a visceral, unplanned, and emotional state of mind. Democrats may or may not be behaving intelligently, but they are behaving sincerely. Their statements are not the product of some Dick Morris-style strategic plan. This stuff wasn't focus-grouped. The Democrats are letting their inner selves out for a romp.

And if you probe into the Democratic mind at the current moment, you sense that the rage, the passion, the fighting spirit are all fueled not only by opposition to Bush policies, but also by powerlessness.

Republicans have controlled the White House before, but up until now Democrats still had some alternative power center. Reagan had the presidency, but Democrats had the House and, part of the time, the Senate. Bush the elder faced a Democratic Congress. But now Democrats have nothing. Even the Supreme Court helped Republicans steal the last election, many Democrats feel. Republicans—to borrow political scientist Samuel Lubell's trope—have become the Sun party and Democrats have been reduced to being the Moon party. Many Democrats feel that

George Bush is just running loose, transforming the national landscape and ruining the nation, and there is nothing they can do to stop him.

Wherever Democrats look, they sense their powerlessness. Even when they look to the media, they feel that conservatives have the upper hand. Conservatives think this is ludicrous. We may have Rush and Fox, conservatives say, but you have ABC, NBC, CBS, the *New York Times*. But liberals are sincere. They despair that a consortium of conservative think tanks, talk radio hosts, and Fox News—Hillary's vast right-wing conspiracy—has cohered to form a dazzlingly efficient ideology delivery system that swamps liberal efforts to get their ideas out.

When they look to the culture at large, many Democrats feel that the climate is so hostile to them they can't even speak up. During the war in Iraq, liberals claimed that millions of Americans were opposed to war, but were afraid to voice their opinions, lest the Cossacks come charging through their door. The actor Tim Robbins declared, "Every day, the airwaves are filled with warnings, veiled and unveiled threats, spewed invective and hatred directed at any voice of dissent. And the public, like so many relatives and friends that I saw this weekend, sit in mute opposition and fear." Again, conservatives regard this as ludicrous. Stand up and oppose the war, conservatives observe, and you'll probably win an Oscar, a National Magazine Award, and tenure at four dozen prestigious universities. But the liberals who made these complaints were sincerely expressing the way they perceive the world.

And when they look at Washington, they see a cohesive corporate juggernaut, effortlessly pushing its agenda and rolling over Democratic opposition. Again, this is not how Republicans perceive reality. Republicans admire President Bush a great deal, but most feel that, at least on domestic policy, the conservative agenda has been thwarted as much as it has been advanced. Bush passed two tax cuts, but on education he abandoned school choice and adopted a bill largely written by Ted Kennedy. On Medicare, the administration has abandoned real reform and embraced a bill also endorsed by Kennedy. On campaign finance, the president signed a bill promoted by his opponents. The faith-based initiatives are shrinking to near nothingness. Social Security reform has disappeared from the agenda for the time being. Domestic spending has increased.

Still, Democrats and liberals see the Bush presidency in maximalist terms. "President Bush's signature on his big tax cut bill Wednesday marked a watershed in American politics," wrote E.J. Dionne of the *Washington Post*. "The rules of policymaking that have applied since the end of World War II are now irrelevant." The headline on a recent Michael Kinsley column was "Captialism's 'Deal' Falls Apart," arguing that the Bush administration had revoked the social contract that had up to now shaped American politics.

In short, when many liberals look at national affairs, they see a world in which their leaders are nice, pure-souled, but defenseless, and they see Republicans who are organized, devious, and relentless. "It's probably a weakness that we're not real haters. We don't have a sense that it's a holy crusade," Democratic strategist Bob Shrum told Adam Clymer of the *New York Times*. "They play hardball, we play softball," Gore campaign manager Donna Brazile added. Once again, Republicans think this picture of reality is delusional. The Democrats are the party that for forty years has labeled its opponents racists, fascists, religious nuts, and monsters who wanted to starve grannies and orphans. Republicans saw what Democrats did to Robert Bork, Clarence Thomas, and dozens of others. Yet Democrats are utterly sincere. Many on the left think they have been losing because their souls are too elevated.

When they look inward, impotence, weakness, high-mindedness, and geniality are all they see.

Earlier this year, Robert Kagan published a book, *Of Paradise and Power: America and Europe in the New World Order*. Kagan argued that Americans and Europeans no longer share a common view of the world. Americans are from Mars, and Europeans are from Venus. The essential reason Americans and Europeans perceive reality differently, he argued, is that there is a power gap. Americans are much more powerful than Europeans, and Europeans are acutely aware of their powerlessness.

Something similar seems to be happening domestically between Republicans and Democrats. It's not just that members of the two parties disagree. It's that the disagreements have recently grown so deep that liberals and conservatives don't seem to perceive the same reality. Whether it is across the ocean or across the aisle, powerlessness corrupts just as certainly as power does. Those on top become overly self-assured, emotionally calloused, dishonest with themselves, and complacent. Those on the bottom become vicious. Sensing that their dignity is perpetually insulted, they begin to see their plight in lurid terms. They exaggerate the power of their foes. They invent malevolent conspiracy theories to explain their unfortunate position. They develop a gloomy and panicked view of the world.

Republicans are suffering from many of the maladies that afflict the powerful, but they have not been driven into their own emotional ghetto because in their hearts Republicans don't feel that powerful. Democrats, on the other hand, do feel powerless. And that is why so many Democratic statements about Republicans resemble European and Middle Eastern statements about America.

First, there is the lurid and emotional tone. You wouldn't know it listening to much liberal conversation, but we are still living in a country that is evenly divided politically; the normal rules still apply; our politics is still a contest between two competing but essentially valid worldviews; power tends to alternate between the two parties, as one or the other screws up or grows stale.

But if you listened to liberal rhetoric, you would think America was convulsed in a Manichean struggle of good against evil. Here, for example, is the liberal playwright Tony Kushner addressing the graduating seniors at Columbia College in Chicago. This passage is not too far off from the rhetoric one can find in liberal circles every day:

> And this is what I think you have gotten your education for. You have presumably made a study of how important it is for people—the people and not the oil plutocrats, the people and not the fantasists in right-wing think tanks, the people and not the virulent lockstep gasbags of Sunday morning talk shows and editorial pages and all-Nazi all-the-time radio ranting marathons, the thinking people and not the crazy people, the rich and multivarious multicultural people and not the pale pale grayish-

white cranky grim greedy people, the secular pluralist people and not the theocrats, the misogynists, Muslim and Christian and Jewish fundamentalists, the hard-working people and not the people whose only real exertion ever in their whole parasite lives has been the effort it takes to slash a trillion plus dollars in tax revenue and then stuff it in their already overfull pockets.

Second, there is the frequent and relentless resort to conspiracy theories. If you judged by newspapers and magazines this spring, you could conclude that a secret cabal of Straussians, Jews, and neoconservatives (or perhaps just Richard Perle alone) had deviously seized control of the United States and were now planning bloody wars of conquest around the globe.

Third, there is the hypercharged tendency to believe the absolute worst about one's political opponents. In normal political debate, partisans routinely accuse each other of destroying the country through their misguided policies. But in the current liberal rhetoric it has become normal to raise the possibility that Republicans are *deliberately* destroying the country. "It's tempting to suggest that the Bush administration is failing to provide Iraq with functioning, efficient, reliable public services because it doesn't believe in functioning, reliable public services—doesn't believe they should exist, and doesn't believe that they can exist," writes Hendrik Hertzberg in the *New Yorker*. "The suspicion will not die that the administration turned to Iraq for relief from a sharp decline in its domestic political prospects," argue the editors of the *American Prospect*. In *Harper's* Thomas Frank calls the Bush budget "a blueprint for sabotage." He continues: "It seems equally likely that this budget document, in both its juvenile rhetorical tricks and its idiotic plans for the nation, is merely supposed to teach us a lesson in how badly government can misbehave."

In this version of reality, Republicans are deviously effective. They have careful if evil plans for everything they do. And these sorts of charges have become so common we're inured to their horrendousness—that Bush sent thousands of people to their deaths so he could reap government contracts for Halliburton, that he mobilized hundreds of thousands of troops and spent tens of billions of dollars merely to help secure favorable oil deals for Exxon.

Sometimes reading through this literature one gets the impression that while the United States is merely attempting to export Western style democracy to the Middle East, the people in the Middle East have successfully exported Middle Eastern-style conspiracy mongering to the United States.

Now it is true that you can find conservatives and Republicans who went berserk during the Clinton years, accusing the Clintons of multiple murders and obsessing over how Vince Foster's body may or may not have been moved. And it is true that Michael Savage and Ann Coulter are still out there accusing the liberals of treason. The Republicans had their own little bout of self-destructive, self-pitying powerlessness in the late 1990s, and were only rescued from it when George W. Bush emerged from Texas radiating equanimity.

But the Democratic mood is more pervasive, and potentially more self-destructive. Because in the post-9/11 era, moderate and independent voters do not see reality the way the Democrats do. Bush's approval ratings are at about 65 percent, and they have been far higher; most people do not see him as a malevolent force, or the figurehead atop a conspiracy of corporate moguls. Up to 80 percent of Americans supported the war in Iraq, and large majorities still approve of the effort, notwithstanding the absence so far of WMD stockpiles. They do not see that war as a secret neoconservative effort to expand American empire, or as a devious attempt to garner oil contracts.

Democrats can continue to circulate real or artificial tales of Republican outrages, they can continue to dwell on their sour prognostications of doom, but there is little evidence that anxious voters are in the mood to hate, or that they are in the mood for a political civil war, or that they will respond favorably to whatever party spits the most venom. There is little evidence that moderate voters share the sense of powerlessness many Democrats feel, or that they buy the narrative of the past two and a half years that many Democrats take as the landscape of reality.

And the problem for Democrats, more than for Republicans, is that they come from insular parts of the country. In university towns, in New York, in San Francisco and Los Angeles, and even in some Democratic precincts in Washington, D.C., there is little daily contact with conservatives or even with detached moderates. (In the Republican suburban strongholds, by contrast, there is daily contact with moderate voters, who almost never think about politics except just before Election Day.) So the liberal tales of Republican malevolence circulate and grow, are seized upon and believed. Contrary evidence is ignored. And the tone grows more and more fevered.

Perhaps the Democrats will regain their equanimity. Perhaps some eventual nominee will restore a temperate tone. The likeliest candidates—Kerry, Gephardt, Edwards, and Lieberman—are, after all, sensible men and professionally competent. But if the current Democratic tone remains unchanged, we would be on the verge of another sharp political shift toward the Republicans.

In 1976, 40 percent of Americans were registered Democrats and fewer than 20 percent were registered Republicans. During the Reagan era, those numbers moved, so that by 1989, 35 percent of Americans were registered Democrats and 30 percent were registered Republicans. During the Bush and Clinton years Democratic registration was basically flat and Republican registration dipped slightly to about 27 percent.

But over the past two years, Democratic registration has dropped to about 32 percent and Republican registration has risen back up to about 30 percent. These could be temporary gyrations. But it's also possible that we're on the verge of a historic moment, when Republican registration surpasses Democratic registration for the first time in the modern era.

For that to happen, the economy would probably have to rebound, the war on terror would have to continue without any major disasters, and the Republicans would have to have some further domestic legislative success, such as prescription drug benefits, to bring to the American voters. And most important, Democrats would have to remain as they are—unhappy, tone deaf, and over the top.

DISCUSSION QUESTIONS

1. *What would you do?* As an adviser to the Democrats, draft a strategy for the party. Should the party pursue a liberal agenda? Should it seek a more centrist course? Perhaps some combination of the two? What are the advantages of your plan—i.e., why do you think this would work better than an alternative? Do the terrorist attacks and aftermath of September 11, 2001, have any impact on your proposed strategy, or would your advice have been the same prior to those events?

2. Brooks and Teixeira lay out very different cases: Brooks that the Democratic party is self-destructing, Teixeira that it is on the verge of recapturing the White House. Whose argument do you find more persuasive? Why?

3. If the country is divided fairly evenly between opposing political views, would it be better for the nation if one side had a chance to implement its plan without compromise? That way, the public could judge whether the plans of that side worked or were failures. In other words, if each side gets a little of what it wants, or if control of Congress and the presidency were split between the parties, would that simply have the effect of dragging out the political division even longer because neither side would feel it had a real chance to implement its policies?

4. Should party leaders (or a president) primarily view their leadership responsibilities as finding common ground between opposing sides or as staking out a firm position and refusing to deviate from that position? If you believe a party should do each of these but at different times, under what conditions would each of these approaches be most appropriate?

13   Interest Groups: A Force for Change or the Status Quo?

In his famous essay *Federalist* 10, future president James Madison expressed concern about the "mischief of factions." It was natural, he argued, for people to organize around a principle or interest they held in common, and the most common motivation for organizing such factions was property—those who had it versus those who did not, creditors versus lenders. The danger in such efforts, however, was that a majority faction might usurp the rights of a minority. In a small direct democracy, where a majority of the people could share a "common passion," the threat was very real. Expand the geographic size of the country, however, and replace direct democracy with a system of elected representatives, separation of powers, and checks and balances, and the threat diminished. The likelihood of any one faction appealing to a majority of citizens in a large republic governed by representatives from diverse geographic regions was remote. To Madison, factions were a natural outgrowth of the differences between people, and the only way to eliminate factions would be to eliminate liberty. Eliminating factions might not be possible or desirable, but the mischief of factions could be controlled with a system of representation based upon varied constituencies that embraced multiple, diverse interests. From the competition of diverse interests would arise compromise and balanced public policy.

Madison's concerns about interests and particularly organized interests have resonated throughout American history. At various times in the U.S., the public has seemed to become especially concerned with the power of interests in politics. Political scientists refer to this as the "ideals vs. institutions" gap—there are times when "what is" is so different from what Americans believe "should be," that pressure mounts to reform lobbying laws, campaign regulations, business practices, and so on. Positions on these issues do not always neatly sort out into the typical liberal and conservative categories. For example, a Democratic senator (Russ Feingold) and a Republican senator (John McCain) joined forces to lead the effort for campaign finance reform, but liberal and conservative groups joined forces in 2003 to challenge the constitutionality of some of the new law's limits on interest group campaign advertising. Similarly, hostile reaction to the Federal Communication Commission's decision in 2003 to allow big broadcasters to serve even larger shares of the national television market came from the left as well as the right, both of whom saw some political danger in this new concentration of broadcasting power.

Was Madison right about the benefits that would emerge from the competition of interests? In the following excerpt from "The Group Basis of Politics," Earl Latham answers with an emphatic "yes!" Despite the popular criticism of "special" interests that seem to taint the political process with their dominant influence, Latham argues that such groups have been a common and inevitable feature of American government. Groups form to give individuals a means of self expression and to help individuals find security in an uncertain world. In fact, the uncertainty of the social environment, and the resulting threat to one's interests, is a chief motivation for groups to form and "taming" this environment is a central concern for group members. Rather than leading to a system ruled by a few dominant powers, Latham suggests the reality is much more fluid. Although it is true that groups that are highly organized are likely to be more powerful, Latham argues that "organization begets counterorganization." The ascendancy of one group will prompt other groups to form to advance their cause. Defeated groups can always try again: "Today's losers may be tomorrow's winners." Groups that lose in the legislature may have more luck with a bureaucratic agency or in a courtroom. There are, in short, multiple avenues of influence and many roads to political success for organized groups, and there are no permanent winners or losers.

Jonathan Rauch disagrees. He views with pessimism the ever-expanding number of interest groups in the political process. Whether groups claim to represent narrow economic interests or a broader public interest, Rauch does not see balance and compromise as the result of their competition in the political arena. Rather, he sees a nation suffering from "hyperpluralism," or the explosion of groups making claims on government power and resources. When elected officials attempt to reduce budget deficits or to establish new priorities and refocus expenditures, they are overwhelmed by the pressures of a wide range of groups. As a result, government programs are never terminated or restructured; tough budget cuts or tax changes are rarely made; and a very rich democratic country and its government becomes immobile. Rather than the dynamic system of change and compromise envisioned by Latham, Rauch sees a system characterized primarily by inertia because of the power of groups to prevent government action.

EARL LATHAM
The Group Basis of Politics: Notes for a Theory

The chief social values cherished by individuals in modern society are realized through groups. These groupings may be simple in structure, unicellular, so to speak, like a juvenile gang. Or they may be intricate meshes of associated, federated, combined, consolidated, merged, or amalgamated units and sub-units of organization, fitted together to perform the divided and assigned parts of a common purpose to which the components are dedicated. They may operate out of the direct public gaze like religious organizations, which tend to have a low degree of visibility. Or they may, like Congress and many other official groups, occupy the front pages for weeks at a time. National organizations are usually conspicuous; indeed, so much is this so at times that they tend to divert the eye from the great number of groups which stand at the elbow of the citizen of every small town. Everywhere groups abound, and they may be examined at close range and from afar.

* * *

So far, we have been concerned with the nature of the structure of society and its principal communities, and with the composition and classification of the group forms which are basic to both. They have been held still, so to speak, while they were being viewed. But they do not in fact hold still; they are in a state of constant motion, and it is through this motion and its interactions that these groups generate the rules by which public policy is formulated and the community is to be governed.

It is necessary now to consider the impulses which animate the group motion and produce these penetrating and far-reaching results.

To consider further a point which has been made, groups organize for the self-expression and security of the members which comprise them. Even when the group is a benevolent, philanthropic association devoted to the improvement of the material and spiritual fortunes of people outside its membership—a temperance or a missionary organization, for example—the work towards this goal, the activity of the organization, is a means through which the members express themselves. Satisfaction in the fulfillment of the received purposes of the group is an important element in keeping groups intact, as Barnard has shown. Indeed, if these satisfactions are not fulfilled, the group suffers loss of morale, energy, and dedication. It is for this reason that military organizations and the civil authorities to which they are responsible seek to inculcate in the soldier some sense of the general purposes for which force by arms is being employed, in an attempt to identify the soldier's personal purpose with that of the community he serves. The soldier then can fulfill his own purposes in combat, as well as those of various groups in the country whose uniform he bears.

At the same time, security is an object of every group organization if security is understood only in its elemental sense of the survival of the group itself in order to carry forward its mission. At the very least, the interest of security means the maintenance of the existence of the group. In different groups one or the other of these impulses—self-expression or security—will predominate.

Self-expression and security are sought by the group members through control of the physical and social environment which surrounds each group and in the midst of which it dwells. It is an elemental fact that environments are potentially dangerous to every group, even as homes are potentially dangerous to the members of the household, as the statistics of accidents in the home will attest. The military battalion runs the risk of being shot up. The church, new or old, runs the risk of losing its members to other and competing claims of interest and devotion. The businessman runs the risk of losing his profit or his customer to his rival. The philanthropic organization devoted to good works often regards other agencies in the same field with a venomous eye. Councils of social agencies in large cities are sometimes notorious for the rancor with which the struggle for prestige and recognition (i.e., self-expression and security) is conducted among them. Every group, large and small, must come to terms with its environment if it is to endure and to prosper.

There are three modes by which this is done. First, the environment may be made safe and predictable by putting restraints upon it. Jurisdictional fights between unions may be explained in this way. Jurisdictional fights are battles in which each claimant union seeks to make an environment for itself in the area of dispute, but to exclude its rival from this environment. On the employer side, the Mohawk Valley Formula was a pattern of actions in a planned sequence by which employers, if they followed it, could break union movements. The objective of this formula was to discredit each union and its leadership and to enlist the support of the townspeople on the side of the plant; it thus was a concerted plan to make an environment unfavorable to the success of unions. One overcomes the hostility in the environment most directly by destroying the influence which creates the hostility.

Second, the environment may be made safe and predictable by neutralizing it. In the propaganda war of giant world powers, the effort is ceaseless to neutralize the effects of propaganda with counterpropaganda so as to render the international environment favorable, or at least not hostile—that is, neutral. The Atlantic and Pacific Tea Company similarly bought a great deal of advertising space in newspapers all over the country to counteract the expectedly unfavorable impressions created by a Department of Justice action against it under the anti-trust laws. The object, among other purposes, was to make the customer-inhabited environment of the business enterprise favorable if possible, neutral at the least, concerning the merits of the charges against it.

Third, the environment may be made safe and predictable, and therefore secure, by conciliating it and making it friendly. Even where there is no manifest hostile influence, a credit of good will may be accumulated by deeds and words which reflect favorably upon the doer. It is true that concessions to a potential hostile force may work sometimes, and again they may not. In the struggle of free nations with the dictatorships, appeasement did not succeed in producing that conciliation which was hoped for it. Nonetheless, politicians are constantly at work making friends and increasing votes by performing favors of one kind or another. Friendliness towards soap is generated on the radio by endless broadcasts of simple tales of never-ending strife and frustration. And during the Second World War advertising by business enterprises was a means of cultivating and keeping goodwill for the products advertised, even though there was no market for them because of the wartime restrictions on production.

All of these are methods by which the environment in which groups dwell is made safe and predictable to them, and therefore secure. And because the relations of people are myriad and shifting, subject to cycles of deterioration and decay, because the environment itself changes with each passing hour, there is a ceaseless struggle on the part of groups to dominate, neutralize, or conciliate that part of their environment that presses in upon them most closely. In this struggle, there is an observable balance of influence in favor of organized groups in their dealings with the unorganized, and in favor of the best and most efficiently organized in their dealings with the less efficiently organized. Strong nations tend to take advantage of the weak, and imperial powers to take advantage of their colonies. Or, to put it another way, organization represents concentrated power, and concentrated power can exercise a dominating influence when it encounters power which is diffuse and not concentrated, and therefore weaker.

The classic struggle of farmers against business enterprise is a case in point, the latter at first being more efficiently organized, and able (before the farmer became "class conscious") to gain advantages which the farmers thought exorbitant, under conditions which the farmers found offensive. But organization begets counterorganization. The farmer organizes in the American Farm Bureau Federation or the National Grange, and uses his influence with the legislatures to write rules to his advantage. In some states of the Middle West, for example, legislation even prescribes the terms of contracts for the sale of farm equipment. But the organized farmer pays little attention to the tenant and the share-cropper, and they in turn experience an impulse to organize for their own advantage. The history of the development of farmers' organizations is instructive; the whole program of farm subsidies which has evolved in the last twenty years may be seen as an effort on the part of the farmer (organized for the purpose) to make himself independent of the vicissitudes of the business economy, that is, to take himself out of the environment which he can control only imperfectly, and to insulate himself against economic adversity.

In the constant struggle of groups to come to terms with their environments, one other phenomenon of group politics may be noted. Simple groups tend to become more complex. And the more complex they become, the greater is the tendency to centralize their control. The structure of the business community in 1950 is different from that of 1860 precisely in that relatively simple forms of business organization have become complex—have gone through federations, combinations, reorganizations, mergers, amalgamations, and consolidations in a growing tendency to rationalize the complexity and to integrate the elements in comprehensive structures. Monopolies, combinations, cartels, giant integrated enterprises are characteristic of a mature phase of the evolution of group forms. Furthermore, the history of federal administration amply shows that the tendency of simple forms of organization to become complex by combination and to develop centralized bureaucracies to cope with this complexity is to be observed among official groups as well as among the groups, like the CIO and the American Legion, which dwell outside the domain of public government.

* * *

The struggle of groups to survive in their environments and to carry forward the aims and interests of their members, if entirely uninhibited, would produce violence and war. Social disapproval of most of the forms of direct action, however, reduces this struggle to an effort to write the rules by which groups live with each other and according to which they compete for existence and advantage. Thus, in the development of mature institutions of collective bargaining from the raw material of unorganized workers, the time comes when violence, disorder, and force are put to one side as the normal aspect of labor relations and the conduct of negotiations occupies the energies of the leaders. In the relations of nations to each other, there has been a persistent effort to substitute diplomacy and the rule of law for war as the arbiter of the differences among national groups. As groups come to put away gross forms of coercion in their dealings with each other, by equal degree the area widens within which the behavior of each is subject to codification by rules. The struggle for advantage, for benefits to the group, for the self-expression and security of its members, tend then to concentrate upon the writing of the rules. Among the forms which the rules may take are statutes, administrative orders and decrees, rules and interpretations, and court judgments.

* * *

The legislature referees the group struggle, ratifies the victories of the successful coalitions, and records the terms of the surrenders, compromises, and conquests in the form of statutes. Every statute tends to represent compromise because the very process of accommodating conflicts of group interest is one of deliberation and consent. The legislative vote on any issue thus tends to represent the composition of strength, i.e., the balance of power among the contending groups at the moment of voting. What may be called public policy is actually the equilibrium reached in the group struggle at any given moment, and it represents a balance which the contending factions of groups constantly strive to weight in their favor. In this process, it is clear that blocks of groups can be defeated. In fact, they can be routed. Defeated groups do not possess a veto on the proposals and acts that affect them. But what they do possess is the right to make new combinations of strength if they are able to do so—combinations that will support a new effort to rewrite the rules in their favor. This process of regrouping is fully in accord with the American culture pattern, which rates high in the characteristics of optimism, risk, experimentalism, change, aggressiveness, acquisitiveness, and colossal faith in man's ability to subdue and bend nature to his desire. The entire process is dynamic, not static; fluid, not fixed. Today's losers may be tomorrow's winners.

In these adjustments of group interest, the legislature does not play the part of inert cash register, ringing up the additions and withdrawals of strength; it is not a mindless balance pointing and marking the weight and distribution of power among the contending groups. * * * Legislators have to be approached with a certain amount of deference and tact; they may be pressured, but some forms of pressure will be regarded as too gross. The Congressman, like men everywhere, comes to his position bearing in his head a cargo of ideas, principles, prejudices, programs, precepts, beliefs, slogans, and preachments. These represent his adjustment to the dominant group combination among his constituents. * * *

The function of the bureaucrat in the group struggle is somewhat different from that of the legislator. Administrative agencies of the regulatory kind are established to carry out the terms of the treaties that the legislators have negotiated and ratified. They are like armies of occupation left in the field to police the rule won by the victorious coalition. * * * The defeated coalition of groups, however, does not cease striving to wring interpretations favorable to it from the treaties that verbalize its defeats. Expensive legal talent is employed to squeeze every advantage which wit and verbal magic can twist from the cold prose of official papers; and the regulatory agencies are constantly besought and importuned to interpret their authorities in favor of the very groups for the regulation of which they were originally granted. This campaign against unfavorable rules which losing coalitions of groups address to the bureaucrats appointed to administer them is, of course, in addition to their constant effort to rewrite the rules in their favor through compliant legislators. Where the balance of power is precarious, the law will remain unsettled until the balance is made stable. * * *

* * *

JONATHAN RAUCH

The Hyperpluralism Trap

Anyone who believes Washington needs to get closer to the people ought to spend a little time with Senator Richard Lugar, the Indiana Republican. "Take a look at the people coming into my office on a normal Tuesday and Wednesday," Lugar said in a speech not long ago. "Almost every organization in our society has a national conference. The typical way of handling this is to come in on a Monday, rev up the troops, give them the bill number and send them up to the Hill. If they can't get in on Tuesday, strike again on Wednesday. I regularly have on Tuesday as many as fifteen constituent groups from Indiana, all of whom have been revved up by some skillful person to cite bills that they don't understand, have never heard of prior to that time, but with a score sheet to report back to headquarters whether I am for or against. It is so routine, it is so fierce, that at some point you [can't be] immune to it."

This is the reality of modern government. The rhetoric of modern politics, alas, is a little different. Take today's standard-issue political stem-winder, which goes something like this: "I think perhaps the most important thing that we understand here in the heartland . . . is the need to reform the political system, to reduce the influence of special interests and give more influence back to the kind of people that are in this crowd tonight by the tens of thousands." That stream of boilerplate is from Bill Clinton (from his election-night speech), but it could have come from almost any politician. It's pitched in a dominant key of political rhetoric today: *standard populism*—that is, someone has taken over the government and "we" must take it back, restore government to the people, etc. But who, exactly, are those thousands of citizens who troop weekly through Senator Lugar's suite, clutching briefing packets and waving scorecards? Standard populism says they are the "special interests," those boils on the skin of democracy, forever interposing themselves between the American people and the people's servants in Washington.

Well, fifty years ago that analysis may have been useful, but not anymore. In America today, the special interests and "the people" have become objectively indistinguishable. Groups are us. As a result, the populist impulse to blame special interests, big corporations and political careerists for our problems—once a tonic—has become Americans' leading political narcotic. Worse, it actually abets the lobbying it so righteously denounces.

Begin with one of the best-known yet most underappreciated facts of our time: over the past three or four decades we have busily organized ourselves into interest groups—lobbies, loosely speaking—at an astonishing rate. Interest groups were still fairly sparse in America until about the time of World War II. Then they started proliferating, and in the 1960s the pace of organizing picked up dramatically.

Consider, for instance, the numbers of groups listed in Gale Research's *Encyclopedia of Associations*. The listings have grown from fewer than 5,000 in 1956 to well over 20,000 today. They represent, of course, only a small fraction of America's universe of interest groups. Environmental organizations alone number an estimated 7,000, once you count local clean-up groups and the like; the Washington

Blade's resource directory lists more than 400 gay groups, up from 300 at the end of 1990. Between 1961 and 1982 the number of corporate offices in Washington increased tenfold. Even more dramatic was the explosion in the number of public-interest organizations and grass-roots groups. These barely existed at all before the 1960s; today they number in the tens of thousands and collect more than $4 billion per year from 40 million individuals, according to political scientist Ronald Shaiko of American University.

Well, so what? Groups do many good things—provide companionship for the like-minded, collect and disseminate information, sponsor contests, keep the catering industry solvent. Indeed, conventional political theory for much of the postwar period was dominated by a strain known as *pluralism*, which holds that more groups equals more representation equals better democracy. Yet pluralism missed something. It assumed that the group-forming process was self-balancing and stable, as opposed to self-feeding and unstable. Which is to say, it failed to grasp the danger of what American University political scientist James Thurber aptly calls *hyperpluralism*.

In economics, inflation is a gradual increase in the price level. Up to a point, if the inflation rate is stable, people can plan around it. But if the rate starts to speed up, people start expecting more inflation. They hoard goods and dump cash, driving the inflation still faster. Eventually, an invisible threshold is crossed: the inflation now feeds on its own growth and undermines the stability of the whole economic system.

What the pluralists missed is that something analogous can happen with interest groups. People see that it pays to organize into groups and angle for benefits, so they do it. But as more groups make more demands, and as even more hungry groups form to compete with all the other groups, the process begins to feed on itself and pick up momentum. At some point there might be so many groups that they choke the political system, sow contention and conflict, even erode society's governability. That's hyperpluralism. And if it is less destabilizing than hyperinflation, it may be more insidious.

The pattern is most visible in smaller social units, such as local school districts, where groups colonize the curriculum—sex education for liberals, values instruction for conservatives, recycling lessons for environmentalists, voluntary silent prayer for Christians. But even among the general population the same forces are at work. Fifty years ago the phrase "the elderly" denoted a demographic category; today, thanks largely to federal pension programs and the American Association of Retired Persons (AARP), it denotes a giant and voracious lobby. In the 1930s the government set up farm-subsidy programs, one per commodity; inevitably, lobbies sprang up to defend each program, so that today American agriculture is fundamentally a collection of interest groups. With the help of group organizers and race-based benefits, loose ethnic distinctions coalesce into hard ethnic lobbies. And so on.

Even more depressing, any attempt to fight back against the proliferating mass of subdivision is foiled by the rhetoric of standard populism and its useful stooge: the special interest. The concept of a "special interest" is at the very core of standard populism—the "them" without which there can be no "us." So widely accepted is this notion, and so useful is it in casual political speech, that most of us talk routinely about special interests without a second thought. We all feel we know a special interest when we see one, if only because it is a group of which we are not a member. Yet buried in the special interest idea is an assumption that is no longer true.

The concept of the special interest is not based on nothing. It is, rather, out of date, an increasingly empty relic of the time of machine politics and political bosses, when special interests were, quite literally, special. Simply because of who they were, they enjoyed access that was available to no one else. But the process of everyone's organizing into more and more groups can go only so far before the very idea of a special interest loses any clear meaning. At some point one must throw up one's hands and concede that the hoary dichotomy between special interests and "us" has become merely rhetoric.

According to a 1990 survey conducted for the American Society of Association Executives, seven out of ten Americans belong to at least one association, and one in four Americans belongs to four or more. Practically everyone who reads these words is a member of an interest group, probably several. Moreover, formal membership tallies omit many people whom we ordinarily think of as being represented by lobbies. For example, the powerful veterans' lobbies enroll only perhaps one-seventh of American veterans, yet the groups lobby on behalf of veterans as a class, and all 27 million veterans share in the benefits. Thus the old era of lobbying by special interests—by a well-connected, plutocratic few—is as dead now as slavery and Prohibition. We Americans have achieved the full democratization of lobbying: influence-peddling for the masses.

The appeal of standard populism today comes precisely from the phony reassurance afforded by its real message: "Other people's groups are the special interests. Less for them—more for you!" Spread that sweet manure around and the natural outgrowth is today's tendency, so evident in the Clinton style, to pander to interest groups frantically while denouncing them furiously. It is the public's style, too: sending ever more checks to the AARP and the National Rifle Association and the National Federation of Independent Business and the National Wildlife Federation and a million others, while railing against special interests. Join and join, blame and blame.

So hyperpluralism makes a hash of the usual sort of standard populist prescription, which calls for "the people" to be given more access to the system, at the expense of powerful Beltway figures who are alleged to have grown arrogant or corrupt or out of touch. Activists and reformers who think the answer to democracy's problems is more access for more of the people need to wake up. Uncontrolled access only breeds more lobbies. It is axiomatic that "the people" (whatever that now means) do not organize to seek government benefits; lobbies do. Every new door to the federal treasury is an opportunity for new groups to queue up for more goodies.

Populists resolutely refuse to confront this truth. Last year, for example, Republicans and the editors of the *Wall Street Journal* campaigned fiercely—and successfully—for new congressional rules making it easier for legislators and groups to demand that bottled-up bills be discharged from committee. The idea was to bring Congress closer to "the people" by weakening the supposedly high-handed barons who rule the Hill. But burying the Free Christmas Tree for Every American Act (or whatever) in committee—while letting members of Congress say they *would* have voted for it—was one of the few remaining ways to hold the door against hungry lobbies clamoring for gifts.

A second brand of populism, *left-populism*, is even more clueless than the standard brand, if that's possible. Many liberals believe the problem is that the wrong groups—the rich, the elites, the giant corporations, etc.—have managed to outorganize the good guys and take control of the system. One version of this model was elaborated by William Greider in his book *Who Will Tell the People*. The New Deal legacy, he writes, "rests upon an idea of interest group bargaining that has gradually been transformed into the random deal-making and permissiveness of the present. The alterations in the system are decisive and . . . the ultimate effects are anti-democratic. People with limited resources, with no real representation in the higher levels of politics, are bound to lose in this environment." So elaborate is the Washington machine of lobbyists, consultants, P.R. experts, political action committees and for-hire think tanks, says Greider, that "powerful economic interests," notably corporations and private wealth, inevitably dominate.

What's appealing about this view is the truism from which it springs: the wealthy enjoy a natural advantage in lobbying, as in almost everything else. Thus many lobbies—even liberal lobbies—are dominated by the comfortable and the wealthy. Consider the case of environmental groups. Anyone who doubts they are major players in Washington today need only look at the massive 1990 Clean Air Act, a piece of legislation that business gladly would have done without. Yet these groups are hardly battalions of the disfranchised. "Readers of *Sierra*, the magazine of the Sierra Club, have household incomes twice that of the average American," notes Senior Economists Terry L. Anderson of the Political Economy Research Center. And *The Economist* notes that "in 1993 the Nature Conservancy, with $915 million in assets, drew 73 percent of its income from rich individuals." When such groups push for emissions controls or pesticide rules, they may be reflecting the priorities of people who buy BMWs and brie more than the priorities of people who buy used Chevies and hamburger. So left-populism's claim to speak for "the people" is often suspect, to say the least.

The larger problem with left-populism, however, is its refusal to see that it is feeding the very problem it decries. Left-populism was supposed to fix the wealth-buys-power problem by organizing the politically disadvantaged into groups: unions, consumer groups, rainbow coalitions and so on. But the strategy has failed. As the left (the unions, the environmentalists) has organized ever more groups, the right (the bosses, the polluters) has followed suit. The group-forming has simply spiralled. This makes a joke of the left-populist prescription, which is to form more "citizens' groups" on the Naderite model, supposedly reinvigorating representative democracy and giving voice to the weak and the silenced. Greider proposes giving people subsidies to spend on political activism: "Giving individual citizens the capacity to deploy political money would inevitably shift power from existing structures and disperse it among the ordinary millions who now feel excluded."

Inevitably, it would do no such thing. Subsidies for activism would perforce go straight into the waiting coffers of (what else?) interest groups, new and old. That just makes matters worse, for if one side organizes more groups, the other side simply redoubles its own mobilization ad infinitum. That escalating cycle is the story of the last three decades. The only winner is the lobbying class. Curiously, then, left-populism has come to serve the very lobbying elites—the Washington lawyers and lobby shops and P.R. pros and interest group execs—whom leftists ought, by rights, to loathe.

The realization that the lobbying class is, to a large extent, both entrepreneurial and in business for itself has fed the third brand of populism, *right-populism*. In the right-populist model, self-serving political careerists have hijacked government and learned to manipulate it for profit. In refreshing contrast to the other two brands of populism, however, this one is in touch with reality. Washington *is* in business for itself, though not only for itself. Legislators and lobbies have an interest in using the tax code to please their constituents, but they also have an interest in churning the tax code to generate campaign contributions and lobbying fees. Luckily for them, those two imperatives generally coincide: the more everyone hunts for tax breaks, the more lobbying jobs there are. Right-populism has tumbled to the fact that so-called public interest and citizens' groups are no more immune to this self-serving logic of lobbying—create conflict, reap rewards—than is any other sort of professional lobby.

Yet right-populism fails to see to the bottom of the problem. It looks into the abyss but flinches. This is not to say that term limits and other procedural fine-tunes may not help; such reforms are no doubt worth trying. But even if noodling with procedures succeeded in diluting the culture of political careerism, it would help (or hurt) mainly at the margins. No, tinkering with the process isn't the answer. What we must do is go straight at the beast itself. We must attack and weaken the lobbies—that is, the *people's* lobbies.

It sounds so simple: weaken the lobbies! Shove them aside, reclaim the government! "It's just that simple," twinkles Ross Perot. But it's not that simple. Lobbies in Washington have clout because the people who scream when "special interests" are attacked are Medicare recipients defending benefits, farmers defending price supports, small businesses defending subsidized loans, racial groups defending set-asides and so on. Inherently, challenging these groups is no one's idea of fun, which is why politicians so rarely propose to do it. The solution is to strip away lobbies' protections and let competition hammer them. In practice, that means:

Balance the Federal Budget

It is a hackneyed prescription, but it is the very first thing we should do to curtail the lobbies' ability to rob the future. Deficits empower lobbies by allowing them to raid the nation's scarce reserves of investment capital. Deprived of that ability, they will be forced to compete more fiercely for money, and they'll be unable to steal from the future.

Cut the Lobbies' Lifelines

Eliminate subsidies and programs, including tax loopholes, by the hundreds. Killing a program here or there is a loser's game; it creates a political uproar without actually making a noticeable difference. The model, rather, should be the 1986 tax reform measure, which proved that a wholesale housecleaning really is possible. Back then, tax loopholes were cleared away by the truckload. The trick was—and is—to do the job with a big package of reforms that politicians can tout back home as real change. That means ditching whole Cabinet departments and abolishing virtually all industry-specific subsidies. Then go after subsidies for the non-needy—wholesale, not retail.

Promote Domestic Perestroika

Lobbies live to lock benefits in and competition out, so government restraints on competition should be removed—not indiscriminately, but determinedly. President Carter's deregulation of transportation industries and interest rates, though imperfectly executed, were good examples. Air travel, trucking, and rail shipping are cheaper *and* safer. The affected industries have been more turbulent, but that's exactly the point. Domestic competition shakes up interest groups that settle cozily into Washington.

Encourage Foreign Competition

This is most important of all. The forces that breed interest groups never abate, and so fighting them requires a constant counterforce. Foreign competition is such a counterforce. Protection invariably benefits the industries and groups with the sharpest lobbyists and the fattest political action committees; stripping away protection forces them to focus more on modernizing and less on lobbying.

No good deed, they say, goes unpunished. We sought to solve pressing social problems, so we gave government vast power to reassign resources. We also sought to look out for ourselves and bring voices to all of our many natures and needs, so we built countless new groups to seek government's resources. What we did not create was a way to control the chain reaction we set off. Swarming interest groups excited government to perpetual activism, and government activism drew new groups to Washington by the thousands. Before we knew it, society itself was turning into a collection of ravenous lobbies.

Why was this not always a problem? Because there used to be control rods containing the chain reaction. Smoke-filled rooms, they were called. On Capitol Hill or in Tammany Hall, you needed to see one of about six people to have any hope of getting what you wanted, and those six people dispensed (and conserved) favors with parsimonious finesse. Seen from today's vantage, smoke-filled rooms and political machines did a creditable job of keeping a lid on the interest group frenzy—they just didn't do it particularly fairly. That's why we opened up access to anyone who wants to organize and lobby, and opened up power to subcommittee chairs and caucus heads and even junior legislators. In doing so, we abolished the venal gatekeepers. But that was only the good news. The bad news was that we also abolished the gate.

No, we shouldn't go back to smoke-filled rooms. But the way forward is harder than it ever was before. The maladies that now afflict government are ones in which the public is wholly, enthusiastically implicated. Still, there are sprigs and shoots of encouragement all around. There was the surprisingly strong presidential bid of former Senator Paul Tsongas, which built something of a constituency for straight talk. There's the rise of a school of Democrats in Congress—among them Senator Bob Kerrey and retiring Representative Tim Penny—who are willing to drag the White House toward sterner fiscal measures. There was the Clinton-led triumph of NAFTA last year. Those developments show promise of a political movement that is counter-populist yet also popular. Maybe—is it too much to hope?—they point beyond the desert of populism.

DISCUSSION QUESTIONS

1. *What would you do?* Placing restrictions on interest-group activities is difficult because of the constitutional protections afforded to these groups. The Constitution guarantees the people the right to assemble and to petition government regarding their grievances, and it also guarantees freedom of speech. All these are the essence of interest-group activity. Nonetheless, many Americans are uneasy with the influence wielded by interest groups. Imagine you are a staffer for a senator elected on a platform that promised to limit the power of "special interests" in politics. The senator has asked you to draft a position paper outlining some possible restrictions on interest-group activity. Would these restrictions create constitutional difficulties?

2. Among the many forms of interest-group activity, campaign contributions seem to provoke some of the harshest criticisms. Is this reasonable? Is there any reason to be more concerned about campaign contributions than about lobbying, lawsuits, funding research, or any other activities groups employ to pursue their causes?

3. Rauch complains that interest groups slow down the policy-making process, but isn't this what the Framers of the Constitution intended? Is the interest-group system as portrayed by Rauch a danger to democracy, or is it in fact implementing the principles implicit in the Constitution?

14 Regulating the Media

When the unthinkable happens, people search for reasons. This seems to be all the more true when young people are involved in the formerly unthinkable actions. Whether it is a rash of suicides or incidents of violence at schools, or some other tragedy, public sensibilities are shocked. Politicians, recognizing the unease in the public, attempt to discern what led to these incidents and how they might be prevented in the future. Frequently, the world of popular culture is seen as one potential cause of this undesirable behavior and proposals to regulate the content of media messages emerge. In the past, these proposals might have dealt primarily with books and magazines, but today the net is cast more broadly to include music, films, television, video games, and the Internet.

In one sense, this concern about media content is a variant of the concerns about biases in media content and the possible effects of that bias. Critics on the left argue that news coverage is slanted toward conservative viewpoints, because media corporations are not willing to alienate potential advertisers and the upscale clientele these advertisers seek. They also complain that media corporations, as parts of much larger companies involved in many different industries, are inherently going to limit the topics they cover. This self-censorship is also a concern of conservative critics. They complain that journalists, especially at the most elite news organizations, are overwhelmingly liberal and that this inevitably affects what stories they cover and how they cover them. Like those federal officials concerned about the impact of "messages" in popular culture, critics on the left and right worry that "biased" media content has a deleterious impact on their favored political views. All three—federal officials, liberal critics, and conservative critics—are convinced that the information presented by the media affects what individuals who read, view, or listen to that information do.

Are federal restrictions on content or mandatory labeling of content reasonable? Wendy Kaminer states strongly that they are not. No matter how these regulations might be dressed up, Kaminer sees the cloak of censorship, pure and simple. Kaminer argues that there are several problems with the effort to regulate the media. First, commercial speech is constitutionally protected unless it is false, misleading, or promotes illegal activity. Very little of the questionable media—violent video games, for instance—would fall into any of these categories. Second, such restrictions would put federal bureaucrats into the position of deciding what is and is not acceptable content. Third, there is little evidence that media exposure produces the harms alleged by critics. Lastly, and perhaps most worrisome to Kaminer, is the so-called slippery slope argument: "Censorship campaigns often begin with a drive to protect children (or women), but they rarely end there."

A "typical, out-of-touch liberal response" sums up the spirit of Michael Massing's reaction to Kaminer's analysis. Massing suggests that Kaminer simply dismisses the concerns of millions of parents, charging that she refuses to even acknowledge that we as a society should have any interest in what young people see and hear. As for Kaminer's specific arguments, outlined above, Massing is unconvinced. Regarding the slippery slope and fears of federal bureaucrats, Massing suggests that Kaminer paints a highly unrealistic and unlikely scenario. And what about the research on the link between media exposure and subsequent behavior? Massing asserts that there may be no smoking gun, but there does appear at least to be some puffs of smoke that are worthy of further study rather than dismissive commentary. Simply because one fears the broader agenda of those inveighing against media messages—and Massing believes this is one of Kaminer's primary motivations—one should not ignore the research that suggests there might well be some effect of media consumption on attitudes and behavior.

In her response, Kaminer defends her arguments. Despite Massing's suggestion that she opposes even industry self-regulation, Kaminer asserts that she is untroubled by such efforts unless they are done under the duress of government threats. She also suggests that the suggestive link that Massing sees in the media research is much weaker than he contends. On the other hand, the slippery slope is much more real than Massing allows, and Kaminer provides some examples to suggest that her worries are not far-fetched. Finally, and perhaps most important for Kaminer, is the question of who decides what speech is harmful. Complaining that Massing ignores this issue altogether, she voices skepticism that "Massing and I, let alone society, could reach consensus on the ideal media diet for America's youth."

WENDY KAMINER
Toxic Media

Like Claude Rains in *Casablanca*, Al Gore is shocked!, shocked! that the entertainment industry is marketing violent material to minors. Countering Hollywood's macho entertainments with some macho rhetoric of his own, he gave the industry six months to "clean up its act" and declare a "ceasefire" in what he apparently sees as the media's war against America's children.

No one should be surprised by the vice president's threat to impose government regulations on the marketing of popular entertainments, which immediately followed the issuance of a new Federal Trade Commission (FTC) report on the subject. As his choice of running mate made clear, Gore is positioning himself as the moral voice of the Democratic Party—replete with Godliness and a desire to cleanse the culture. With a concomitant promise to protect ordinary Americans from rapacious corporations, Gore is an early twenty-first-century version of a nineteenth-century female Progressive—a God-loving social purist with a soft spot for working families and, not so incidentally, women's rights.

Many Victorian women's rights activists, like Frances Willard of the Women's Christian Temperance Union and Julia Ward Howe, enthusiastically supported the suppression of "impure" or "vicious" literature, which was blamed for corrupting the nation's youth. "Books are feeders for brothels," according to the notorious nineteenth-century anti-vice crusader Anthony Comstock, for whom the nation's first obscenity law was named. Gun violence is fed by violent media, Al Gore,

Joseph Lieberman, and others assert. The new FTC report was commissioned by President Clinton immediately after the 1999 shootings at Columbine High. That was when centrist politicians (and commentators) were touting the new "common-sense" view of youth violence: It was caused by both the availability of firearms and the availability of violent media. Gun control would be complemented by culture control.

So in June 1999, two Democratic senators, Lieberman and the usually thoughtful Kent Conrad of North Dakota, joined with Trent Lott and John McCain in proposing federal legislation requiring the labeling of violent audio and visual media. These requirements, which were to be enforced by the FTC, were amendments to the cigarette labeling act. (When politicians revisit their bad ideas, critics like me repeat themselves. I discussed this proposed bill and the bipartisan drive to censor in a November 23, 1999, *American Prospect* column, "The Politics of Sanctimony.")

Advocates of censorship often charge that media can be "toxic" (as well as "addictive") like tobacco and other drugs. By describing whatever film or CD they disdain as a defective product, they undermine the view of it as speech. (We should regulate pornography the way we regulate exploding Ford Pintos, one feminist antiporn activist used to say; she seemed to consider *Playboy* an incendiary device.) In endorsing Internet filtering programs, Gore has remarked that minors should be protected from "dangerous places" on the Internet—in other words, "dangerous" speech. Some Web sites should effectively be locked up, just as medicine cabinets are locked up to protect children from poisons, the vice president remarked at a 1997 Internet summit.

Once you define violent or sexually explicit media as toxic products, it is not terribly difficult to justify regulating their advertising, at least, if not their distribution and production. Commercial speech generally enjoys constitutional protection, but as advocates of marketing restrictions assert, the First Amendment does not protect false or misleading advertising or ads promoting illegal activities. That's true but not necessarily relevant here. Campaigns marketing violent entertainment to children may be sleazy, but they don't promote an illegal activity (the sale of violent material to minors is not generally criminal); and they're not deceptive or unfair (many popular entertainments are just as bad as they purport to be). Ratings are not determined or mandated by the government (not yet, anyway), so why should it be a federal offense for industry executives to violate the spirit of their own voluntary codes?

Effective regulation of media marketing campaigns would require new federal legislation that would entangle the government in the production of popular entertainments. What might this legislation entail? Ratings and labeling would be mandatory, supervised by the FTC (or some other federal agency), and any effort to subvert the ratings system would be a federal offense. Testifying before the Senate Commerce Committee on September 12, Lieberman promised that regulation of the entertainment industry would focus on "how they market, not what they produce," but that promise ignores the effect of marketing considerations on content.

Some may consider the decline of violent entertainments no great loss, imagining perhaps that slasher movies and violent video games will be the primary victims of a new federal labeling regime. But it's not hard to imagine a docudrama about domestic abuse or abortion, or a coming-of-age story about a gay teen, receiving the same restricted rating as a sleazy movie about a serial murderer. In any case, a stringent, federally mandated and monitored rating and labeling system will not enhance parental control; it's a vehicle for bureaucratic control. Federal officials, not parents, will determine what entertainment will be available to children when they devise and enforce the ratings.

Some claim that federal action is justified, nonetheless, by an overriding need to save lives. At the September 12 hearing inspired by the FTC report, several senators and other witnesses vigorously condemned the entertainment industry for "literally making a killing off of marketing to kids," in the words of Kansas Republican Sam Brownback. He called upon the industry to stop producing the entertainments he abhors. Lieberman charged that media violence was "part of a toxic mix that has turned some of our children into killers." Lynne Cheney, former head of the National Endowment for the Humanities, declared that "there is a problem with the product they market, no matter how they market it." Democratic Senator Fritz Hollings proposed giving the Federal Communications Commission the power to impose a partial ban on whatever programming it considers violent and harmful to minors.

What all this hyperbolic rhetoric obscured (or ignored) was the dearth of hard evidence that violent media actually turns "children into killers." In fact, the FTC study on which would-be censors rely found no clear causal connection between violent media and violent behavior. "Exposure to violent materials probably is not even the most important factor" in determining whether a child will turn violent, FTC Chairman Robert Pitofsky observed. The most he would say was that exposure to violent media "does seem to correlate with aggressive attitudes, insensitivity toward violence, and an exaggerated view of how much violence occurs in the world."

This is not exactly a defense of media violence, but it may present a fairly balanced view of its effects, which do not justify limitations on speech. Living in a free society entails a commitment not to prohibit speech unless it clearly, directly, and intentionally causes violence. If violent entertainment can be regulated by the federal government because it allegedly causes violence, so can inflammatory political rhetoric, like assertions that abortion providers kill babies. Anti-abortion rhetoric probably has even a clearer connection to violence than any violent movie, but both must be protected. If Disney can be brought under the thumb of federal regulators, so can Cardinal Law when he denounces abortion as murder.

It's unfortunate and ironic that apparently amoral corporations, like Disney or Time Warner, stand as champions and beneficiaries of First Amendment rights. As gatekeepers of the culture, they're not exactly committed to maintaining an open, diverse marketplace of ideas. Indeed, the de facto censorship engineered by media conglomerates may threaten public discourse nearly as much as federal regulation. And neither our discourse nor our culture is exactly enriched by gratuitously violent media.

But speech doesn't have to provide cultural enrichment to enjoy constitutional protection. We don't need a First Amendment to protect popular, inoffensive speech or speech that a majority of people believe has social value. We need it to protect speech that Lynne Cheney or Joseph Lieberman consider demeaning and degrading. Censorship campaigns often begin with a drive to protect children (or women), but they rarely end there.

MICHAEL MASSING AND WENDY KAMINER

Toxic Media versus Toxic Censorship

MICHAEL MASSING WRITES:

Anytime a public official issues a peep of protest about the violent fare on television, a chorus of liberal voices rises in denunciation. The most recent instance came in September, when the Federal Trade Commission (FTC) issued a report criticizing the marketing of movies and music with violent content to young people. Citing the report, both Al Gore and Joe Lieberman blasted Hollywood. And the response from liberal commentators was furious.

Gore's "frenzied and often self-contradictory posturing about Hollywood," Frank Rich wrote in the *New York Times,* provided "a creepy, if G-rated, preview of coming attractions depicting what his administration may be like at its opportunistic and pandering worst." Richard Rhodes, on the *Times*'s op-ed page, derided "moral entrepreneurs" who were "at it again, pounding the entertainment industry for advertising its Grand Guignolesque confections to children." *The Nation* accused the two Democratic candidates of making "a deft feint to the right, enlisting the Federal Trade Commission for blatantly partisan purposes."

And in her *American Prospect* piece "Toxic Media," Wendy Kaminer sneeringly dismissed Gore as a "God-loving social purist" with "a desire to cleanse the culture." Gore and others who share his concern about violent programming, she argued, are nothing less than "advocates of censorship."

Kaminer and company seem to see themselves as brave upholders of free speech in the face of vote-hungry politicians. In fact, they represent a new orthodoxy among liberals, who, wrapping themselves in the First Amendment, airily dismiss an issue of genuine concern to millions of American parents.

Needless to say, any talk of restricting what can or cannot appear on television does raise free-speech concerns. But it also involves what we as a society think is appropriate for young people to see and listen to. Any serious consideration of the issue must attempt to balance these competing interests. Yet Kaminer and the rest refuse even to acknowledge the conflict.

Kaminer grudgingly admits that "neither our discourse nor our culture is exactly enriched by gratuitously violent media." Nonetheless, she will brook no restriction of any sort on what appears on television. No limits on the hours during which violent programs can be shown. No ratings system to help parents decide what their children should watch.

No restrictions (even voluntary ones) on the marketing practices of entertainment companies. She rejects mere criticism of the movie industry as a form of censorship. No matter how many slasher films Hollywood turns out, and no matter how often they are advertised on TV, Kaminer contends, we must grin and bear it. Let's examine her arguments.

The Slippery Slope

"Living in a free society," Kaminer writes, "entails a commitment not to prohibit speech unless it clearly, directly, and intentionally causes violence. If violent entertainment can be regulated by the federal government because it allegedly causes violence, so can inflammatory political rhetoric, like assertions that abortion providers kill babies. Anti-abortion rhetoric probably has even a clearer connection to violence than any violent movie, but both must be protected. If Disney can be brought under the thumb of federal regulators, so can Cardinal [Bernard] Law when he denounces abortion as murder."

This seems absurd. Nobody in the current debate is even remotely talking about imposing restrictions on political speech; anyone who did would be tarred and feathered. To make such an argument shows how far the new orthodox will overreach to make their point.

Ratings Can Be Abused

"Some may consider the decline of violent entertainment no great loss," Kaminer writes, "imagining perhaps that slasher movies and violent video games will be the primary victims of a new federal labeling regime. But it's not hard to imagine a docudrama about domestic abuse or abortion, or a coming-of-age story about a gay teen, receiving the same restricted rating as a sleazy movie about a serial murderer. In any case, a stringent, federally mandated and monitored rating and labeling system will not enhance parental control; it's a vehicle for bureaucratic control. Federal officials, not parents, will determine what entertainment will be available to children when they devise and enforce the ratings." While any rating system must necessarily reflect subjective judgments, the type of abuses Kaminer here warns of seem far-fetched. And while government bureaucrats may be involved in devising a ratings system, it is parents who ultimately decide what their kids will watch. Certainly many parents are grateful for whatever help they can get in determining what is appropriate fare for their children.

The Data Are Inconclusive

Like many other liberal critics, Kaminer questions the very idea that exposure to violent media negatively affects young people. The FTC study on which "would-be censors rely," she writes, "found no clear causal connection between violent media and violent behavior. 'Exposure to violent materials probably is not even the most important factor in determining whether a child will turn violent, FTC Chairman Robert Pitofsky observed. The most he would say was that exposure to violent media 'does seem to correlate with aggressive attitudes, insensitivity to violence and an exaggerated view of how much violence occurs in the world.' "

It is undoubtedly true that exposure to media violence is not the most important factor in determining whether a child becomes violent. Most young people who watch shoot-'em-ups on TV are not going to go out and re-enact them in real life.

Nonetheless, one would think that the correlations Pitofsky cited—to aggressive attitudes and insensitivity to violence—would seem serious enough to warrant concern. Indeed, for more than thirty years now, the data about those effects have been accumulating. In 1972 the U.S. surgeon general's office conducted a comprehensive review of the existing research and found that televised violence contributes to anti-social behavior. Ten years later, the National Institute of Mental Health conducted another review and came to a similar conclusion. Between 1990 and 1996, the American Medical Association, the American Psychological Association, the American Academy of Pediatrics, and the American Academy of Child and Adolescent Psychiatry all concluded that TV violence fosters aggressive behavior in the real world. Clearly, millions of parents believe this, as evidenced by their fitful struggles to exercise some control over what their kids watch.

In light of this, it's hard to understand the zeal with which Kaminer and her colleagues dismiss criticism of the entertainment industry—until one considers the broader context in which it is occurring. Traditionally, the fight against media violence has been led by conservatives—William Bennett and Bob Dole, Jerry Falwell and the Christian Coalition. In the process, they have pushed an agenda that goes well beyond concern for the mental health of young people; rather, they seem to be trying to impose on society their own narrow moral vision. If the Christian Coalition got its way, we would find not only bludgeonings and beheadings barred from the airwaves but also sexual couplings, off-color jokes, family dysfunction, and everything else deemed unwholesome by right-wing standards. Anxiety over this seems to underlie Kaminer's concerns about the slippery slope. Such worries, however, should not lead to a blithe rejection of the research showing the potential negative consequences of violent programming.

So what is to be done? I agree with Kaminer that ratings systems are flawed—not, however, because they are instruments of bureaucratic control, but because they're not very effective. With the sleaze of contemporary culture so pervasive, it's hard for even the most determined parents to shield their kids, especially when so many Americans with children are forced to work long hours.

Nor are tightened controls over marketing the answer. The debate over the recent FTC report misses the real point. It's not the commercials that are the problem but the movies themselves. It's the endless flood of gratuitously violent films and misogynistic music lyrics that pose the real threat to young kids, and until something is done to restrict the flow, the harmful fallout will continue.

Certainly one does not want to encourage direct government intervention. The prospect of new laws or executive orders declaring what can and cannot appear on TV or in movie theaters and record stores does pose a threat to free speech. But speaking out against violent media does not. As First Amendment advocates themselves are quick to assert, the best antidote to bad speech is more speech. Public figures should continue to criticize and pressure Hollywood to stop producing such noxious fare. If enough voices are raised in protest, the movie studios might finally respond. Kaminer regards this as censorship, but aren't politicians who speak up on such matters exercising their own First Amendment rights? Well, it might be argued, if there's a market for this type of programming, shouldn't entertainment companies be free to provide it? To a degree, yes. But at the same time, society has a right to demand a certain level of responsible behavior by the entertainment industry, especially where young people are concerned.

Tobacco provides a good analogy. Cigarettes are legal but also lethal. At one point, they were widely advertised on TV. But in the late 1960s, as evidence of their toxicity mounted, public-interest groups began demanding more controls. The Federal Communications Commission reacted by calling for more counteradvertising, in the form of commercials dramatizing the health risks associated with smoking. In response, the tobacco companies—realizing the threat such commercials posed to their profits—agreed not to advertise their products on TV. And cigarette commercials have remained off the air ever since.

If Kaminer were writing back then, she would probably criticize such actions as infringing on the free-speech rights of the tobacco companies. Most Americans, though, would applaud such measures as helping to safeguard the nation's health.

No one, of course, would argue that violent movies pose as much of a threat to the nation's health as tobacco does. But the research studies that have accumulated over the years—together with the commonsense concerns of many parents—more than justify the calls on the entertainment industry to exercise greater restraint. And it would help if liberal critics joined in the campaign. If matters are left to the Bennetts and Falwells, the effort to clean up the media could take a troubling direction. At the very least, it's time for liberals to give up their reflexive disdain and recognize that the issue is a serious one requiring vigorous debate.

WENDY KAMINER RESPONDS:

Michael Massing sure is mad at me. It's probably anger, not bad faith, that leads him to misrepresent my views so grossly. I did not and would not foolishly condemn mere criticism of media content as censorship (I began my own writing career as a book critic and generally believe that nothing and no one should be protected from critics.) My column condemned Al Gore, Joe Lieberman, and other politicians for threatening to impose governmental controls on the entertainment industry if it continues to produce films, video games, or CDs that they don't like. Massing may disagree that proposed federal restrictions on how entertainments are marketed will affect what entertainments are produced, but he can hardly equate demands for legal restrictions on marketing campaigns with mere "criticism" of marketing techniques or content.

Massing dismisses recent attacks on the media by politicians from both parties as mere peeps of protest. That's not how I'd characterize a series of Senate hearings and legislative proposals aimed at curbing media violence. (It's not just marketing techniques that are being targeted, as testimony at the recent Senate Commerce Committee hearing made clear.) Consider the 1996 Communications Decency Act (CDA) prohibiting "indecency" on the Internet, signed into law by President Clinton and invalidated by the Supreme Court not long after. Was that merely another "peep"? After the CDA was struck down, Congress and the president tried again to criminalize speech in cyberspace with the Child Online Protection Act, which was recently struck down by a federal appeals court. It sought to prohibit commercial dissemination of Internet speech deemed "harmful to minors."

Who decides precisely what speech is harmful to minors? Massing ignores this troubling question at the heart of all censorship debates. He says that restrictions on media involve what "we as a society think is appropriate for young people to see and listen to," and I can only respond, "Who's we?" Our diverse society is deeply divided over questions about sexual morality, race discrimination, militarism, vengeance, and gun ownership. Are minors morally corrupted or energized and informed by rap? We, "as a society," disagree. I doubt that even Massing and I, let alone society, could reach consensus on the ideal media diet for America's youth.

To some extent, this does leave us at the mercy of industry executives. A sophisticated critique of my position would have likened the power of media conglomerates to the power of government and elaborated on the problem of de facto censorship. As I noted in my column, a marketplace controlled by a few media giants is not exactly free and receptive to diverse or unsettling ideas. So my own opposition to government control of the media doesn't reflect any illusions about the quality of discourse that a laissez-faire approach produces. I do think that media critiques are important (and protected by the First Amendment, of course), and I did not oppose voluntary controls by the entertainment industry. How could I? Media executives are in the business of controlling content and marketing, as are editors of magazines like *The American Prospect*. But I do question the voluntary nature of ratings systems instituted under threats of government control.

Advocates of regulation argue that restrictions on content are justified because the proliferation of violent entertainments constitutes a national emergency: In their view, violent images are direct causes of violent behavior. Pornography causes rape, according to some feminists; sex education causes teenage pregnancy, Jerry Falwell and Phyllis Schlafly have suggested; violent video games, CDs, and films cause high school shootings and other horrors, Michael Massing and many others believe. Indeed, it has become conventional wisdom that violent entertainments cause violent behavior.

Massing and I will not resolve the debate about the relationship between images and behavior in this brief exchange. (Interested readers can find a critique of the literature on violence in "Blaming the Media," by Marjorie Heins, in the fall 2000 issue of the *Media Studies Journal*.) But I do want to stress, again, that the Federal Trade Commission found only a correlation, not a causal relationship, between imaginary and actual violence. Massing observes reasonably that this correlation is cause for "concern," but he's wrong to assume that concern about the effects of violent entertainment justifies regulation of the entertainment industry. The preservation of free speech requires much more than concern; it requires evidence that speech presents actual and more or less immediate dangers—not mere speculation or even educated guesses about its consequences. Violent entertainment may be a problem for society, but it is not a problem that law can solve, so long as we value free speech. If the government could regulate any speech that provoked concern, it could regulate any unsettling or offensive speech; it could, and undoubtedly would, regulate dissent.

Massing dismisses as absurd my suggestion that government regulation of popular entertainments could affect political speech. Either he has an exceedingly narrow definition of "political" or he knows nothing of past and present censorship campaigns. Put aside the view of many people that rap music (which so offends many members of Congress) is political and consider less controversial examples instead. Efforts to protect children (and women) from sex and violence in the media routinely target political speech. Filtering software installed or proposed for use in public schools and libraries across the country is notorious for blocking discussions of homosexuality, abortion, and AIDS prevention, among other political subjects. Censorship crusades in public schools have targeted writers like Maya Angelou, John Steinbeck, Margaret Atwood, E.M. Forster, and other authors whose works can fairly be called political. During the mid-1990s, a public-school teacher in Colorado was fired for showing Bernardo Bertolucci's antifascist film *1900* to a class of high school seniors; the firing was upheld by the Colorado Supreme Court.

People who dare to suggest restricting political speech risk being "tarred and feathered," Massing confidently asserts. Not quite. Some ascend to the nation's highest courts; others are elected to Congress and state legislatures. Is it unrealistic to believe that anti-abortion rhetoric might be restricted? State laws prohibiting protests outside abortion clinics, establishing no-speech "buffer zones," have been passed and upheld by the Supreme Court. (The legality of buffer-zone legislation passed in Massachusetts and approved by the state's highest court has recently been questioned in a surprise decision by a federal district court.) It's also worth noting that Congress has very nearly passed a constitutional amendment criminalizing flag burning. The amendment, which was passed several times by the House and very narrowly defeated in the Senate, remains a serious threat. It's hard to imagine a clearer effort to censor political speech, but advocates of a flag-burning amendment are usually re-elected to Congress, not run out of town on a rail.

Massing may regard these efforts as irrelevant to crusades against violent entertainments, but that's a bit like suggesting that discrimination against one stigmatized group of people has nothing to do with discrimination against another. What threatens First Amendment freedoms more than any isolated instance of censorship is the unifying rationale of all censorship campaigns: the presumption that "bad" speech directly causes "bad" behavior and that government officials should be empowered to distinguish good speech from bad. It's not the slippery slope I fear. (That has always seemed like an inapt metaphor to me.) It's the specter of bureaucrats and politicians armed with scythes, hacking through an open field.

DISCUSSION QUESTIONS

1. *What would you do?* Ratings systems for movies and video games, as well as warning labels about lyrics, have been voluntarily implemented by these respective industries. Imagine you are a U.S. senator who has initiated an investigation into the reliability of voluntary labels and ratings systems. Would you support federal oversight of these systems that would impose penalties for ratings or labels deemed to be inaccurate? What factors might affect your decision?

2. Why do you suppose there is a rating system for movies but not for books and magazines? If there were a choice between no ratings at all and expanding ratings to include books and magazines, which would you prefer? What would be the pros and cons of each option? Do you think that having ratings affects the kinds of movies (and potentially books and magazines) that are made?

3. Many critics of the film and video game industries argue that without pressure from politicians, these industries would have never implemented ratings systems and warning labels. Do you believe that exerting such pressure is a proper role for politicians or do you agree with Kaminer that such a role is dangerous?

15 Government and the Economy: Tax Policy and the Budget

The centerpiece of the Bush Administration's economic policy is a program of tax cuts. President Bush has aggressively pursued this course and has so far succeeded in getting two major initiatives through Congress. In June 2001 Bush signed a law that lowered taxes by about $1.35 trillion over eleven years, mainly by reducing marginal tax rates, increasing certain deductions and credits, and gradually eliminating the estate tax (at the end of this eleven-year period many of these taxes are scheduled to return, unless Congress acts in the meantime to make the cuts permanent). And in May 2003, Bush signed into law another $350 billion tax cut.

Critics of the 2001 and 2003 tax cuts argue that the benefits go mainly to the wealthy and that the lower revenues will make it difficult to fund crucial programs such as prescription-drug benefits and social security reform. The Center for Budget and Policy Priorities argues that the average taxpayer would receive only a few hundred dollars in relief. Supporters respond that the wealthy already pay a disproportionate *share* of taxes (the top 1 percent of earners pays 35 percent of all income taxes; the top 25 percent of earners pays 83 percent of all income taxes, according to the Heritage Foundation) and should benefit accordingly, and that long-term economic growth is the key to future revenues.

The empirical argument for tax cuts, outlined in the Mitchell reading, is that they stimulate economic growth by letting people keep more of their money, which they can then save and invest. Individuals are much better than the government at deciding how this money can best be used, Mitchell maintains, so lower taxes are better for economic growth in the long run. Higher economic growth, in turn, raises standards of living and produces more tax revenue. Mitchell notes that tax cuts, if they are to be effective, should encourage economically productive behavior and not be aimed at short-term stimulus effects.

Reich, who served as Secretary of Labor under President Clinton, offers a different perspective. Reich notes that the Democrats have been largely unsuccessful in stopping Bush's tax cuts; he is especially unhappy about the elimination of the estate tax, which he claims benefits only the very wealthiest families. He urges the Democrats to respond by proposing a cut in the payroll tax—the 15.3 percent tax on wages that employers and workers split. The payroll tax is especially regressive since it applies to the first dollar of earnings and is mostly phased out once income exceeds a ceiling (in 2003, most of the payroll tax applies to only the first $87,000 in income). The result is that someone who makes $10,000 pays a much higher percentage of her income in payroll taxes than someone who makes $1 million. Reich wants the Democrats to pit the payroll tax directly against the estate tax; it's a debate, he thinks, that the Republicans would have a hard time winning.

ROBERT B. REICH
Whose Tax Cuts?

I'm welcoming myself back to the *Prospect* by declaring a holiday on the payroll tax. Starting as soon as possible, you'll be relieved of payroll taxes on the first $20,000 of your annual income. The tax holiday will last two years. Ballpark cost to the government: $700 billion. We'll pay for it by repealing Bush's estate tax cut, which will also cost around $700 billion. Are you with me? All we have to do is convince Democrats it's a smart move and strike fear in the hearts of enough Republicans to get it passed and signed. We'll start in January when Congress reconvenes.

Bush has a different plan, of course. His goal is to make his whopping $1.35 trillion tax cut permanent. Republicans love forcing Democrats to vote for or against tax cuts. It puts Democrats into a Republican box. Bush did it last year and it worked. But having lost both houses of Congress, Democrats should have learned their lesson. Avoid the Republican box. Instead, force Republicans into a Democratic box. Make them choose between a payroll tax cut for more than 130 million American working families, worth about $5,000 to each family, or a tax cut for the richest 2 percent of American families, worth millions to each of their do-nothing kids. If Republicans are too dumb to choose a payroll tax cut over an estate tax cut, Democrats should blast them. Use it as ammo for 2004. Make it a central part of the Democratic message. Yell about it on television, radio. Bellow about it from rooftops.

Everyone hates taxes, but the payroll tax has got to be the worst. Four out of five American workers pay more in payroll taxes than they do in income taxes. The payroll tax is also regressive as hell—poorer workers pay proportionately more than richer ones. It's paid out of the very first dollar earned, all the way up to a threshold that's now roughly $80,000. After that, nothing. (Wealthy earners pay only the tiny Medicare portion of the payroll tax on all their earnings.) So the very rich get finished paying almost all their payroll taxes early in the year. Bill Gates is done a few minutes past midnight, New Year's Eve. True, poorer retirees get back more each year from Social Security and Medicare than richer retirees, relative to the yearly payroll taxes they contributed when they worked. But poorer retirees don't live nearly as long as richer ones. So, overall, the system's still regressive.

A larger and larger portion of federal revenues have been coming from payroll taxes. At the end of World War II, it was only 2 percent. Now it's 37 percent. That's because most major tax cuts of the past twenty-five years have been heavily tilted toward the rich. The biggest tax increase has been the payroll tax, which rose substantially in the 1980s.

The estate tax is almost a mirror image of the payroll tax. Ninety-eight percent of American families don't come near it. Half of all estate taxes collected by the federal government in 1999 came from 3,300 family estates. That's less than two-tenths of 1 percent of American families. A quarter of all estate taxes came from just 467 families, each of which was worth more than $20 million. I mean, we're not even talking about the upper-middle class. We're talking about the super, super rich.

Besides, a payroll tax cut will be a boon to the economy, stimulating more spending just when we need it. If you hadn't noticed, we're in one of the most anemic recoveries on record—so anemic about dead. The Federal Reserve can't kick-start the economy even after twelve rate cuts. The reason is that we still have a lot of productive capacity that's not being used because there aren't enough customers for all the goods and services that can be produced. Bottom line: Business won't invest a penny more in new equipment or new jobs until consumers buy more.

The best way to get consumers to buy more is to put more money in their pockets. And the easiest way to do this is by cutting payroll taxes. There's a bonus. Because employers will no longer have to pay their share, they'll have an extra incentive to keep more people on their payrolls. The Bush estate tax cut, on the other hand, has virtually no stimulative effect on the economy. It gives more money to a handful of rich families that already spend as much as they want. And most of the estate tax cut won't happen for years anyway.

Anyone worried that a payroll tax cut will hurt Social Security or Medicare doesn't understand federal budgeting. Every tax dollar the government collects is the same as every other dollar. Repeal the estate tax cut and the federal government gains $700 billion, making up for the $700 billion it loses by cutting the payroll tax for two years. Forget the "trust funds." They're just a matter of accounting.

Framing it as a choice between the two cuts also serves a larger purpose. It draws public attention to the scandal of the widening gap of income and wealth in America over the past two decades. After-tax incomes of the top 1 percent of American families have risen more than 150 percent, while the vast majority of families in the middle have barely gained ground. America hasn't experienced this degree of inequality in more than eighty years.

Part of the wideninggap is due to a shift in economy, away from standardized production and good unionized jobs and toward constant innovations requiring more specialized knowledge. But it's also the cosnequence of government policies that have favored the rich and powerful while doing little or nothing to help everyone else through the transition. The Bush estate tax cut is Exhibit A.

The choice between the two tax cuts also shows which party favors people who work for a living. The payroll tax penalized work; cutting it rewards work. By contrast, the estate tax was enacted to prevent family dynasties whose heirs would never need to work. Cutting the estate tax rewards idleness.

So there you have it: a clear choice that speaks volumes. Democrats had no message in 2002 and paid the price. Bush had a tax cut and a war on terrorism. You can't fight something with nothing. If Democrats want to win back at least one chamber of Congress and have a fair chance of regaining the White House two years from now, they'll have to fashion a tough but humane foreign policy and a plan to get the economy moving. Most importantly, they'll need to remind Americans what's at stake: a democratic society that offers the world a model of equity and opportunity or one that's run by and for the people at the top. Some choice.

DANIEL J. MITCHELL

Nine Simple Guidelines for Pro-Growth Tax Policy

Economic growth occurs when people work more, save more, and invest more. These are the behaviors that increase national income and boost the nation's wealth. People do not produce more simply because the government has a balanced budget. Nor do they increase their levels of work, saving, or investment just because the government gives them a check, even if it is in the form of a tax rebate. To ensure that national income increases and to encourage the efficient use of national resources, lawmakers should focus on fiscal policy options that improve incentives to engage in productive behavior, recognizing the following facts.

1. **Not all tax cuts are created equal.** Certain tax cuts help the economy, because they improve incentives to earn more income and create wealth. Lowering tax rates on productive behavior is the key to good tax policy. Taxes are essentially a "price" imposed on different activities. When the cost is prohibitive (that is, when tax rates are high), the activity being taxed is discouraged. Lower tax rates on work, saving, and investment encourage additional economic growth. By contrast, other tax cuts may have no effect on growth. Giving all taxpayers $500, for instance, does not increase their incentives to earn more income or engage in productive behavior and will thus do nothing to increase national income.

2. **The change in tax rates matters, not the size of a tax cut.** Public policy debate frequently focuses on the size of a tax package, but this can be very misleading. Providing an annual "rebate" to every taxpayer in the country, for instance, would involve a significant reduction in tax revenue but would have no impact on economic growth. By contrast, a small reduction in the capital gains tax would encourage more investment and boost the economy's performance—even though this tax relief would be tiny compared to the tax rebate. Some tax policies can boost growth even without lowering the overall tax burden. A revenue-neutral flat tax, for example, would increase national economic output significantly even though taxpayers as a group have no additional money in their pockets.

3. **Good tax policy leads to a "revenue feedback" as a result of better economic performance.** With good tax policy, the actual reduction in tax revenue is always smaller than the projections produced by static revenue-estimation models. Lower tax rates encourage taxpayers to work more, save more, and invest more. As a result, the national income increases, and the tax base becomes concomitantly larger. This does not mean that all tax cuts pay for themselves. Only in select instances (such as the 1997 capital gains tax-rate reduction) does a tax-rate reduction generate a big enough increase in taxable income to offset the revenue loss associated with a lower tax rate.

4. **Tax cuts do not help the economy by "giving people money to spend."** Although tax cuts allow taxpayers to keep more of their money, this extra money does not materialize out of thin air: The government must borrow it from private credit markets (or, if there is a surplus, return less money to private credit markets). Any increase in private consumer spending generated by a tax cut is offset by a reduction in private investment spending. Thus, there is no increase in total spending, national income, or economic growth.

5. **Consumer spending is a consequence of growth, not a cause of growth.** Some politicians argue that encouraging consumer spending will spur growth. This puts the cart before the horse. Consumers spend when they have disposable income, and faster growth is the only permanent way to increase the level of disposable income.

6. **Good long-term tax policy is the best short-term "stimulus."** Some policymakers claim that good tax policy should be postponed in order to focus on "stimulus." This assumes that consumer spending drives the economy. In fact, the only tax policies that create short-run growth are the ones that also improve long-run growth. Some of these policies (such as tax cuts that attract capital from other nations) can have a pronounced immediate impact. The economic benefits of other equally desirable policies (such as personal income tax-rate reductions) may take effect over a longer period of time.

7. **The size of government matters, not deficits.** So-called deficit hawks mistakenly focus on the symptom of bad fiscal policy and ignore the underlying cause. Taxing and borrowing are two ways to finance government, and both have adverse consequences, as resources are transferred from the productive sector to government. Although some government expenditures, such as providing national security or maintaining a well-functioning legal system, bring societal benefits that compensate for the economy's forgone growth, in many cases, the rate of return on government spending is very low—or even negative.

8. **Supply-side tax cuts lower interest rates.** Financial institutions and other lenders make funds available to borrowers because that is how they make money. But in order to earn a profit, the interest rate charged on loans and other investments must be high enough to compensate for factors such as projected inflation rates and likelihood of default. Taxes also affect interest rates. When tax rates are high, investors must charge a higher interest rate. This explains why interest rates for "tax-free" municipal bonds are about 150 basis points lower than interest rates for comparable debt instruments that are taxable. Reducing the multiple layers of taxation on income that is saved and invested will lower interest rates.

9. **Deficits do not have a significant impact on interest rates.** Interest rates are determined in world capital markets where trillions of dollars change hands every day. Even a large shift in the U.S. government's fiscal balance is unlikely to have a noticeable impact on interest rates. Indeed, interest rates have fallen in the past three years even though the federal government now has a $200+ billion deficit instead of a $200+ billion surplus. This does not mean that higher deficits lead to lower interest rates. Instead, it shows that other factors have a greater impact than deficits. Academic studies have confirmed that there is no significant relationship between fiscal balance and interest rates.

If policymakers want to boost the economy's performance, they should reject big-government policies and, using these nine guidelines, work to lower tax rates on productive activity.

DISCUSSION QUESTIONS

1. *What would you do?* You are the Republican Majority Leader of the Senate, and you have been asked to draft the party's response to a bill that would cut payroll taxes by 50 percent and make up lost revenue by restoring the estate tax. What is your answer? Do you oppose the bill? Why or why not?

2. The normative case for tax cuts, in part, is that taxes aren't the government's money but belong to the people who pay them. As such, criticizing tax cuts as a "give back" ignores the fact that the money is actually going back to its original owners. What do you think of this position?

3. Do you think the tax code should be used to encourage or reward certain types of behavior (buying a house, investing in the stock market)? Why or why not? If you think that this is acceptable, where do you draw the line? What sorts of activities and behaviors should be encouraged?

16 Privatizing Social Security: Who Wins, Who Loses?

Social Security affects tens of millions of Americans; according to the Social Security Administration, over 50 million Americans received some sort of support from the program in 2002. There is wide agreement that the program requires major reform if it is to continue to provide economic security to future retirees and their survivors. Even so, there is much less agreement about what, specifically, should be done. At the heart of the debate are two contrasting perspectives on what the Social Security system is designed to do, both deeply rooted in U.S. political culture. One perspective is that Social Security is a national guarantee of basic income for all individuals in retirement; it is the ultimate "safety net" for the elderly. The other holds that Social Security should be an individualistic program that allows people to make choices about their own retirement. To put it another way, is Social Security a social welfare program, or a social investment program?

For several decades, the libertarian Cato Institute has been arguing that the Social Security system be privatized—that individuals should control their own retirement accounts, and be permitted to make specific decisions about how the account should be invested. In return for foregoing future claims, individuals would be permitted to keep control over their own contributions, which they could then invest in the stock market. Andrew Biggs sets out the case for this, and argues that the market's recent performance should not affect its feasibility. There is, in Cato's view, no alternative, because the entire system is currently structured as an unsustainable pyramid scheme, in which each generation's retirees are funded through the next generation of workers; when the baby boomers begin retiring in 2008, there simply won't be enough people contributing to pay for all the benefits. Allowing people to take responsibility for their own accounts—in effect, eliminating the current "pay as you go" funding—would lower costs, spur savings, and give individuals a much higher rate of return on their contributions. Even with the last three years of poor market performance, workers would still be better off handling their own investments. "The stock market," argues Biggs, "has never lost money over any twenty-year period." Private accounts would save the system, which otherwise will require huge tax increases or harsh benefit cuts.

But others argue that privatizing social security would destroy the program's core, by eliminating a sense of shared sacrifice and collective responsibility. These critics point out that privatization will make social security's revenue-benefits imbalance worse, by reducing current contributions without doing anything about current benefits. Brooke Harrington has a slightly different spin on this issue. She points out that most people lack the skills and knowledge necessary to make good investment decisions. The central problem, she says, is one of "information asymmetries," in which sellers have more information than buyers. Furthermore, some groups of potential investors, such as women or minorities, are more likely to make conservative investment decisions that will hurt their long-term returns, and reduce their economic security under a privatized system. Rather than serving the redistributive and social insurance purposes of the current social security system, privatization would exacerbate existing income and wealth inequalities.

ANDREW G. BIGGS
Stock Market Declines' Effect on the Social Security Reform Debate

Imagine the following deal: You could invest part or all of your Social Security taxes in a personal retirement account. However, your account could hold nothing but stocks, and you would retire during the biggest bear market since the Great Depression. Would you accept such a deal? I would, because even today, personal accounts would increase retirement benefits while giving workers greater ownership and control over their savings.

Slumping stock markets have opponents of personal accounts claiming vindication. The situation shows, they argue, that only a traditional government-run, defined-benefit Social Security program can provide adequate retirement security. As then-Senate Majority Leader Tom Daschle put it on July 12, 2002, "After what's happened in the stock market the last few weeks, we think it's a terrible idea. . . . Imagine if you were retiring this week, with most major stock indexes hitting five-year lows." Indeed, many Americans are sure to be concerned after hearing such comments.

Yet, in judging the risks of long-term market investment based on just a few months or years of returns, these opponents of personal accounts are victims of the so-called law of small numbers—the propensity to believe that a small sample is representative of the larger universe of outcomes. Like those who took a few years of double-digit stock returns in the 1990s and predicted that they signified a future of limitless investment riches, personal account opponents have failed to take an in-depth look at the historical facts regarding stock and bond returns over the long term.

These facts show that, even now, personal accounts would increase benefits and help strengthen Social Security for the future. However had the market's recent performance, a worker retiring today would have begun investing in the late 1950s. The stock market has never lost money over any twenty-year period. Even without diversification, a worker retiring today would have forty years of investment behind him or her to make up for recent losses. A worker just entering the market would have forty years to regain lost ground. There is simply no way recent events can credibly justify a disastrous scenario for personal accounts. Even a worker retiring in the Great Depression would have received a four percent annual return after inflation, and one retiring today would do substantially better.

Personal accounts give workers the opportunity to diversify their investments across hundreds or even thousands of stocks and bonds, reducing the risk that declines in a single company or asset class would severely impact retirement income.

Moreover, longtime horizons provide "time diversification" that smoothes out the short-term volatility of investments in the stock market.

Historically, in almost all cases, workers with diversified market investments would have received substantially higher benefits if allowed to invest part or all of their payroll taxes in personal retirement accounts. Looking forward to Social Security reform proposals already on the table, practically all workers could expect to increase their total retirement incomes by opting to participate in personal accounts, even if they had to give up part of their traditional benefits to do so.

Asset diversification: mixing stocks and bonds. Stocks are risky investments over the short run, varying greatly from year to year. Bonds and other fixed-income investments, while producing lower returns over the long term, provide the year-to-year stability that many investors demand.

For this reason, most financial advisors recommend that investors move from a predominantly stock-based portfolio when they are young to fixed-income investments such as bonds as they near retirement. Younger workers have more time to make up for market losses, as well as more future labor income with which to supplement their savings. A common rule of thumb is that the percentage of stocks in a worker's portfolio should equal "100 minus your age," so that a twenty-year-old would begin his or her working life with 80 percent of savings going into stocks and retire at sixty-five with just 35 percent in equities.

Statistics from 401(k) plans show that most workers stick reasonably close to these guidelines. The average worker aged 60–65 keeps about 40 percent of 401(k) assets invested in stocks and 60 percent put in fixed-income assets such as bonds. A younger worker, by contrast, reverses the mix to 60–40 percent in favor of stocks.

To illustrate the impact of life cycle investing, imagine a sixty-five-year-old average-wage worker retiring today. One year ago, he or she had $100,000 in a personal account and allocated 40 percent to the S&P 500 stock index and 60 percent to the Lehman Brothers aggregate bond index. What would that account be worth today, assuming no additional contributions were made in the last year?

Believe it or not, despite truly awful stock market returns in the past year, the account balance would be virtually unchanged. The loss of 21.6 percent on the stock portion of the portfolio would be almost matched by the 9.9 percent gain on the larger bond portion, for a total year-end loss of just 3.25 percent. In other words, if that worker had started the year with $100,000 in the account, he or she would have ended with $97,288. This loss would reduce monthly retirement income by merely around $15. Moreover, a typical low-income worker aged 60–65 has just 23 percent of his or her 401(k) invested in equities. This low-income worker would have made money over the last year, earning a return of 2.6 percent as gains from the bonds in the portfolio outweighed losses in the stock market.

Any investor would rather make money than lose it, but these results show that even the poor stock market results of the past year would have had just a small impact on a typical worker holding a personal retirement account. As Dallas Salisbury of the Employee Benefit Research Institute remarks, "There is no retirement crisis because of the stock market decline." Workers' retirement accounts are sufficiently diversified that they lost only 5–10 percent on average over the last year, according to the *Los Angeles Times*, with those nearing retirement presumably suffering even smaller declines.

Time diversification: stocks for the long run.

While the relatively small declines despite recent stock market losses may reassure the nervous, what really matters for personal accounts isn't how they would have performed over the last year, or over any single year. For retirement investment, what matters is where you start and where you wind up. What happens in between is much less important. Retirement investing is about the long run, and over the long run, stocks have been remarkably safe investments.

As noted above, most workers diversify their investments between stocks and bonds, moving out of equities as they approach retirement. Personal account opponents, however, often assume that workers have their entire account invested in stocks, maximizing their risk in the event of a market decline.

If that is what account opponents insist on, let's see what it would mean. To illustrate, take a male worker earning the average wage each year, currently around $35,000, and retiring in 2002. Assume that he deposited 3 percent of his wages into a personal account investing exclusively in the S&P 500 stock index. The account balance will be compared to the notional "wealth" he would have accumulated from putting the same amount of money into the current system.

The annual return from Social Security for a single male retiring today is 1.74 percent above inflation, according to the Social Security Administration. This estimate includes all retirement, survivors, and disability benefits. Married couples, particularly those with a single earner, could expect somewhat higher returns. Future retirees can generally expect lower returns than those retiring now.

Even with the recent stock market decline, a single male investing solely in stocks would receive benefits 2.8 times higher than had he "invested" the same amount of money in the current program. Put another way, the recent decline in stock prices means the worker's personal account would be worth the same today as it was worth in 1997. Nevertheless, that worker's Social Security "savings" would be worth today only what the personal account was worth in the late 1980s. It would take a much-larger decline than the one we have seen for a personal account to be a worse "deal" than the current program.

Simulating personal account returns through history.

The Congressional Research Service took a more-wide-ranging look at the issue of market risk and personal retirement accounts, utilizing stock and bond returns dating back to 1927 to simulate how individuals with personal accounts would have fared had accounts been introduced in the past. It is true, as the CRS finds, that stock returns vary greatly from year to year, but this variation takes place at a level *higher* than that provided by Social Security. That is, while a worker could not be sure from historical returns of receiving higher benefits than a person retiring last year or next year, that individual could be reasonably sure of receiving more than if he or she had invested the same amount of money in the traditional pay-as-you-go program. Over the thirty-five different forty-one-year periods the CRS studied, there is not one in which a worker who had invested payroll taxes in stocks would have been better off remaining in the current system. On average, a personal account invested solely in stocks would produce benefits two and one-half times higher than had those same funds been devoted to the traditional pay-as-you-go program.

A mixed portfolio of stocks and bonds was not always better than Social Security, but it nearly always was so. Of the thirty-five different forty-one-year periods studied, in seven of them a worker would have been better off investing payroll taxes in Social Security than in a 60–40 stock-bond portfolio, although the difference is small—an average of just 6 percent.

The relative weakness of a mixed portfolio during the 1970s is attributable to two factors. First, investment returns were low by historical standards, with a slow economy reducing stock returns and high inflation making real bond returns negative from 1970 to 1979. Second, Social Security paid substantially higher returns during that period than it does today or will in the future. Workers retiring in the 1970s received real annual returns from Social Security averaging around 10 percent. Future retirees can expect to receive returns of approximately two percent, depending on their income and marital status. While low market returns are possible in the future, the current Social Security program can never again pay returns similar to those received during the 1970s and before.

Overall, however, a 60–40 stock-bond portfolio would have paid an average of 39 percent more than Social Security, even compared to the higher rates of return the current program has paid in the past. From the late 1970s onward, no individual—including one retiring today—would have been worse off with a personal account than by remaining in the current system. All workers would have received higher benefits by investing in personal accounts, even if their account contained a high proportion of bonds, and many workers would have received much-higher benefits.

These results may understate somewhat the returns from personal account plans such as those from the President's Commission, since the CRS assumes administrative costs of one percent of assets managed, vs. an estimate of 0.3 percent of assets managed by Social Security's independent actuaries for the Commission's account structure. Over a forty-one-year working lifetime, a 0.7 percent increase in the net investment return would raise the final asset accumulation by slightly over 20 percent, further increasing the advantage of personal accounts over pay-as-you-go financing.

Long-run market risk.   Another way to consider stock market risk is to compare the variations in returns over various holding periods. The influential book *Stocks for the Long Run*, by Wharton School finance professor Jeremy Siegel, shows the standard deviation of returns for stocks, bonds, and Treasury bills held for different periods of time. The standard deviation measures the dispersion of statistical data, showing how much individual instances tend to vary from the average for the group.

In the short run, the standard deviation of stock returns is very high, so the return in one year could be very different from that of another. Fixed income investments, by contrast, have lower standard deviations and thus lower risk. Over the long term, though, the standard deviation of stock returns has fallen. The return from holding stock for, say, twenty years does not vary so much, regardless of which twenty-year period of American history you choose. For thirty-year periods, the standard deviation of returns is lower still.

Moreover, for long holding periods, the standard deviation of stock returns is actually lower than for bonds or Treasury bills. That is to say, in a certain sense at least, stocks were *less* risky over the long term than bonds. It is this reduction of the variance of returns over the long run that forms the basis for time diversification and the common advice given younger individuals to hold riskier investments.

WORST-CASE SCENARIOS

Personal-account opponents are quick to point that that, while stocks have high *average* returns, the promise of guaranteed protection against poverty cannot be "averaged out" if some people feast on the rewards of a rich stock account while others cannot afford to eat. Social Security is supposed to be there for everyone, regardless of whether they have good luck or know how to manage investments. Hence, reform opponents are justified in demanding we look not just at the average returns available from personal accounts, but how people would fare if they experienced low returns over their lifetimes.

Another way to look at stock investment for personal accounts, then, is to examine the extremes. If you had a personal account and received below-average returns on your investments, how badly would you have fared?

As expected, stocks have often produced large losses in the short term. For instance, over single-year holding periods, the worst performance from stocks in American history was a loss of 38.6 percent; for bonds in a single year, a loss of 21.9 percent; and for Treasury bills, a loss of 15.6 percent.

Over the long term, however, annual gains and losses offset each other. When stocks are held for ten years, the largest average annual loss was 4.2 percent after inflation. Over twenty years or more, though, stocks have never failed to produce positive returns, with the worst annual return being one percent. Over thirty years, the worst annual return from stocks was a gain of 2.6 percent after inflation.

Bonds actually produced lower worst-case returns over the long run than stocks. The worst thirty-year return from bonds was an annual loss of two percent; for Treasury bills, a loss of 1.8 percent. In other words, the true worst-case scenarios would not have involved stock investment, but holding supposedly "safe" government bonds.

These figures assume that workers hold a diversified portfolio replicating the performance of the stock market as a whole. A worker could lose his or her savings simply by investing the entire portfolio in one of the approximately two hundred public corporations that declare bankruptcy in any given year. It is precisely for this reason that all major personal account-based reform legislation mandates that workers could not invest in single stocks or even in single corporate sectors. Workers with accounts could purchase only highly diversified mutual funds holding dozens, hundreds, or even thousands of stocks and bonds. Some reform plans base their account administration on the Federal Thrift Plan, which gives workers the option to invest in one or more of five stock or bond index funds, coupling simplicity and extremely low administrative costs with high levels of diversification. Hence, while personal account opponents cite the amount a worker might have lost by investing in the NASDAQ index, there is no existing reform legislation that would allow such an investment to take place.

In practice, it would be next to impossible for an individual to lose money. To illustrate, imagine a worker who could invest in either the S&P 500 stock index or in a fund of AAA-rated corporate bonds. Each year, he or she moved his entire portfolio to the investment that would reap the lowest returns for that year. Even after making the worst investment choices possible, if retiring today, the worker still would have had positive net returns on his or her portfolio as a whole.

Short-term investors are right to be concerned about short-term stock market volatility. Long-term investors, such as those saving for retirement, should focus more on long-term returns and long-term volatility. Additionally, over the time frames in which individuals would utilize personal accounts for Society Security, diversified investments in stocks and bonds remain perfectly adequate means to prepare for retirement.

Indeed, review of the evidence shows the hysterical reactions of personal account opponents to recent stock market declines to be wholly overblown. Most workers nearing retirement would have relatively little exposure to stock market risk and thus would have merely experienced small declines in their account values. Most workers who did have large proportions of their accounts invested in stocks would be young, with many years to make up for today's losses. Even workers invested entirely in stocks and retiring precisely when the market had fallen would still have received higher returns than the current Social Security program can produce. Historical evidence shows that even a worker retiring in 1933, when the Great Depression dragged the stock market to its lowest, would have still received a 4 percent average annual return, over twice what today's average worker can expect from Social Security.

Moreover, experience shows that workers can invest their assets wisely to account for stock market risk. In the 1980s and 1990s, millions of new investors entered the market as employers shifted from traditional defined-benefit pensions to employee-controlled defined-contribution accounts. Many of these new investors had little experience with stocks or bonds, but data shows that generally they have made reasonable decisions on how to allocate their assets as they aged. Personal accounts would be designed with new investors in mind, ensuring low costs and adequate diversification so that inexperienced investors would not find themselves losing money due to high administrative fees or inappropriate reliance on merely a few stocks.

Just as importantly, personal accounts give workers the opportunity to stay out of the stock market entirely if they so choose. They could invest solely in corporate or government bonds and still receive higher benefits than by staying in the current program. This stands in contrast to plans in which the government itself would invest the Social Security trust fund in the stock market. Not only would that plan open the fund to political manipulation, it would make workers and retirees subject to stock market risk, whether they desired it or not.

Personal accounts are voluntary, and no worker would be forced to choose one or to invest even a penny in the stock market. Given the relative safety of long-run diversified market investment, there is little reason why individual workers should not be allowed to choose.

Yes, the stock market is risky, and individuals should bear this risk in mind when making investment decisions. Nevertheless, while opponents of personal accounts trumpet the amount that accounts might have lost in the past four years, they decline to discuss how much workers would have gained over the last forty—not just in dollars, but in the security and dignity that comes from ownership and control over one's own retirement wealth.

BROOKE HARRINGTON
Can Small Investors Survive Social Security Privatization?

It has become nearly axiomatic in this country to argue that everything would be better if it were run like a business. In response, government has shifted its mission: If it used to operate like Super Glue, bonding Americans to one another, it is now working more like WD-40, minimizing friction in the pursuit of individual (and corporate) profit.

Social Security is not only the largest government program but the embodiment of the Super Glue approach to politics: the ultimate test case for privatization. The Bush administration proposes to allow contributors to invest a portion of their public Social Security pensions in the stock market. What a coup that would be for the WD-40 contingent.

Privatization proponents rest their proposal on three claims: Social Security funds are comparable to private investments, like IRAs; since most Americans manage their own IRAs, there is no reason they shouldn't manage their public pensions as well; and given the average returns on American stocks, we'd all have much more money at retirement if we could take some of our Social Security fund out of government bonds and put it into the stock market. This shift could be interpreted as the financial equivalent of "bowling alone," Robert Putnam's much-quoted phrase about the decline of community life in the United States. Or you could think of it as the 401(k)-ification of America: The defined-contribution plan has shifted our view of retirement into something that is purely an individual matter, rather than a collective one.

A *New York Times* poll conducted earlier this year indicates that many Americans are increasingly persuaded by these ideas. Despite the market downturn, there has been a marked increase in the percentage of Americans who expect to rely only on their own savings—rather than private pension plans or Social Security—in retirement. Only 15 percent now believe that Social Security will be a primary source of their retirement funds. As one survey participant put it, "These decades to come are going to be more about what you do for yourself, as opposed to what you allow other people to do for you. It's not pro-government, not anti-government, just me myself and I." But while Americans may think they are well prepared to give up a piece of their social safety net, the evidence from recent economic studies suggests otherwise.

The prospect of higher returns is the main attraction of privatization, despite the seemingly insurmountable problems of logistics, costs, and implementation it poses. Belief in this claim seems to be curiously robust, even in the face of the recent stock-market decline and attempts to explain the costs, risks, and problems associated with privatization. People have dollar signs in their eyes, and nothing seems able to dislodge them.

In part, this can be attributed to the increasing displacement of belief in the public good by belief in the marketplace. The movements to bring market forces to the management of public schools, Medicare, and electrical-power transmission are among the most visible recent examples.

The central problem facing these hybrid public-private organizations is "information asymmetry": Market forces can't bring efficiency if there are large information differences among sellers and buyers. The classic example is the purchase of a used car. The seller has more information than the buyer and has no incentive to tell the buyer the truth. Therefore, the buyer may end up (1) buying a lemon or (2) spending a lot of time and money on research, both of which offset the savings from getting a "bargain" on the price.

When you introduce market forces into a formerly public service, you run into all of these problems of information asymmetry and opportunism. Thus, the key question for success in any hybrid is: Are citizens prepared to act as informed consumers?

In the case of Social Security, support for a privatized system rests entirely (and often implicitly) on assumptions about public knowledge and competency with regard to stock investing. But recent studies by economists and finance scholars suggest that Americans really don't understand the risks associated with stock investments and stand a good chance of doing worse financially under a hybrid system than under the current one.

RISK, RETURN, AND TRANSACTION COSTS

In the language of finance, the benefits of a privatized Social Security system depend upon the "equity premium." This is the increased return that investors can get for investing in risky securities such as stocks as opposed to risk-free securities such as Treasury bonds. Investors are compensated for assuming risk; the higher the risk, the greater the compensation.

During the century that just ended, the return on U.S. stock investments has averaged about 11 percent per year. The U.S. Treasury bonds in which Social Security funds are invested returned much less—averaging more like 5 percent per year. Offered a choice between the two investments, the answer seems obvious: Take the higher return.

But of course there is a catch—two catches, in fact. The equity premium is not guaranteed (if it were, there would be no risk). It is just an average return, and some individual investors will actually lose money on stock investments. Not only are the risks of any individual stock unpredictable, but the historical-average return of U.S. stocks may not apply in a given time period. A grinding bear market or high inflation around the time you retire could mean that you have to cash out your portfolio when it's under water. In any case, the historical-average returns involve periods much longer than the relevant individual time frame, which is basically the forty-odd years between the start of one's working life and retirement. That means many of us will not be able to capitalize on long-range returns; as Keynes put it, "in the long run, we are all dead."

A second, related catch is that once investors capture the equity premium, they have to be careful not to give it away to their brokers. Trading stocks incurs transaction costs: Each buy or sell order means paying a commission. These costs can easily eat up all the gains from a profitable investment. Unless the government wants to become the world's first no-commission broker, transaction costs are going to be a serious issue in a privatized Social Security system.

The entire proposition that Social Security participants will come out ahead financially in a privatized system depends on their knowledge of and ability to manage investment risk and transaction costs. The evidence on this subject is not encouraging.

For example, polls conducted to examine Americans' attitudes toward Social Security privatization have shown that it is alarmingly easy to reverse support for the proposal by simply mentioning risk. When questions about privatization are phrased so that they don't mention risk, about 58 percent of Americans support the proposal. But if the questions are rephrased so that they mention risk in any way, the results are reversed: 59 percent of respondents *oppose* privatization.

Studies of actual investor behavior support the polls. Ordinary individuals seem to have a polarized response to risk; they become either very conservative or very risk-seeking. Unfortunately, neither strategy is profitable. Though *on average* risk is compensated by return in the stock market, some risks don't pay off. Rather than being a linear relationship, in which more risk always pays off with higher returns, the risk-return relationship is more like an inverted U-shaped curve: Risks pay off up to a certain point, after which they become a waste of money. As with gambling, most of the fun in investing consists of locating that fine line between risks that pay off and those that don't.

Unfortunately, the vast majority of people guess wrong. Finance professor Terrance Odean has found that the portfolios of average American households and of investment clubs underperform the stock market by about 4 percent annually. In addition, Odean found that Americans trade their accounts excessively, creating high transaction costs. Apparently unaware that they were giving away their profits in the form of commissions, American households turned over their portfolios—that is, sold existing stocks and bought new ones—at the astronomical rate of 75 percent per year. Investment clubs weren't far behind, with a 65 percent annual turnover rate. At the end of the day, they mostly made money for their brokers. There is no reason to expect that Americans would fare any better or trade any less in a privatized system.

Of course, an ultraconservative approach to investing doesn't provide much of an alternative. Several economic studies indicate that the populations most likely to need Social Security in old age—people of color and women—are also the least likely to benefit from a privatized system. For example, a study by economists Nancy Jianokoplos and Alexander Bernasek indicates that women invest too conservatively, putting only 40 percent of their investment dollars into stocks, compared with 46 percent for men. This conservatism doesn't pay off: If a man and a woman start with equal amounts of investment capital (which is of course a highly stylized assumption in itself) and invest it according to the averages over a twenty-year period, that 6 percent difference in allocation results in the woman having 47 percent less money in her retirement fund than the man has. Thus, conservative behavior in a privatized system may not result in more retirement dollars for everyone. For the people who need a nest egg most, privatization may be no better, and perhaps worse, than the current public system.

This difference doesn't have anything to do with innate characteristics of men and women—or of blacks and whites—but rather with lack of exposure to investment opportunities, such as working the kind of job where you get a 401 (k) plan that forces you to learn something about investing. That's how most Americans got into investing in the first place. But the investing bandwagon that swept the country during the 1990s left behind large numbers of women, people of color, and the poor. To correct this problem, the government would have to create a national investor-education program—an undertaking so costly that the Social Security trustees warned against it in 1999, saying that the expenses incurred would almost certainly outweigh the gains from privatization.

PRIVATIZATION: READY OR NOT?

Historically, Social Security has served multiple purposes, providing savings, insurance, and income redistribution in a single program. Privatization would shift the program away from redistribution and toward individual savings. This is part of the larger trend toward distrust of government and detachment from notions of the common good. In this sense, after years of erosion of public-sector institutions and faith in their mission, Americans *are* well prepared for a hybridized Social Security. More than twenty years of retreat from the notion of entitlement has changed our expectations and led many of us to accept the notion that we should individually bear most of the risk and responsibility for funding our retirements.

But all of us are vulnerable to the possibility of bad luck. Privatization would introduce a lottery-like element into the system that undercuts security for everyone. There is no guaranteed profit in the stock market: neither risk seeking nor conservatism reliably pays off, and neither investment professionals nor ordinary Americans have been successful at guessing where stock prices would go. Americans may think that they know something about investing—remember when everyone agreed that you couldn't go wrong in dot-com stocks?—but their confidence, and the confidence of policy makers, is not supported by the evidence.

The evidence suggests that the people who would be most likely to see financial benefit from privatization in the Social Security system are white, male, affluent, and young. Unfortunately, recent polls indicate that these are also the people most likely to say they don't need Social Security and would like to drop out of the program entirely.

The end of Social Security in its purely public form would mean losses for Americans that are not just economic but social. In abandoning the largest and most popular public program that binds us together through its benefits, we would lose an institutional and economic linchpin of our political community. When stacked up against the uncertain financial gains from privatization, the benefits of a public Social Security system look increasingly priceless.

DISCUSSION QUESTIONS

1. *What would you do*? If you had the choice of opting out of the social security system, foregoing any future guaranteed benefits in return for being able to invest your contributions, would you do it? What are the advantages and disadvantages of giving individuals the power to control their own accounts?

2. Social Security is not, at present, means tested: retirees are eligible for benefits no matter how wealthy they are. In 1999, over 2 million retirees received benefits even though their household incomes were over $100,000. What would happen if benefits were means tested? Would this jeopardize the broad public support for the program?

3. Do you think that most people are able to make their own investment decisions? Under a privatized system, should the government guarantee any of these investments? How might such a guarantee affect the decisions that individuals make about where to put their money?

17 Foreign Policy: Nation Building

When terrorists crashed airplanes into the World Trade Center in New York City and the Pentagon in Washington, Americans were stunned and in a state of disbelief. How could this happen? Who was responsible? When President Bush indicated that he was prepared to fight a war on terrorism to ensure that the guilty parties were punished and to prevent any similar incident in the future, he rode a wave of public opinion demanding action. Dislodging the Taliban in Afghanistan was the first leg of this strategy. Changes in domestic security procedures, such as safety and inspection procedures at airports, constituted the second leg. The third leg was a plan to remove Saddam Hussein from power in Iraq. Although his interpretation and analysis were disputed by some observers, the president declared that Iraq not only was a haven for terrorists in general, but also perhaps provided support for the terrorists involved in the events of September 11. The president also declared that, even if not involved in September 11, Iraq was an identifiable risk for supporting future terrorism and creating international turmoil through weapons programs and aggressive stances toward its neighbors. On these stated grounds, the president ordered the U.S. into battle against Iraq. In short order, American troops and their allies had taken control of Bagdahd and chased Hussein from power. The question then became: what next?

In the 2000 presidential campaign, candidate Bush expressed skepticism about the concept of "nation building," suggesting that it stretched the military thin and often got the U.S. bogged down in situations that were unlikely to be resolved by outside forces. After September 11, 2001, however, the president found himself directing nation-building efforts in Afghanistan and Iraq. Although there is some dispute over precisely what nation-building entails, at the minimum most analysts would agree that it means constructing a functioning government that can govern even in a society composed of disparate ethnic, linguistic, religious, and geographical groupings. It also involves building an economic infrastructure and system that will reduce the likelihood of social and political instability. Today, these tasks typically involve the efforts of individuals and governments outside the targeted country as well as individuals and groups within the country. The United States itself has gone through its own nation-building experiences, particularly in the period following the Revolutionary War, the time of the writing of the Constitution, and also in the aftermath of the Civil War. To state the obvious, nation building is difficult.

Marina Ottaway offers a set of principles by which to evaluate and understand nation building. She suggests that we have to have realistic expectations about these efforts at reconstruction. We may hope democracy will result, but it quite possibly will not. We might wish to see nation building accomplished without military force. This, too, she argues, is unlikely. Ottaway also contends that hoping a truly integrated "nation" will emerge will emerge is often wishful thinking—the best that might be achievable is a country in which rival forces are not shooting at each other. Nation building need not become an endless quagmire, though. In her view, clear goals and sufficient resources can prevent nation building from becoming an endless exercise.

Stan Crock and David Pryce-Jones offer different perspectives on the early success of the nation-building effort in Iraq. Crock is very critical of the performance of the Bush administration. Arguing that there are five key questions that must be answered in any nation-building effort, Crock contends that the adminstration chose the wrong answer on each. To Crock, the adminstration understood the appropriate role for neither the military nor civiliians in Iraq, and misunderstood the scope of what was needed for effective nation building as well as how much the Iraqis can solve on their own. Pryce-Jones offers a more positive assessment. In his view, critics have been too quick to rush to judgment about the process of nation building in Iraq and the ultimate success or failure of the initiative. Postwar Iraq is in much better shape than one might have expected, and certainly in much better shape than many doomsday scenarios suggested. Although effective government has yet to be implemented, basic economic and social needs are being resolved. Putting an effective government in place will take time—Pryce-Jones notes that other countries, particularly those recovering from authoritarian or totalitarian rule, have taken many years to develop viable governments. Overall, he suggests that we need to avoid any rush to judgment.

MARINA OTTAWAY
Nation Building

Once, nations were forged through "blood and iron." Today, the world seeks to build them through conflict resolution, multilateral aid, and free elections. But this more civilized approach has not yielded many successes. For nation building to work, some harsh compromises are necessary—including military coercion and the recognition that democracy is not always a realistic goal.

"NATION BUILDING IS A QUAGMIRE"

Not necessarily. Nation building is difficult, but it need not become a quagmire as long as the effort has clear goals and sufficient resources. Compare Somalia and East Timor: The United States and the United Nations stumbled into Somalia without a plan. As a result, what began as a humanitarian mission to feed people starved by rival warlords became a misguided attempt at ad hoc nation building as U.S. troops sought to capture Somali warlord Mohammed Farah Aidid. The United States extricated itself from that quagmire by leaving Somalia to its fate in 1994, and the United Nations later did the same.

In East Timor, by contrast, the international community followed a plan and was not dragged into a situation it could not control. Right from the start, the United Nations sought consensus for nation building by organizing an unprecedented plebiscite on independence from Indonesia. Learning from the mistakes of the

Balkans and elsewhere, peacekeepers (led by Australia) were authorized to use deadly force against pro-Indonesia militias who sought to disrupt East Timor's bid for autonomy through a campaign of violence, looting, and arson. At the time of this writing [October 2002], the East Timorese have democratically elected a new government, which has hired more than 11,000 civil servants and retrained former guerrillas as soldiers for the country's nascent defense force. East Timor is still a construction site, but it is not a quagmire.

"NATION BUILDING IS ABOUT BUILDING A NATION"

No. Nationhood, or a sense of common identity, by itself does not guarantee the viability of a state. In Haiti, for example, citizens already share a common identity, but the state has collapsed nevertheless. Other states are so deeply divided along ethnic (Bosnia), religious (Northern Ireland), or clan (Somalia) lines that forging a common identity is currently out of the question. The international community cannot hope to make Muslims, Croats, and Serbs in Bosnia forget their differences, nor can it compel Catholics and Protestants in Northern Ireland to bridge the religious gulf.

Even successful states are less homogenous than they claim. Many European countries, such as France and Spain, grudgingly have recognized the existence of regional cultures. In the United States, the notion of the melting pot has been debunked, particularly as a new wave of immigrants from the developing world has shunned outright assimilation by forming a mosaic of hyphenated Americans. And contrary to the mythology inherited from nineteenth-century Europe, historical evidence reveals that the common identity, or sense of nationhood, that exists in many countries did not precede the state but was forged by it through the imposition of a common language and culture in schools. The Gauls were not France's ancestors until history textbooks decided so.

Thus, the goal of nation building should not be to impose common identities on deeply divided peoples but to organize states that can administer their territories and allow people to live together despite differences. And if organizing such a state within the old internationally recognized borders does not seem possible, the international community should admit that nation building may require the disintegration of old states and the formation of new ones.

"NATION BUILDING IS A RECENT IDEA"

Absolutely not. Take a look at how the political map of the world has changed in every century since the collapse of the Roman Empire—that should be proof enough that nation building has been around for quite a while. Casting a glance at the nineteenth and twentieth centuries will reveal that the types of nation building with the most lasting impact on the modern world are nationalism, colonialism, and post-World War II reconstruction.

Nationalism gave rise to most European countries that exist today. The theory was that each nation, embodying a shared community of culture and blood, was entitled to its own state. (In reality, though, few beyond the intellectual and political elite shared a common identity.) This brand of nationalism led to the reunification of Italy in 1861 and Germany in 1871 and to the breakup of Austria-Hungary in 1918. This process of nation building was successful where governments were relatively capable, where powerful states decided to make room for new entrants, and where the population of new states was not deeply divided. Germany had a capable government and succeeded so well in forging a common identity that the entire world eventually paid for it. Yugoslavia, by contrast, failed in its efforts, and the international community is still sorting out the mess.

Colonial powers formed dozens of new states as they conquered vast swaths of territory, tinkered with old political and leadership structures, and eventually replaced them with new countries and governments. Most of today's collapsed states, such as Somalia or Afghanistan, are a product of colonial nation building. The greater the difference between the precolonial political entities and what the colonial powers tried to impose, the higher the rate of failure.

The transformation of West Germany and Japan into democratics states following World War II is the most successful nation-building exercise ever undertaken from the outside. Unfortunately, this process took place under circumstances unlikely to be repeated elsewhere. Although defeated and destroyed, these countries had strong state traditions and competent government personnel. West Germany and Japan were nation-states in the literal sense of the term—they were ethnic and cultural communities as well as political states. And they were occupied by the U.S. military, a situation that precluded choices other than the democratic state.

"ONLY WAR BUILDS NATIONS"

Not quite. The most successful nations, including the United States and the countries of Europe, were built by war. These countries achieved statehood because they developed the administrative capacity to mobilize resources and to extract the revenue they needed to fight wars.

Some countries have been created not by their own efforts but by decisions made by the international community. The Balkans offer unfortunate examples of states cobbled together from pieces of defunct empires. Many African countries exist because colonial powers chose to grant them independence. The British Empire created most modern states in the Middle East by carving up the territory of the defeated Ottoman Empire. The Palestinian state, if it becomes a reality, will be another example of a state that owes its existence to an international decision.

Such countries have been called quasi states—entities that exist legally because they are recognized internationally but that hardly function as states in practice because they do not have governments capable of controlling their territory. Some quasi states succeed in retrofitting a functioning country into the legalistic shell. The state of Israel, for example, was formed because of an international decision, and Israel immediately demonstrated its staying power by waging a successful war to defend its existence. But many quasi states fail and then become collapsed states.

Today, war is not an acceptable means of state building. Instead, nation building must be a consensual, democratic process. But such a process is not effective against adversaries who are not democratic, who have weapons, and who are determined to use them. The world should not be fooled into thinking that it is possible to build states without coercion. If the international community is unwilling to allow states to be rebuilt by wars, it must provide the military muscle in the form of a sufficiently strong peacekeeping force. Like it or not, military might is a necessary component of state building.

"NATION BUILDING IS NOT A TASK FOR THE 82ND AIRBORNE"

Maybe not, but it's certainly a task for a strong military force with U.S. participation. Current White House National Security Advisor Condoleezza Rice had a point when she quipped during the 2000 presidential campaign that the 82nd Airborne has more important tasks than "escorting kids to kindergarten." But no one ever said that the primary task of U.S. troops should be babysitting. If the international community does not want to give war a chance by allowing adversaries to fight until someone prevails, then it has to establish control through a military presence willing to use deadly force. And if nation building is in the interests of the United States (as the Bush administration has reluctantly concluded), then the United States must participate in imposing that control.

It is not enough just to participate in the initial effort (in the war fought from the sky), because what counts is what happens on the ground afterward. Newly formed states need long-term plans that go beyond the recent mission statement outlined by one U.S. diplomat: "We go in, we hunt down terrorists, and we go out as if we'd never been there." Even if the United States succeeds in eliminating the last pockets of the Taliban and al Qaeda in Afghanistan, Americans could face another threat in a few years. And although warring armies are no longer active in Bosnia, the country would splinter apart if international troops went home.

The United States does not have to take the central role in peacekeeping operations, but U.S. participation is important because the country is the most powerful member of the international community. Otherwise, the United States sends the message that it doesn't care what happens next—and in doing so, it undermines fragile new governments and encourages the emergence of feuding factions and warlords.

"THE INTERNATIONAL COMMUNITY KNOWS HOW TO BUILD NATIONS BUT LACKS POLITICAL WILL"

It has neither the will nor the way. Many of the nation-building methods used in the past are inconceivable today, but the international community has yet to find effective substitutes. For instance, the first step colonial powers took when engaging in nation building was "pacification," invariably a bloody undertaking described by the British writer Rudyard Kipling as "the savage wars of peace." In today's gentler world of nation building, such violent agreements are fortunately unacceptable. Instead, peacemakers usually try to mediate among rival factions, demobilize combatants, and then reintegrate them in civilian life—a theoretically good idea that rarely works in practice.

Political will for state reconstruction is also in short supply nowadays. That's hardly surprising, given that countries expected to help rebuild nations are the same ones that until recently were accused of neoimperialism. Sierra Leoneans today welcome the British peacekeeping force with open arms and even wax nostalgic about the old days of British rule. But they revolted against British colonialism in the 1950s, and not so long ago, they condemned it as the root cause of all their problems. Should we be surprised that the British are, at best, ambivalent about their role?

And even when the international community demonstrates the will to undertake nation building, it's not always able to figure out who should shoulder the burden. The international community is an unwieldy entity with no single center and lots of contradictions. It comprises the major world powers, with the United States as the dominant agent in some situations and as a reluctant participant in others. In Afghanistan, for instance, the United States wants to have complete control over war operations but refuses to have anything to do with peacekeeping. Meanwhile, the multilateral organization that by its mandate should play the dominant role in peacekeeping and state reconstruction—the United Nations—is the weakest and most divided of all.

* * *

"NATION BUILDING SHOULD BE LIMITED TO STRATEGICALLY IMPORTANT STATES"

Only if anyone can determine which ones they are. "No sane person opposes nation-building in places that count," writes conservative columnist Charles Krauthammer. "The debate is about nation-building in places that don't." But this type of reasoning eventually forced the United States to fight a war in Afghanistan, a country deemed so unimportant after the Soviets departed that it was left to become a battleground for warlords and a safe haven for al Qaeda. In 1994, the United States abandoned strategically insignificant Somalia, too, only to start worrying after September 11, 2001, whether that country had also been infiltrated by terrorist networks.

For most countries, strategic significance is a variable, not a constant. Certainly, some countries, such as China, are always significant. But even countries that appear of marginal or no importance can suddenly become crucial. Afghanistan is not the only example. In the days of the Cold War, countries or regions suddenly became prominent when they were befriended by the Soviet Union. "SALT," then National Security Advisor Zbigniew Brzezinski declared in 1980, "was buried in the sands of the Ogaden"—referring to the cooling of U.S.-Soviet relations when the countries were dragged in to support opposite sides in a war between Ethiopia and Somalia. A few years later, the Reagan administration sent people scrambling for small-scale maps of Lebanon by declaring that Souk el-Gharb, an obscure crossroads town, was vital to U.S. security.

The lesson by now should be clear: No country is so insignificant that it can never become important. So, by all means, let us focus our efforts only on strategically important countries, as long as we can predict which ones they are. (Good luck.)

"THE GOAL OF NATION BUILDING IS A DEMOCRATIC STATE"

Let us not indulge in fantasy. It is politically correct to equate state reconstruction with democracy building. Indeed, the international community has a one-size-fits-all model for democratic reconstruction, so that plans devised for Afghanistan bear a disturbing resemblance to those designed for the Democratic Republic of the Congo (DRC). This model usually envisages a negotiated settlement to the conflict and the holding of a national conference of major domestic groups (the *loya jirga* in Afghanistan and the Inter-Congolese Dialogue in the DRC) to reach an agreement on the structure of the political system, followed by elections. In addition to these core activities, the model calls for subsidiary but crucial undertakings, beginning with the demobilization of former combatants and the development of a new national army, then exending to reforming the judiciary, restructuring the civil service, and establishing a central bank—thus creating all the institutions deemed necessary to run a modern state.

This model is enormously expensive, requiring major commitments of money and personnel on the part of the international community. As a result, this approach has only been implemented seriously in the case of Bosnia, the only country where the international community has made an open-ended commitment of money and power to see the job through to the end. Six years into the process, progress is excruciatingly slow and not even a glimmer of light is waiting at the end of the tunnel. But elsewhere in the world, including Afghanistan, the international community prescribes this model without providing the resources. The most obvious missing resource in Afghanistan is a robust international peacekeeping force.

STAN CROCK
Bush Is Flunking Reconstruction 101

His team proved it knew how to defeat Iraq militarily. Too bad, it appears to have not much clue about succeeding at nation building.

If the Bush Administration's performance in postwar Iraq were a pop quiz in Reconstruction 101, the White House would be flunking right now. It has failed to absorb some of the basic tenets of nation building, and, along with the Iraqi people, it's paying a steep price. Can the Bushies still salvage this postwar scenario and pass the final exam? Perhaps. But so far, the paucity of clear thinking from the administration is disturbing.

First, the good news—though not all of it thanks to Team Bush's efforts. The worst fears for Iraq—mass starvation, bloody reprisals, oil fields ablaze, a refugee crisis, and a push for independence by Kurds or Shiites—haven't materialized. Joseph Collins, a top Pentagon official overseeing reconstruction, notes that cities such as Mosul, Irbil, and Basra have better water or electricity services than before the war, and are in far better shape than Baghdad—though reporters tend to be in Baghdad and see the worst of it.

Still, it's far from clear that Washington can overcome the greatest stumbling block: a fundamental ambivalence inside the White House toward nation building. Without the fortitude and discipline required to reconstruct Iraq, the U.S. could be facing a very cold peace in the Middle East.

Let's take a look at the quiz so far and the administration's answers:

Question 1: Should an invading/liberating country deploy a large force of military police at the start of a conflict so that immediately after major combat is over, the police can fill the security vacuum and maintain order in ways that regular soldiers cannot?

The Administration's answer: No. The correct answer: A painfully obvious yes.

This is a no-brainer. But it's clear from the near-anarchy in Baghdad that the U.S. wasn't ready with a sufficient MP force. Previous examples of nation building—from Germany and Japan after World War II to Haiti, Somalia, Bosnia, Kosovo, and Afghanistan—all show that a police force is needed to provide security in the wake of military action.

Calls are now coming for bringing in an international police corps, but a great deal of time, property, and goodwill have been lost because of the failure to have cops on the beat right away. Unless police, judges, and a civil administration are put in place quickly, the military occupation "creates a window of opportunity you're never able to seize," says James Dobbins, a former special envoy in Afghanistan, Kosovo, Bosnia, Haiti, and Somalia, and one of several Rand official who recently completed a study of past U.S. reconstruction efforts.

Question 2: Should the civilian occupation leader focus on playing a low-key coordinator role or display the clout that a Douglas MacArthur or Lucius Clay showed after World War II?

The Administration answer: Low-key coordinator role.

The correct answer: Duh. Again, painfully obvious—someone with muscle and clear authority is the right choice. In the predictably chaotic atmosphere following combat, a leader who can take charge, rather than just mediate among various agencies, is critical. The appointment of L. Paul Bremer, who is to have authority over "anybody who does anything," as one administration official puts it, is intended to correct that flaw in the game plan.

The shift suggests that the administration can learn. But it also may indicate that Defense Secretary Donald Rumsfeld and the rest of the administration simply won't listen to people familiar with this kind of process. They insist on trying to reinvent the wheel every time—and that creates costly mistakes.

Question 3: Should an occupying force announce an exit strategy early on?

The administration's answer: Yes.

The correct answer: No.

You don't want people intent on undermining your efforts to wait in the weeds on the assumption you'll leave soon and give them the chance to pounce. That's the danger of saying the U.S. will stay as long as necessary, but not one day longer, as Rumsfeld puts it.

He and the rest of the Administration evidently think this is a clever formulation of policy, since it's echoed so frequently. It may assuage domestic political concerns, since voters don't want troops in Iraq forever. And it may be a sop to Islamic sensibilities about having U.S. troops in the Middle East for an extended period.

Still, Rummy, think this through: The second part of the statement—not a day longer—reflects an unseemly desire to cut and run. And that's sending the wrong message to a key audience: potential malefactors inside and outside Iraq. They may take from this that America hasn't changed a whit since Lebanon or Somalia, that a little terror or some combat casualties will send the U.S. packing.

"Exit strategies and departure timetables are inconsistent with success," says Dobbins. "We have done it quickly, and we have done it well. But we have never done it quickly and well." He adds that no successful U.S. postwar occupation has ever taken less than five years.

What's needed is a firm declaration that the U.S. is going to be there for the long haul to give everyone time to adjust to a new reality. Worried about the resilience of the Baath Party, Deputy Defense Secretary Paul Wolfowitz told the *Washington Post* that the U.S. will be in Iraq for a long time. But there are few indications whether others, particularly political guru Karl Rove, agree.

Question 4: Does peacekeeping require more, about the same, or fewer ground troops than actual combat?

The administration's answer: Fewer.

The correct answer: Don't answer that, because it's not yet clear.

In Somalia, the number of troops shrank from 20,000 to 2,000 as the mission shifted from humanitarian assistance to democratization, which Dobbins considers a broader mission. That was a disaster, as students who've read *Black Hawk Down* know.

Just by virtue of its size, Iraq may require a much larger presence than the two divisions—30,000 troops—the Pentagon is assuming it will need. *A Washington*

Times analysis shows that NATO put a force of more than 50,000 into Bosnia, a country of fewer than 5 million people, while Iraq is five times bigger. The per capita number of soldiers in Kosovo was even higher. Either calculation would dictate a ground force far larger than was involved in combat in the Iraq war.

Extra credit question: Which is more important in reconstructing a war-torn country, effectiveness or legitimacy?

The administration's answer: That's up to the Iraqis.

The correct answer: Effectiveness, because it can produce a legitimacy of its own. Before any shots were fired, administration officials struggled over whether reconstruction should be essentially unilateral (more effective, less legitimate) or multilateral (bring in the U.N., which would add legitimacy).

That tension remains, but it's cast a little differently. Now it's a question of whether the coalition should make some crucial decisions about Iraq's future (be effective) or defer to Iraqis (more legitimate—but extended lead times could make this approach less effective over the long term).

The Bush team has to make decisions quickly about currencies, tariffs, commercial legal codes, and the structure of the Iraqi oil industry. It has to accept the status of an occupying power, so that someone has the legal authority to sign contracts, let in direct foreign investment, negotiate foreign debt payments and forgiveness, and do a host of other things that will bring tangible benefits rapidly to the Iraqi people.

It won't do to wait for the desultory U.N. Security Council process to label the U.S. an occupying power. If Washington does bring positive change and shows quite visibly that Iraqi petrodollars are benefiting the Iraqis, that will bring legitimacy.

Nor can the U.S. wait until a formal Iraqi government is created. That would take too long, especially now that Bremer has decided to delay creating an interim government. An elected government should be postponed until a free press blossoms and lays the foundation for robust debate, and until political parties have a chance to form and organize. That would enable a broad spectrum of politicians—from Shiite clerics imported from Iran to the Iraqi Communist Party to leaders of the Iraqi National Congress—to build grass-roots support.

It's fine in the meantime to use existing ministries and officials not tainted by their closeness to the Saddam Hussein regime. Just get key goals done.

IT'S YOUR JOB. My fear is that all the talk about deferring issues to the Iraqis reflects continuing ambivalence in the administration about nation building. It's troubling to note, for example, the scheduled closing next fall of the Army War College's peacekeeping institute, the only school of its kind in the U.S. military.

Mr. President, Mr. Rumsfeld, suck it up. You decided to go in. You now have obligations and opportunities. Accept them. The guidance from history is clear. Successful nation building in Iraq will require a long-term commitment. It's the only chance you have to pass the final exam.

DAVID PRYCE-JONES
A Little Patience Please

IRAQ WON'T LOOK LIKE OUR TOWN OVERNIGHT

The absolute monarchs of the op-ed pages and television commentary predicted fearful outcomes to the Iraqi Freedom operation—hundreds of thousands of casualties on all sides, Baghdad razed, the Muslim world in an uproar, every Arab an Osama bin Laden. Well, things haven't turned out like that. President Bush and his administration explained what they would do, and did it. Unwilling to give credit where credit is due, the absolute monarchs have moved on to predict fresh fearful outcomes—a Khomeinist dictatorship of the Shia ayatollahs, an intifada against the American "occupation," every Arab once again an Osama bin Laden. What is most striking in this immense failure: the bias against the administration, the ignorance, or the contrast with the professionalism of the military?

When a totalitarian regime is overthrown, the very first likelihood is the settling of scores. In 1945 concentration-camp survivors killed their S.S. guards when they could. In Budapest during the revolution of 1956, the crowds hanged Communist secret policemen on lampposts. In a final showdown with the Communists, even the newly democratic Boris Yeltsin left many dead when his tanks shelled the Moscow White House.

Since the days of the British, moreover, every previous change of regime in Iraq has involved mayhem and murder. Nothing of the kind has occurred so far in Iraq. Under Saddam Hussein, Arabs massacred Kurds and drove them out of Mosul and Kirkuk, stealing their homes and property. Reclaiming what is rightfully theirs, the Kurds have not killed those who so maltreated them. In Basra, the mob caught a notorious secret-police chief; they did not lynch him as they might have, but handed him over to the British. The families of victims are often able to name and identify the Baathist secret policemen and torturers who committed crimes against them. Many of them expressed their feelings by looting whatever of the former regime's real or symbolic property was within reach, but they have not taken the law into their own hands in revenge killings. That is remarkable, and grounds for hope.

Life is instead approaching normality. Former general Jay Garner and his staff of several hundred have teamed up with Iraqi officials and technicians. The electricity supply will soon be fully restored in all major cities, and with it comes clean water and the purification of sewage. There is no hunger; markets are operating. Gas stations are open. Schoolchildren no longer have to glorify Saddam in class. The regular police force is back at work, in new uniforms, armed and using weapons handed to them by Americans to enforce good conduct. Military lawyers are trying to establish interim criminal and civil codes. Economists are debating what the post-Saddam currency ought to be.

Administration is not government, and in that respect Iraq is still a political vacuum. For reasons that seem to have to do with departmental in-fighting in Washington, the United States did not prepare for an Iraqi government-in-waiting. Power is therefore lying in the streets—to adopt the famous phrase coined for the Bolshe-viks in 1917—and someone has only to pick it up. All sorts of contenders with all sorts of credentials have rushed forward, each with claims to be representing one or another of the ethnicities and religious sects which make up the kaleidoscope of Iraq. Some of these contenders are at the national level—for instance Ahmad Chal-abi, leader of the Iraqi National Congress, and known to have the Pentagon's back-ing but also the blocking of the State Department—others at regional or city levels. Out of the blue, one Muhammad Mohsen Zubaidi appointed himself mayor of Bagh-dad and set up so many committees to deal with municipal issues that the military has put a stop to his activities.

Other contenders still are tribal elders or sheikhs accustomed to authority and respect. The traditional Kurdish leaders Jalal Talabani and Massoud Barzani speak for their people, and make it clear that Kurds expect to be rewarded for their loyalty to the coalition, as well as their restraint towards a Turkey unhappy to see the Kurds enjoying freedom. For the past decade, they have shown themselves capable of run-ning Iraqi Kurdistan at least as democratically as the Turks run Turkey: not per-fectly, but not too imperfectly either.

Representing only about a fifth of the population, Sunni Muslims have hitherto governed Iraq. Baathist ideology began as an unholy compound of Communism and Nazism, and ended as the justification of Sunni rule over everyone else. For the Sunni minority, the downfall of Saddam is a calamity marking the end of their su-premacy, and putting them in fear of their lives at the hands of those they op-pressed. A would-be Sunni successor to Saddam needs the unusual credential of having stood up to Saddam, and enough civic courage to tell his fellow Sunnis how blindly cruel they have been while in power. Had the State Department been able to find such a paragon, an Iraqi government-in-waiting might have accompanied the Marines.

In Iraq, Shia outnumber Sunnis by about three to one. In neighboring Iran, Aya-tollah Khomeini and his successors have attempted to widen Shi'ism into some sort of universal Islamist weapon against the West, in particular the American "Great Satan." To Saddam, the Shia were fanatics in the grip of religious frenzy, and as a precaution he banned traditional Shia processions and rituals in their holy cities of Karbala and Najaf. The State Department evidently views the Shia much as Sad-dam did. Mercilessly persecuting their own Shia minority, the Saudis also con-tribute to this unspoken coalition to keep Shia down everywhere.

The fall of Saddam gives the Iraqi Shia a sense of freedom and power, for the first time in their history. Large numbers of the faithful took to the streets to revive their traditional processions and rituals, in which they flagellate themselves and mutilate themselves with swords and knives. The blood-drenched spectacle con-firmed everything the State Department dreads. Some spokesman from the Hawza—a seminary which acts as the main Shia powerhouse in Karbala—then openly declared, "We want to establish an Islamic, Shia state, the same as hap-pened in Iran." Secretary of defense Donald Rumsfeld quickly declared that the United States was not prepared to see Iranian-style dictatorship replace Saddam's dictatorship. Gen. Garner takes the same line.

Iran has sent representatives and undercover agents to work for an Iraq in Shia hands. The media monarchs draw the instant conclusion that another Shia extremist state must be in the making. But the Shia are not in fact a bloc of undifferentiated fanatics. Their ayatollahs depend on genealogy and learning for authority. The most authoritative is Grand Ayatollah Ali Sistani in Najaf, a man well into his seventies. First he advised everyone not to resist the coalition, and then he declared he would not "interfere in the type of government the Iraqi people wish to choose." Other ayatollahs have followers or factions but their political ambitions and capacities for violence cancel each other out.

In a further division, many Shia—including Ahmad Chalabi and most of the INC—have a Western secular outlook. It is not clear whether the State Department objects to Chalabi because of his personality, his career, or the fact that he is a Shia rather than a Sunni. By luck rather than judgment, this hostility toward him may still turn out to be for the best. Should he in the end be the man to pick up the power lying in the streets, he will have done so on his own, not as an American stooge.

It hardly takes a Locke or a Montesquieu to see that the coherent way to fill the political vacuum is to convene a constituent assembly. Every ethnic and religious entity should send its representatives, some of whom no doubt will be self-selected, and a few may well try to be wreckers. Time and patience are the prerequisites for reaching agreement to share power among so many identities and interests. Gen. Garner speaks of a process lasting a few months, after which he will be handing responsibility for government over to Iraqis. Chalabi and the intellectuals of the INC hope that a constituent assembly will come up with the blueprint for a federal system of government, but expect that the details won't be settled for at least two years.

Nazi Germany took ten years to become a Federal Republic, and Russia is still shaking off some of the Soviet legacy after more than a decade. Iraq will do well to match that sort of timescale. American forces will have to stay for as long as it takes to preserve the peace and guarantee the workability of the new government. Of course in the event that someone from whatever background picks up power to make himself another Supreme Leader at the expense of everyone else, then all bets are off, and for once the media might be right to expect the worst.

DISCUSSION QUESTIONS

1. *What would you do?* As president, you ask your advisers to assess the advantages and disadvantages of a nation-building effort in Iraq. One set of advisers favors a large-scale effort in which the United States would be a leader, commit substantial financial resources and personnel, and be prepared to stay involved in Iraq for up to ten years. In the long-term, they suggest, this will enhance the image of the United States in the Middle East. Another set of advisers argues that the U.S. effort should be limited in scope and designed to extract the United States from Iraq in a short amount of time, perhaps a year. Rather than a lead effort, the United States should let the United Nations lead the effort

in Iraq and pay most of the costs. A long-term effort led by the United States, they contend, would produce resentment toward the United States. A third set of advisers argues that the United States should not get involved in nation building at all, that such efforts need to be entirely internal to Iraq for them to have legitimacy and credibility. Unless the Iraqis are allowed to work out their problems like Americans were after the Civil War, they will always feel that their government and system is a puppet of the United States. What questions do you ask these advisers to help you make a decision?

2. If Ottaway's analysis is right, what should we expect from nation-building efforts? According to the information presented by Crock and Pryce-Jones, have expectations been met in Iraq?

3. Pryce-Jones and Crock were writing while the postwar reconstruction effort in Iraq was relatively young. From what you have heard, read, or seen about nation building in Iraq more recently, does Pryce-Jones's optimism or Crock's pessimism about the adminstration's nation-building effort seem more warranted?

4. In general, do you believe the United States should be engaged in nation-building activities? If not, why not? Are there any risks for the United States if it does not get involved? If you believe the United States should be engaged in nation building, how would you determine when it should or should not be involved?

Permissions Acknowledgments

Biggs, Andrew G. "Stock Market Declines' Effect on the Social Security Reform Debate" in *USA Today Magazine*, vol. 131, no. 2696 (May 2003), pp. 28–30. Reprinted from *USA Today Magazine* (May 2003), copyright 2003 by The Society for the Advancement of Education, Inc.

Broder, David S. "Dangerous Initiatives: A Snake in the Grass Roots," in *The Washington Post* (March 26, 2000), p. B1. © 2000, The Washington Post Writers Group. Reprinted with permission.

Brooks, David. "A Federalism Worth Fighting For," in *The Weekly Standard*, vol. 8, no. 41 (June 30, 2003), pp. 23–26. Copyright *The Weekly Standard*. Reprinted by permission.

Carlson-Thies, Stanley, and Barry Lynn. "The Faith-Based Initiative Two Years Later: Examining Its Potential, Progress and Problems," excerpts from a discussion organized by the Pew Forum on Religion and Public Life and held at The Brookings Institution (March 5, 2003). Reprinted by permission of The Brookings Institution and The Pew Forum on Religion and Public Life.

Cohn, Jonathan. "Roll Out the Barrel: The Case Against the Case Against Pork" in *The New Republic* (April 20, 1998), pp. 19–23. Reprinted by permission of *The New Republic*, © 1998 The New Republic, Inc.

Crock, Stan. "Bush Is Flunking Reconstruction 101," in *Business Week Online* (May 19, 2003). Reprinted from the May 19, 2003, issue of *Business Week* by special permission, copyright © 2003 by The McGraw-Hill Companies, Inc.

Emery, Noemie. "Too Much History," in *The Weekly Standard* (June 2, 2003), pp. 26–29. Copyright *The Weekly Standard*. Reprinted by permission.

Firestone, David. "A Nation at War: Paying for the War: Senate Rolls a Pork Barrel into War Bill," in *The New York Times* (April 9, 2003), p. B11. Copyright © 2003 by The New York Times Co. Reprinted by permission.

Glassman, James. "Reform the Electoral College, Don't Toss It," in *The American Enterprise*, vol. 12, no. 2 (March 2001). Reprinted with permission of *The American Enterprise* magazine.

Graglia, Lino A. "Revitalizing Democracy," in *Harvard Journal of Law and Public Policy*, vol. 24, no. 1 (Fall 2000), pp. 165–77. Reprinted by permission.

Hamilton, Marci. "Are Federalism and the States Really Anti-Civil Rights as Liberals Often Claim?" in FindLaw's Writ (January 2, 2003). This column originally appeared on FindLaw.com. Reprinted by permission.

Harrington, Brooke. "Investor Beware: Can Small Investors Survive Social Security Privatization?" in *The American Prospect*, vol. 12, no. 16 (September 10, 2001), p. 20. Reprinted with permission from *The American Prospect*, Volume 12, Number 16: September 10, 2001. The American Prospect, 5 Broad Street, Boston, MA 02109. All rights reserved.

Isaacs, John. "Congress goes AWOL," in *Bulletin of the Atomic Scientists*, vol. 59, no. 3 (May/June 2003), pp. 20–21, 72. Reprinted with the permission of the *Bulletin of the Atomic Scientists*.

Kaminer, Wendy. "Toxic Media," in *The American Prospect*, vol. 11, no. 22 (October 23, 2000), pp. 36–37. Reprinted with permission from *The American Prospect*, Volume 11, Number 22: October 23, 2000. The American Prospect, 5 Broad Street, Boston, MA 02109. All rights reserved.

Latham, Earl. "The Group Basis of Politics: Notes for a Theory," in *American Political Science Review*, vol. 46, no. 2 (June 1952), pp. 376, 385–89, 390–92. Reprinted with the permission of Cambridge University Press.

Massing, Michael, and Kaminer, Wendy. "Toxic Media vs. Toxic Censorship," in *The American Prospect*, vol. 12, no. 1 (January 1–15, 2001), pp. 22–24. Reprinted with permission from *The American Prospect*, Volume 12, Number 1: January 1–15, 2001. The American Prospect, 5 Broad Street, Boston, MA 02109. All rights reserved.

Mitchell, Daniel J., Ph.D. "Nine Simple Guidelines for Pro-Growth Tax Policy," in *The Heritage Foundation Executive Memorandum*, no. 867 (March 21, 2003). Reprinted by permission.

Newfield, Jack. "The Right's Judicial Juggernaut," in *The Nation*, vol. 275, no. 11 (October 7, 2002), pp. 11, 13–16. Reprinted with permission from the October 7, 2002, issue of *The Nation*.

Ornstein, Norman. "No Need to Repeal the Electoral College," in *State Legislatures*, vol. 27, no. 2 (February 2001), pp. 12–16. Copyrighted by the National Conference of State Legislatures. Reprinted by permission.

Ottaway, Marina. "Nation Building," in *Foreign Policy* (September/October 2002), pp. 16–18, 20, 22. Reprinted by permission.

Paige, Sean. "Rolling Out the Pork Barrel," in *Insight on the News* (January 4, 1999), pp. 32–33. Reprinted with permission of *Insight*. Copyright 2003 News World Communications, Inc. All rights reserved.

Ponnuru, Ramesh. "1984 in 2003?" in *The National Review*, vol. 55, no. 10 (June 2, 2003), pp. 17–18. © 2003 by National Review, Inc., 215 Lexington Avenue, New York, NY 10016. Reprinted by permission.

Presser, Stephen B. "The Role of the Senate in Judicial Confirmations," from *The Federalist Society* (May 8, 2003). Reprinted by permission.

The Progressive [Editors]. "Casualties of War," in *The Progressive*, vol. 67, no. 1 (January 2003). Reprinted by permission from The Progressive, 409 E. Main St., Madison, WI 53703.

Pryce-Jones, David. "A Little Patience, Please," from *The National Review*, vol. 55, no. 9 (May 19, 2003), pp. 28, 30, 32. © 2003 by National Review, Inc., 215 Lexington Avenue, New York, NY 10016. Reprinted by permission.

Rauch, Jonathan. "The Hyperpluralism Trap," in *The New Republic* (June 6, 1994), pp. 22–25. © 1994 by Jonathan Rauch. Reprinted by permission.

Reich, Robert B. "Whose Tax Cuts?" in *The American Prospect*, vol. 13, no. 22 (December 18, 2002). Reprinted with permission from *The American Prospect*, Volume 13, Number 22: December 18, 2002. The American Prospect, 5 Broad Street, Boston, MA 02109. All rights reserved.

Rosen, Jeffrey. "Our Discriminating Court," in *The New Republic* (April 16, 2001), p. 24. Reprinted by permission of *The New Republic*, © 2001 The New Republic, Inc.

Sarasohn, David. "Taking (Back) the Initiative," in *The Nation* (June 18, 2001), pp. 19–22. Reprinted with permission from the June 18, 2001, issue of *The Nation*.

Schlesinger, Arthur Jr. "The Imperial Presidency Redux," in *The Washington Post* (June 28, 2003), p. A25. Reprinted by permission of the author.

Schlesinger, Arthur Jr. "Not the People's Choice," in *The American Prospect*, vol. 13, no. 6 (March 25, 2002), pp. 23–27. Reprinted with permission from *The American Prospect*, Volume 13, Number 6: March 25, 2002. The American Prospect, 5 Broad Street, Boston, MA 02109. All rights reserved.

Sullivan, Kathleen M. "What's Wrong with Constitutional Amendments?" from *New Federalist Papers: Essays in Defense of the Constitution*, by Alan Brinkley, Nelson W. Polsby, and Kathleen M. Sullivan (W. W. Norton & Company, 1997), pp. 61–67. © 1997 by the Twentieth Century Fund, Inc. Used by permission of W. W. Norton & Company, Inc.

Teixeira, Ruy. "Deciphering the Democrats' Debacle," in *The Washington Monthly*, vol. 35, no. 5, (May 2003), pp. 8–13. Reprinted with permission from *The Washington Monthly*. Copyright by Washington Monthly Publishing, LLC, 773 15th St. NW, Suite 520, Washington, DC 20005.

United States House of Representatives Committee on the Judiciary, "Statement of Hon. George Allen, Former Member of Congress and Former Governor of Virginia," from "Hearing Before the Subcommittee of the Constitution Proposing an Amendment to the Constitution of the United States to Provide a Procedure by Which the States May Propose Constitutional Amendments," One Hundred Fifth Congress, Second Session on H.J. Res. 84, March 25, 1998, Serial No. 86.

United States Senate Committee on Government Affairs, "Report to the Ranking Minority Member," from GAO-02-42 Department of State: Status of Achieving Key Outcomes and Addressing Major Management Challenges, December 7, 2001.

United States Supreme Court. Justice Clarence Thomas, Dissent, from *Barbara Grutter v. Lee Bollinger, et al.* (2003), No. 02-241, 2002 U.S. Briefs 241.

United States Supreme Court. Timothy A. Nelson, Frances P. Kao, Eric J. Gorman, and Amy M. Gardner, "Brief of the Clinical Legal Education Association as Amicus Curiae Supporting Respondents," February 18, 2003, from *Barbara Grutter v. Lee Bollinger, et al.* (2003), No. 02-241, 2002 U.S. Briefs 241.

Wilson, James Q. "What Government Agencies Do and Why They Do It," from *Bureaucracy: What Government Agencies Do and Why They Do It* (Basic Books, 1989), pp. 113–17, 120–21, and 134–36. Copyright © 1989 by PERSEUS BOOKS GROUP. Reproduced with permission of PERSEUS BOOKS GROUP in the format Textbook via Copyright Clearance Center.